D0886983

German Realpolitik
and
American Sociology

German Realpolitik
and
American Sociology

An Inquiry into the
Sources and Political
Significance of the
Sociology of Conflict

James Alfred Aho

Lewisburg
Bucknell University Press
London: Associated University Presses

This work grew out of a dissertation,
Sociology and Conflict, © 1971 by James A. Aho.

Associated University Presses, Inc.
Cranbury, New Jersey 08512

Associated University Presses
108 New Bond Street
London W1Y OQX, England

Library of Congress Cataloging in Publication Data
Aho, James Alfred, 1942-
German realpolitik and American sociology.

Bibliography: p.
Includes index.
1. Social conflict. 2. Sociology—History.
3. Political sociology. I. Title.
HM136.A32   301.6'3   73-21229
ISBN 0-8387-1453-6

PRINTED IN THE UNITED STATES OF AMERICA

To my father—for a sense of discipline and the ability to finish a task once started.
To my mother—for the capacity to trust my own sensibilities.

Contents

Acknowledgments

1 Introduction 13

2 The German Historians and the Sociologists
of Conflict 25

3 The Sociologists of Conflict on Conflict
within the State 61

4 German Intellectual Sources in American
Social Science 88

5 The Early Life and Careers of Ward, Small,
Park, and Bentley 112

6 Lester F. Ward's Sociology of Conflict 130

7 Albion Small's Sociology of Conflict 162

8 Robert E. Park's Sociology of Conflict 203

9 Arthur F. Bentley's Sociology of Conflict 241

10 Sociology and Conflict 279

Appendix: Letter from Everett C. Hughes to
    James Aho, July 8, 1970   315

Bibliography   320

Name Index   335

Subject Index   340

Acknowledgments

I wish to thank the following publishers and persons for having given me permission to quote from published works:

AMS Press, Inc., for excerpts from *Reminiscences of an American Scholar* by John Burgess. Reprinted with permission of AMS Press, Inc., copyright 1966.

Charles H. Hapgood for excerpts from *A Victorian in the Modern World* by Hutchins Hapgood. Reprinted with permission of Charles H. Hapgood, copyright by Harcourt Brace and World, Inc., 1939.

Harcourt Brace Jovanovich, Inc., for excerpts from *Politics* by Heinrich von Treitschke and abridged and introduced by Hans Kohn. Reprinted with permission of Harcourt Brace Jovanovich, Inc., copyright 1963.

Macmillan Publishing Co., Inc., for excerpts from *Race and Culture* by Robert E. Park and edited by Everett C. Hughes. Reprinted with permission of Macmillan Publishing Co., Inc., copyright 1950.

Oxford University Press for excerpts from *The Quest*

Acknowledgments

vellianism by Friedrich Meinecke and translated by Douglas Scott. Reprinted with permission of Yale University Press, copyright 1957.

I would like briefly to acknowledge some of the many persons who have helped me in the writing of this book. First of all I would like to thank Richard Ogles of the Department of Sociology at Washington State University who, through his constant exhortation and example, taught me never to become alienated from my work. Any analytical skills demonstrated in the following pages are due in large measure to his teaching and guidance. For the stimulating discussions out of which the idea to conduct research in this area originally arose, I would like to thank Andreas Maris Van Blaaderan, also of the Department of Sociology at Washington State. For his reading of an earlier version of the manuscript and his insightful criticisms thereon, thanks are due to Raymond Muse, Chairman of the History Department at Washington State. For their personal letters relating to Robert Park, I would like to thank both Everett C. Hughes and Ms. Winifred Raushenbush. For her patient help in translating parts of the work and correspondence of Ludwig Gumplowicz, Gustav Ratzenhofer, and Franz Oppenheimer, I am indebted to Mrs. James Kirk of the Department of Foreign Languages at Idaho State University. For their searching through the unpublished papers of Park, Albion Small, Lester Ward, and Arthur Bentley, I would like to thank respectively the manuscript librarians at the University of Chicago, Brown University, and the Lilly Library at Indiana University. Finally, for her critical reading of the manuscript, patience, and constant moral support I would like to thank my wife, Margaret. Without the assistance of these people this book would not have been possible.

German Realpolitik
and
American Sociology

1

Introduction

Perhaps it is natural that as a novel intellectual perspective becomes institutionalized into the daily routine of university and governmental life, its proponents tend to forget their forebears. Maybe it is inevitable that as a philosophical outlook held by outsiders to the academic community evolves into a scientific paradigm defining the boundaries of an exclusive and honored profession, its official historians begin to ignore those events of its past that are inconsistent with the public image it seeks to present. At least so it seems to be with sociology. For here is almost a classic example of a theoretical point of view originally promulgated by German Jews, talented dilettantes, and disillusioned Protestant ministers that was only grudgingly granted admittance into nineteenth-century university curricula, but that in less than a century arose to the stature of the "intellectual common denominator" of a substantial portion of American scholarly thought. And significantly, as this success story has unfolded, there have developed pressures within the sociological Establishment making it difficult for critical students to inquire into the more disreputable aspects of its past.

Since 1940 there have appeared a number of histories of sociology that have received the profession's imprimatur. However, possibly because the most notable of these efforts have been written by scholars of unmistakably optimistic liberal persuasion, as textbooks for consumption by young aspirants to the profession who hold the same prejudices, they have avoided serious discussion of the darker pessimistic and anti-liberal basis of sociological thought. American sociology, they say, has its roots in English liberalism and Darwinism, French socialism, and in the liberal neo-Kantianism of Max Weber and Georg Simmel. When names such as Gustav Ratzenhofer, Ludwig Gumplowicz, Lester Ward, and Albion Small are mentioned, they are given only cursory treatment as provocative but essentially irrelevant deviants from the main "scientific" line of sociological development.

It is my intention to present an altogether different picture of the situation. Instead of arguing that sociology grew out of the reflections of bouyant English and French reformists and free thinkers, I hypothesize that it arose from same ground of spiritual despair and nihilism that has come to be associated with much of the great literature of nineteenth-century Europe. It received its nourishment from the same soil that gave rise to Ibsen's dramas, Kafka's short stories, the sagas of Tolstoy, and the philosophies of Schopenhauer and Nietzsche. I submit that sociology received its initial impetus and early formulation in the German slough of romantic despondency, and that at least its original theories of social discord, those of the "sociologists of conflict"—Gumplowicz, Ratzenhofer, and Franz Oppenheimer,[1] were written within the same tradition of political cynicism that informed the world views of

---

1. Hereafter, when the phrase "sociologists of conflict" is used, unless otherwise specified, it refers exclusively to these three persons.

the most outspoken apologists for German military conquest—Treitschke, Moltke, and Bernhardi. I trace how this same political doctrine of Machiavellianism, or "realpolitik" as it will henceforth be called, penetrated the thinking of the American sociologists Ward, Small, Robert Park, and Arthur Bentley through their contact with German *Sozialwissenschaft*, and came to be employed by them in their interpretation of social phenomena in America.

An Anticipation of the Findings

The mode of analysis that contemporary intellectual historians have dubbed realpolitik, is considered by authorities to have found its most sophisticated formulation in the writings of the three Prussian historians, Hegel, Leopold von Ranke, and Heinrich von Treitschke. Perhaps it is for this reason that, to my knowledge at least, commentators on American sociology, a field that prides itself on being able to clearly distinguish its product from that of historiography, have thus far not seriously studied the proposition that sociology's own categories can be ultimately traced back to a style of thought that flourished among the proponents of the Prussian historical school.

It is, of course, true that all those who have told the story of sociology's development speak confidently of (especially) Ward's and (somewhat less so) of Small's intellectual indebtedness to what I call the sociologists of conflict. Yet, with few exceptions, these same persons maintain that the doctrines of Oppenheimer, Ratzenhofer, and Gumplowicz are examples of what they call "social Darwinism." While it is recognized that there is some ambiguity as to the precise meaning of "social Darwinism," such a classification may entail overlooking the fact that the German sociologists of conflict, their American counterparts, and indeed most who write in the tradition of German realpolitik, speak of conflict as something quite different from what has been claimed about the silent, unconscious "struggle" for existence that presumably takes place universally among all plants and animals. While this point will be considered in much more depth later, the characteristic German ability to distinguish between natural and human phenomena finds expression in the views of virtually every scholar whose work will be reviewed in the following pages, that social conflict and political domination are relationships that can occur only among conscious, goal-directed *persons*, and not for instance among different species of vegetation in an ecological community.

The tendency to classify the sociologists of conflict and their American students as social Darwinists, contains the further danger of missing the crucial point that at least in regard to its sociology of conflict, American sociology can not justifiably argue that it arose from strictly liberal intellectual circles. It is well known, for example, that Hegel, Ranke, and Treitschke, the Prussian historians who first attempted to apply Machiavellianism to modern political affairs, were outspoken opponents of liberalism. Moreover, although Oppenheimer, Ratzenhofer, and Weber may have been advocates of reform, they were above all nationalists who believed that liberalism was one of the main causes of the social problems they were seeking to resolve. And apparently, one of the prime motives underlying Bentley's, Ward's, Small's, and Park's excursions into Teutonic scholarship was a vague feeling that, as it had been promulgated by Rousseau and Jefferson, liberalism simply could not effectively address the social issues of their day.

Consistent with their aliberal perspective, none of these persons saw coercion as Hobbes might have done, as a form of interaction characteristic of exclusively "natural," presocial man. On the contrary, to them, all political domination, including coercion, was an inevitable attribute of human social life. Or they did not argue, as liberals might, that force or even the extensive use of violence is incompatible with social unity and civilization. Rather, they hypothesized that social unity itself, finding expression at higher and higher levels of morality and reason, grows naturally out of social conflict. Conflict, they theorized, gives rise to the state, to legal systems, to that institution called "class stratification," to bureaucracy, and finally even to culture.

This is not to say, however, that the American and German sociologists of conflict viewed the dynamics of conflict through the rose-colored glasses of sentimentality. Later on, it will be seen that they were very cognizant of the fact that conflict is not something that can, as those of more liberal political persuasion might submit, always be overcome by dialogue at the table of reason. As power struggles, they recognized that conflicts are often decided on the basis of the quite irrational factor of which party has access to the more sophisticated tools of violence.

This example of the continuity that links these particular latter nineteenth and early twentieth-century German and American sociologists into a single intellectual tradition should not be considered an isolated phenomenon. In the following chapters, it is pointed out how this specific case of cultural assimilation was merely a small incident in a vast American scholarly movement, wherein literally thousands of budding literati sailed overseas to attend graduate school in the German universities of Berlin, Heidelberg, and Göttingen. One generally ignored consequence, both of this impressive intellectual migration plus the coincident systematic effort to translate German philosophy and history into English, was that all of the American social sciences that became professionalized during this time, including institutional economics, sociology, political science, and history, received many of their basic assumptions and theoretical impetus from their German counterparts.

While the main part of this book is devoted to describing the significant place that German *Realpolitik* held in the social theorizing of the four early American sociologists, it is also shown how the notions of conflict that were developed by Oppenheimer, Ratzenhofer, and Gumplowicz were not naively borrowed by them and then applied *in toto* to the American scene. Just as apparently there was a concerted borrowing of provocative ideas that promised to shed some light on political goings-on in America, there was a simultaneous, if unconsciously selective, treatment of German scholarship based upon Ward's, Small's, Park's, and Bentley's own unique backgrounds. In particular, it will be seen that these four individuals consistently rejected any pessimism that might follow as a consequence of employing realpolitik in an unrelenting way to explain social interaction. I interpret this finding by invoking the hypothesis that American culture, especially prior to the First World War, was imbued with a peculiar optimism; an ethic that held that at least here in the New World there is sufficient opportunity for men to overcome the adversities of their environment and achieve as much individual and/or collective progress as they desire. It is argued that the American sociologists of conflict were socialized into this hopeful outlook, and as a result they found themselves unable to understand the foreboding attitude that Gumplowicz, Ratzenhofer, and Oppenheimer sometimes adopted toward history.

The hypothesis that in America there has been a widespread belief in the possibility of individual success and social advance is a source of controversy in professional circles. Yet it has had for its adherents some of the most eminent of American sociologists and historians, from Frederick Jackson Turner, David Potter, and Walter Prescott Webb to Carl Becker, Robert K. Merton, and even C. Wright Mills.[2] Naturally, there is little consensus among them concerning the precise source of this peculiar optimistic creed. For example, Turner and his most reknown student, Becker, believe that the experience of living on a boundless frontier of free land gave to a substantial stratum of individualistic American farmer-entrepreneurs an air of "unbridled hopefulness." On the other hand, while Webb and Mills speak in a similar manner of the vast amount of "land without proprietors," Potter claims that it was America's "social abundance" that was the decisive variable conditioning the confidence with which its citizens have traditionally confronted the future. However, in spite of the differences in opinion regarding the probable causes of this nineteenth-century American ethic, commentators agree that it is alien to European culture, with its long past of serfdom, paternal-

2. The following list by no means exhausts the authors who have had occasion to make reference to America's presumably optimistic cultural outlook: Frederick Jackson Turner, *The Frontier in American History* (New York, Chicago & San Francisco: Holt, Rinehart & Winston, Inc., 1967); Richard Hofstadter and Seymour Martin Lipset, eds., *Turner and the Sociology of the Frontier* (New York: Basic Books, Inc., 1968) contains clarifications, criticisms, and extended applications of Turner's hypothesis to other settings; David M. Potter, *People of Plenty: Economic Abundance and the American Character* (Chicago: University of Chicago Press, 1954); Walter Prescott Webb, *The Great Frontier* (Boston: Houghton Mifflin Co., 1952); Carl Becker, *The United States: An Experiment in Democracy* (New York: Harper & Bros., 1920); Robert K. Merton, *Social Theory and Social Structure* (Glencoe, Ill.: Free Press, 1963), pp. 136-39; 166-70. Merton's "success theme in American culture" is identical to the above authors' descriptions of the theme of optimism; C. Wright Mills, *White Collar: The American Middle Classes* (New York: Oxford University Press, 1956), pp. 3-9; 259-72.

istic rule, feudalism, and constant border strife. And it is such a belief that I impute to Ward, Small, Park, and Bentley, to give some meaning to their shared revulsion to German pessimism.

This important consideration aside, it is difficult not to observe that since the Second World War, particularly since America, as a "Great Power," has become increasingly involved in the mundane political affairs of the world, there has been a discernible movement on the part of American sociology to extricate, not selectively but completely, all aspects of realpolitik from its conceptualizations of social conflict. Although the meaning of such a shift in theoretical perspective could comprise the subject matter for several independent investigations, the last part of this book is devoted to speculation concerning some possible reasons for it.

For present purposes, it is sufficient to emphasize in this regard that in the whole tradition of realpolitik there exists a sort of faith, as it were, in the mutual reasonableness of the opponents, and therefore in the constructive, indeed civilizing aspects of power struggles altogether. Power struggles do not, according to this point of view, necessarily lead to the extermination of the vanquished, for this would not be to the economic advantage of the victor. And after all, say the proponents of realpolitik, enemies do not engage in conflict simply for the sake of fighting, but rather for some concrete purpose. Theirs is the conscious attempt to realize some clearly defined goal, and not a subconsciously motivated aggression to rid themselves of frustration or to reduce some psychological disequilibrium.

Since World War II, however, sociologists seem to have "lost" the assurance they once had; that struggles for power are both effective and essential means to realize moral, cultural, and civilized ends. Instead, they have involved themselves in sophisticated efforts to debunk realpolitik by claiming, for instance, that social conflict is caused more by nonrational "tensions," than by cold assessments of the anticipated profits to be had from fighting. Generally speaking, they have tended to avoid the whole subject of strategic thinking and have expended their energies on postulating the basic processes of tension reduction to prevent especially war and revolution from breaking out.

The Approach to the Problem

This is not a comprehensive textbook in social theory. The research contained herein was motivated by much more than a desire to simply attain a type of "objectivity" through the maintenance of a skeptical and critical attitude toward historical and biographical data. My original goal was to elucidate the controversy that has been raging in sociology for nearly twenty years, concerning the proper stance it should adopt toward the issues of order and conflict, consensus and coercion. There has been a conscious attempt throughout the following chapters then to derive those generalizations from the reported findings that will help clarify and perhaps even resolve the questions that have formed the basis for this debate.

The reader should be cautioned, therefore, that while the sociologies of each of the Germans and their American followers are interesting in their own right, I have not sought to describe each of them in their uniqueness as distinct from those of their fellows. Rather, I have attempted to reconstruct the continuities or parallels in their thinking about social conflict that seem to unite them into a single overall paradigm.

It is for this same reason that I have chosen to ignore completely the writings of such influential early American sociologists as William Graham Sumner, Edward A. Ross, Thorstein Veblen, and Charles Horton

Cooley. In the first place, with the exception of
Sumner, none of these persons even developed a comprehensive sociology of conflict. Thus, however significant their sociologies might be in other respects, they
are surely irrelevant for the stated objects of this
monograph. Sumner, on the other hand, while an acknowledged authority on the subject of conflict, was
left out of consideration because his work seems to fall
into quite another intellectual tradition than that in
which Bentley, Ward, Small, and Park wrote; namely,
social Darwinism. And a scholarly interpretive understanding of his thinking is available that links him not
to German political economy, but with the Englishman
Herbert Spencer.[3]

Aside from these points, Ward, Small, Park, and
Bentley comprise an important focus for research in
their own right because of the sway they held, particularly over early developments in American sociology.
While Ward has been spoken of as the father of the
American welfare state,[4] Bentley completed what is
considered by many to be the seminal American work
on government. And although Albion Small is generally lauded for his administrative genius, his theory of
conflict presented in the *General Sociology* has been
hailed by none other than Harry Elmer Barnes as the
most significant contribution to political sociology issued between the period of Calhoun's *Disquisition on
Government* and Bentley's *Process of Government*.[5]
Lastly, there is Robert Park, whose place in the history
of sociology can be characterized in all of its eminence
by simply designating him the founder of the "Chicago
School." Through his classroom leadership and author-

3. Richard Hofstadter, *Social Darwinism in American Thought* (New York:
G. Braziller, 1959).
4. For example, see Henry Steele Commager, ed., *Lester Ward and the Welfare State* (Indianapolis & New York: Bobbs-Merrill Co., 1967.)
5. Harry Elmer Barnes, "The Place of Albion Woodbury Small in Modern
Sociology," *AJS* XXXII (July, 1926): 43.

ship of what later became the profession's most widely read textbook, Park established the approximate boundaries of the modern study of race relations, human ecology, and urban sociology, including deviant behavior.

No sociologist of knowledge can be satisfied with merely presenting a description of a theory in its abstract form. His singular task is to determine the precise meaning that this theory has had for its expositors by carefully situating them in their appropriate linguistic milieu. He seeks to explain the similarities in thinking and perception among men by tracing them back to conditions they have shared in their early lives and institutional careers. Among the variables that are held to be crucial in the formation of a scholar's cultural product, the audience for whom he writes stands out with particular importance. Evidence presented later will suggest that in their lectures, books, and articles, Ward, Small, Park, and Bentley were all speaking to the members of a reference group that I will designate by the term "local society."

During the end of the nineteenth century, those who (like the four American sociologists) identified with local society, experienced a sometimes vague, but clearly recognizable fear that their prestige and political influence were being decisively threatened by the "captain of industry" and the impoverished East European immigrants who were then streaming to America's shores. Interpreting the danger to their status as constituting an attack on the hallowed values of local democracy, political decency, and private property, members of local society became avid participants in that early twentieth-century reactionary movement that today is known as "Progressivism." Four of the most emphatic ideologists for the Progressive movement were Small, Park, Ward, and Bentley. In attempting to give expression to the social problems of America as viewed from the eyes of local society, these men came to draw upon the teachings of others whose insight and scholarship they explicitly admired, and who seemed to be addressing similar difficulties in their own countries; namely, Gumplowicz, Ratzenhofer, and Oppenheimer. As a result their characterizations of contemporary American social strife came to be posed in essentially the same harshly realistic terms as those employed by the German proponents of real-politik. As I will demonstrate in the next two chapters, realpolitik was not a unique creation of the German-speaking sociologists. In fact it was originally culti-vated by the Prussian historians, who as advocates of military virtues are today associated with the worst of German higher learning.

What follows, then, is an attempt to understand, in a disciplined manner, the sociologies of conflict of four of the fathers of American sociology. It is an attempt to exploit the methods and theory of sociology, plus the structural and biographical data offered by history to gain a better picture of sociology's stand in regard to the questions of power and conflict in social life. Above all, however, it is an attempt to point out some of the events in sociology's past that its practitioners would otherwise prefer to ignore.

No value judgements are intended that, for instance, contemporary sociology should return to the formula-tions of its founders. The apparent naiveté of these political "realists" in a number of respects will im-mediately reveal itself to readers who have lived dur-ing a century of total war and revolution. On the other hand, the almost concerted effort, it would seem, by some to avoid the categories developed in a rudimen-tary way by the sociologists of conflict—categories that could otherwise elucidate many modern-day social problems—suggests the need to at least consider their contributions to be more than simply pedagogical ar-tifacts.

2

The German Historians and the Sociologists of Conflict

Although modern sociology is primarily an American institution, both in terms of its form and content, it was born in Europe. And not just anywhere overseas, but in Germany. Perhaps the greatest sociologist of his time was a German-speaking Polish Jew, living in Austria, by the name of Ludwig Gumplowicz. A devoted family man, a Stoic in the classic sense, and a prolific writer, Gumplowicz stimulated the development of an intellectual movement that it is the object of the following chapters to describe. He taught Gustav Ratzenhofer and influenced Franz Oppenheimer, and his ideas can easily be found in the political writings of Georg Simmel and Max Weber. And through these persons, his sociology even made excursions to America, expressing itself in the work of Lester Ward, Albion Small, Robert Park, and Arthur Bentley.

Naturally, like any other significant intellectual worker, Gumplowicz was a product of his time and the cultural pressures that played upon him. In fact even his foremost contribution, his theory of the origin of the state, was a more or less formalized rehashing of what had long been appreciated in German scholarship, particularly by Georg Wilhelm Friedrich Hegel, Leopold von Ranke, and Heinrich von Treitschke. But ignoring Hegel for the moment, these men were historians, and Gumplowicz was as vigorously opposed to historical inquiry as the historians were to sociology. How then can one justifiably claim that Gumplowicz's sociology was anticipated by several of the most illustrious names in German historiography?

In my view, Gumplowicz took issue not so much with the substantive content of history, as he did with the *method* of analyzing social life that was being espoused by the history faculties of the German universities during his time; namely, historicism. A brief outline of the basic position of historicism will allow the reader to form a correct picture of what it was about history that Gumplowicz disliked.

The historicists believed that while the proper study of natural phenomena entailed inferences from empirical observations to general statements, human history that is comprised of unduplicable acts of individual free will must be submitted to a radically different approach. To understand the historical behavior of governments, the content of legal systems, or the economic life of a people, each must be reduced to a characterization of its unique intention or purpose.[1] Thus did Karl Savigny, the noted Prussian jurist, argue that the German people, a community with its own separate character, can borrow legal precedents from the Roman Empire or from France only by sacrificing the Fatherland's national integrity. Or it was submitted by the national economists at Berlin University that as the German system of production and exchange had

1. For a scholarly characterization of historicism, see Georg Iggers, *The German Conception of History* (Middletown, Connecticut: Wesleyan University Press, 1968).

unconsciously evolved out of the true spirit of its folk, then it would be morally unjustified to arbitrarily impose upon their affairs the alien British theory of Smithian economics.[2]

A second component of Prussian historicism was its position that it is not sufficient for a true understanding of history merely to describe in a detached and disinterested way, the external correlations between events. In order to comprehend its unique essence, the analyst must at crucial times "psychologically enter" into the object of study itself. For example. Wilhelm Dilthey, who was an outspoken opponent of a positivist approach to history, believed that getting at the "truth" of a metaphysical system involved one's coming to sympathetically understand (*Verstehen*) it. But this necessitates not only the empirical description of its content, but more importantly, a reconstruction of the emotional impulses (*Erlebnis*) from which this content arose.[3]

Both of these aspects of historicism, its emphasis on particularism and its subjectivism, were vigorously rejected by Gumplowicz. Under the spell of Newtonian physics and Darwinian biology, he proposed instead that sociology devote itself exclusively to attempting to discover universal laws, statements that could explain the historical development of all races and states, in spite of their individual differences. Furthermore, he argued that the only basis for the substantiation of

2. For a classic study of the relationship between sociology and history, see Albion W. Small, *Origins of Sociology* (Chicago: University of Chicago Press, 1925).

3. For a detailed characterization of Dilthey's methodology, see Carlo Antoni, *From History to Sociology: The Transition in German Historical Thinking,* trans. and ed. by Hayden V. White (Detroit: Wayne University Press, 1959). Besides the Iggers volume, one can also find a competent account of historicist methodology in Talcott Parsons, *The Structure of Social Action* (Glencoe, Illinois: Free Press, 1949).

such laws can be objective observation and not private experience.[4]

Gumplowicz paid for his stubborn insistence that social science be modeled after natural science, by stimulating the wrath of the historicists. Consequently, when they did not publicly ignore his writings altogether, they attacked them for being overly mechanistic and abstract. Often too, they generalized their denunications to include the whole of sociology itself, successfully resisting the attempts by those misguided enough to label their work "sociology" (many of whom were Jews anyway, as the cases of Simmel, Oppenheimer, and Gumplowicz indicate) to occupy established university chairs.[5]

But over and above all the methodological argumentation, beyond the fact that the faculties of history were understandably fearful lest intruders armed with a foreign dogma threaten their monopoly over the correct approach to Truth, there is an unmistakable similarity in the substantive content of the political theories of the German sociologists, Oppenheimer, Ratzenhofer, and Gumplowicz, and those of the historians.

---

4. Gumplowicz asks, "Can such laws be stated for social phenomena as well; in a word; are there social laws? We ought to answer in the affirmative if there are social phenomena which constantly occur together or in the same order, so that we may ascribe them to, . . . a 'law,' as we do physical phenomena. That the mutual development of social groups, the formation of social communities, their development and their decay so occur, history and experience prove undeniably. Hence, we may direct investigation in the social domain with a view to formulating the social laws of those events." Ludwig Gumplowicz, *The Outlines of Sociology,* trans. by Frederick W. Moore, ed. and intro. by Irving Louis Horowitz (New York: Paine- Whitman, 1963) p. 145. This volume is hereafter referred to as *Outlines.* See also Ibid. pp. 145-60 for the author's surprisingly sophisticated critique of historicism and his less impressive list of "social laws."

5. This opposition has been noted by a variety of writers. Theodore Abel, *Systematic Sociology in Germany* (New York: Octagon Books, Inc., 1965) attempts to show that the delimited systematic sociologies of Georg Simmel, Leopold von Wiese, Alfred Vierkandt, and Max Weber, which were posed in

The German Historians and Realpolitik

This substantive similarity in writing about politics on the parts of both the Prussian historians and the sociologists of conflict will hereinafter be called realpolitik.[6] To the proponents of realpolitik, the state in its essence (*Staatsräson*) is organized power over a territory, rather than an institution whose sole purpose is to protect individual rights and property. As this is the case, then the state is said to arise and grow not out of voluntary contracts among its subjects, but against their collective will as another group conquers them and forces them into obedience. From this perspective, the proper study of the state entails a description of the uses and dynamics of power. And a realistic analysis of this capacity clearly demonstrates that regardless of the ends, for instance freedom, culture, or equality, that are purportedly pursued in political affairs by either states or parties, the means they employ are identical; the ultimate technique being violence.

such a way as to effectively eliminate the opposition of the historians, were not so much the result of fundamental theoretical differences between the two fields, but rather the result of professional jealousies. In this regard, consider the imperialistic sociology proposed by Ratzenhofer, "[Sociology is devoted to history] for it furnishes the bulk of material for making out the social process. . . . [But history] has, to be sure, proved to be in vain, because. . .[it] lacks the essence of science. . . . At bottom the true goal of history is sociology. Whatever falls outside this purpose belongs in the realm of art and ideals." Gustav Ratzenhofer, *Soziologie: Positive Lehre von den Menschlichen Wechselbeziehungen* (Leipzig: F.A. Brockhaus, 1907), quoted in Albion W. Small, "Ratzenhofer's Sociology," *AJS* XII (Jan., 1908): 436. See Gumplowicz, *Outlines* pp. 87-90 for his picturesque description of "sociology's triumphant struggle" against history.

6. For an excellent discussion of realpolitik that contrasts it with liberal political thinking, see Francis W. Coker, *Recent Political Thought* (New York: Appleton-Century-Croft, 1934), pp. 433-59. The interested reader is also referred to the politically motivated, but well-documented monograph by Westel W. Willoughby, *Prussian Political Philosophy* (New York: D. Appleton & Co., 1918).

Because of its emphasis upon the struggle for dominance over a territory, this manner of political thinking has been said by some to have been significantly
influenced by Darwin's work. But for purposes of explaining the rise of realpolitik in general, much less
the German sociologies of conflict, giving to Darwin
such an important role may be misleading. After all,
the three most notable proponents of realpolitik, Hegel,
Ranke, and Treitschke, were lecturing on the subject
long before the publication of Darwin's *Origin of the
Species*. This is not to say that Darwinist thought held
absolutely no sway over the minds of Gumplowicz, Ratzenhofer, and Oppenheimer. But the fact of the matter
is simply that realpolitik found written expression
prior to and independently from Darwin's writings. Indeed, according to some historians, realpolitik was not
even synthesized with Darwinism until about 1865,
and then in the work of American aristocrats in an attempt to justify slavery. The second noteworthy effort
to interpret human history in biological terms was carried out not by a German, but by the Englishman
Bagehot in 1870. But as realpolitik was quite well developed by this time, this suggests that Darwin may
have been used more as a source of evidence, rather
than as a completely unique background theorist by
the Germans.[7]

According to Friedrich Meinecke,[8] a student of
Treitschke, a close friend of Max Weber, and himself
one of the last great German political realists, the
father of modern German realpolitik was none other

---

7. For views on this subject similar to these, see Robert C. Binkley, *Realism
and Nationalism: 1852-1871* (New York: Harper & Bros. Pub., 1935).

8. Friedrich Meinecke, *Machiavellism,* trans. by Douglas Scott (New York:
Frederick A. Praeger, 1965). For other authoritative accounts of this intellectual movement see, Hans Kohn, *The Mind of Germany: The Education of
a Nation* (New York: Harper & Row, 1960); Iggers, *The German Conception
of History.*

than the sixteenth-century Italian philosopher, Nicolai Machiavelli. It was Machiavelli, says Meinecke, and not Darwin, who inspired three generations of German scholars to reduce the passion and idealism of politics to the earthy level of the uses and abuses of power.

Machiavellianism was discovered by German intellectuals in the course of their negative reaction to classical Enlightenment liberalism, which they held to be responsible for the destructive anarchy of the French Revolution and thus the "stabilizing" period under Napoleon. In their search for something peculiarly German to admire, an idea or an institution that would set the German folk apart from the vulgar democratization and bourgeoisie totalitarianism of the West, they turned to Prussia. Without question, here was a state that, with its novel mixture of traditional-bureaucratic rule and its statesman-generals, was organized in a manner consistent with the true historical destiny of Germany. In the course of his escapades, Napoleon had taken it upon himself to "liberate" several German kingdoms from feudal aristocracy. It was Prussia in 1816 that in turn freed them from foreign occupation, an event that convinced even the most liberal of German patriots that Prussia was a worthy leader of the German Empire.

One of the foremost liberals-turned-admirer of the militaristic state of Prussia was Georg Wilhelm Friedrich Hegel. Called by Herbert Marcuse[9] the semi-official philosopher of Prussia for his implication in the *Philosophy of Right* that *it* is the fullest exemplification of the Idea of Right in history,[10] Hegel lauded its use of force as a means to insure both domestic tranquility

9. Herbert Marcuse, *Reason and Revolution: Hegel and the Rise of Social Theory* (London: Routledge, Kegan & Paul Ltd., 1968). The following characterization of Hegel is indebted to both Meinecke and Marcuse.

10. Georg Wilhelm Friedrich Hegel, Hegel's *Philosophy of Right,* trans. and ed. by T. M. Knox (New York: Oxford University Press, 1952).

and international peace. In fact, he came ultimately to believe that only through force was social order possible at all. Although he continued to light candles every July 14 to celebrate the French Revolution, Hegel always found it difficult to derive social unity and corporate action from a voluntary contract between Rousseau's rational individuals alone. The state, he argued, citing the case of revolutionary France, can neither be guaranteed nor explained by the contract among individuals, for out of the irreconcilable conflict of particular interests characteristic of civil society can come no unity.[11] Drawing upon his observations of Prussian domestic and foreign policy and agreeing with a position that was to be elaborated upon some fifty years later by the German sociologists of conflict, Hegel concluded that social order must come from without those subject to it. It must be "imposed upon the particulars, as it were, against their will."[12]

If social order and the state can not logically be derived from atomic individuals, then neither can the relations between states be judged in terms of individual morality. Justice between states is different than that between individuals, being an issue of power and thus ultimately resolvable in war.[13] Therefore, in defending

11. Says Hegel, "If the state is confused with civil society and its specific end is laid down as the security and protection of property and personal freedom, then the interest of the individuals as such becomes the ultimate end of their association, and it follows that membership of the state is something optional. But the state's relation to the individual is quite different from this. Since the state is mind objectified, it is only as one of its members that the individual himself has objectivity, genuine individuality, and an ethical life." Ibid., p. 156.
12. Georg Wilhelm Friedrich Hegel, "Report to the Debate of the 1817 Estates of Württemberg." *Schriften zur Politik und Rechtsphilosophie,* ed. by Georg Lasson (Leipzig: 1913), quoted in Marcuse, *Reason and Revolution,* p. 174.
13. According to Hegel, "It entirely depends on the circumstances, the combination of power . . . whether the interest and justice that are endangered

its own rights from the claims of others, it is perfectly legitimate, indeed it is a moral duty, for the state to use any tool that is practical. As Hegel said at one time: "There can be no question here of any choice of means. A situation in which poison and assassination have become customary weapons, is not compatible with soft countermeasures."[14]

Even if international disputes involve the possible employment of violence, war is not, according to Hegel, destructive of civilized values. In fact, again anticipating the position of the German sociologists, he felt that war is one of the best ways by which the moral well-being of nations can be preserved. If this is true, then

> war is not to be regarded as an absolute evil and as a purely external accident, which itself has some accidental cause. . . . [Rather] war has the higher significance that by its agency, . . . the ethical health of peoples is preserved in their indifference to the stabilization of finite institutions. Just as the blowing of the winds preserves the sea from the foulness which would be the result of a prolonged calm, so also corruption in nations would be the product of prolonged, let alone 'perpetual' peace. . . . [T]his fact appears in history in various forms, e.g. successful wars have checked domestic unrest and have consolidated the power of the state at home.[15]

On the basis of these considerations, then, there is some justification for designating Hegel as the founder of modern German realpolitik. However, it would be misleading not to temper this assessment by adding

should be defended with all the might of power; in that case, however, the other part would also be able to plead a right and justice on its side, for it also possesses that very opposed interest which is producing the collision and thus a right too. And the war . . . now has the task of deciding . . . which of the rights shall give way to the others." Georg Wilhelm Friedrich Hegel, "Freiheit und Schicksal," ed. by Heller, Reclams Bibliothek, Germany, quoted in Meinecke, *Machiavellism,* p. 357.

14. Quoted in Meinecke, *Machiavellism,* p. 358.

15. Hegel, *Philosophy of Right,* pp. 209-10.

that the concluding section of the *Philosophy of Right,* a book in which he presented several of his most Machiavellian proposals, is given over to a discussion of the Idea of Right becoming manifest in the World Spirit of Reason to which the rights of sovereign states are apparently to be made subordinate. Thus, while the state, he says, can not be made to answer to the moral expectations of private individuals, it is, it seems, to be held responsible to some sort of universal ethical system. And to this extent, it is as difficult to believe that Hegel would have condoned the use of any conceivable mechanism of violence in the name of the state's rights as it is for the liberal philosopher Kant to be thought of in these terms. Possibly for this reason, Hegelian philosophy found itself under attack from the fervidly nationalistic Prussian historians following his death, the University of Berlin becoming a focus of academic conflict between the philosophy and history professors in Germany.

Cultivated originally by only a few prophetic individuals, realipolitik, cleansed of its Hegelian idealism, became the common denominator of political thinking in Germany coincidently with the forcible unification of the German *Bund* under Prussian arms from 1815 to 1866. Many of the proponents of realpolitik were disillusioned one-time liberals who had come to believe like Hegel years before, that only Prussia had the sufficient might to give political reality to their ardent nationalistic dreams. For many of the university students and professors who participated in the pathetic failure of the 1848 "revolution" to consolidate Germany on the basis of liberal ideas, the outstanding success of the Prussian Army to achieve what they had not, could not be ignored. Through their espousals of realpolitik, in such organs as the *Preussiche Jahrbücher,* such newly confirmed believers as Droysen, Sybel, Baumgarten, Dahlmann, and Ranke all played active roles in attempting to legitimize Prussian power politics to the

Fatherland. The military state in turn expressed its debt to these men for their efforts by subsidizing various institutions as the world reknown *Monumenta Germaniae Historica* that helped make the Prussian universities a necessary place of study for aspiring young historians.

A classic example of the active participation of university scholars in the movement toward national unification is given in Leopold von Ranke. Although known among American historians primarily for his methodology of the document, Ranke became, during his editorship of the *Historisch-Politische Zeitschrift*, the official spokesman for realpolitik in Germany.[16]

Ranke, like Hegel before him, argued that the essential characteristic of the state is its capacity to maintain its own independence even when threatened.[17] But, while Hegel philosophized about the Idea of mind and state, Ranke generally avoided such metaphysical accounts and devoted himself instead to developing what he thought was an empirically based hypothesis concerning the actual origin of political relations. For this reason, a comparison of his work with that of the German sociologists of conflict has perhaps even more relevance for the stated purposes of this chapter than the previous review of Hegelian political theory.

In Ranke's view, while the meaning of the state is sovereign independence, no state in historical fact has ever come into existence of its own accord, independently of other states. Rather, as the example of his Germany showed, nations have always made their de-

16. The following account of Ranke is indebted to Theodore H. Von Laue, *Leopold Ranke: The Formative Years* (Princeton, New Jersey: Princeton University Press, 1950). Hereafter this volume is referred to as *Ranke*.

17. "Between state and power in themselves there is perhaps no difference for the idea of a state originates in the idea of a certain independence which cannot be maintained without the corresponding power." Leopold von Ranke, *Preussicher Geschichte*, 12 vols. (Munich: Historische Komission Beider Bayerischen Academie der Wissenschafter, 1847-1848), quoted in Meinecke, *Machiavellism,* p. 385.

mands for sovereignty within the context of other already existing states.[18] But, as the latter are attempting to preserve their own territorial claims, they can not, without denying their own nature, voluntarily cede to upstart nations their arguments for political independence. The legal right to statehood, then, has throughout history been forcibly seized from existing states against their wills.[19] The historical milieu out of which nation states have come into being, therefore, has not been abstract reason and debate, as liberal thinking would have it, but violence and war. "War is the father of all things," Ranke once said making reference to Heraclitus. "Out of the clash of opposing forces in the great hours of danger—fall, liberation, salvation—the decisive new developments are born."[20]

Using a different path than this sometime antagonist, the philosopher Hegel, the historiographer Ranke still arrived at exactly the same theoretical location. In concluding that war has not been a destructive occurrence in the past, but really a means to progress, Ranke, like Hegel, was putting forth a position

18. As he describes it: "Ever since powers have been established on earth, endeavoring to realize, to represent, and to promote those general ideas which involve the destiny of the human race, it would seem that no nation is any longer allowed to develop itself by the unrestrained exercise of its own innate strength and genius." Leopold von Ranke, *The History of the Serbian Revolution,* trans. by Mrs. Alexander Kerr (London: H. G. Bohn, 1835), quoted in Von Laue, *Ranke,* p. 85.

19. "Friedrich: The world, as we know, has been parcelled out. To be somebody you have to rise by your own efforts. You must achieve independence. Your rights will not be voluntarily ceded to you. You must fight for them. . . .

Carl: And from war, from victory, you now want to derive also the forms of internal political organization?

Friedrich: Not exactly, not directly, but their modifications. The position of the state depends upon the degree of independence it has attained. It is obliged therefore, to organize all its internal resources for the purpose of self-preservation. This is the supreme law of the state." Leopold von Ranke, "Political Dialogues," trans. by Theodore H. Von Laue, *Ranke,* p. 157.

20. Leopold von Ranke, *Sammtliche Werke* XXIV (Leipzig: Duncker & Humblot, 1875-1900), quoted in Von Laue, *Ranke,* p. 86.

that was soon to be developed in a much more detailed manner by Gumplowicz, Ratzenhofer, and Oppenheimer. "...[T]he central idea of the human race; ..." as he saw it, "[resides in the fact] that in the conflicts which occur between the opposing interests of states and nations, more and more potent forces are constantly arising which cause the universal element to be altered and adapted, and are repeatedly giving it a new character."[21]

In spite of the obvious fact of Ranke's positive appreciation of the import of international violence for social change, the father of German historical methodology was accustomed to color his otherwise realistic portrayals of politics with poetic references to divine forces. For him, war was not simply a bloody rite, a contest devoid of any transcendent meaning. On the contrary, "it is infinitely false to see in the wars of historical powers only the play of brutal force. No state ever existed without a spiritual meaning. In power itself lies a spiritual genius, with a life of its own...."[22] And to this extent, a thoroughgoing realpolitik, a Machiavellianism emptied of virtually all sentimentalism had to wait for the coming of his most famous student, Heinrich von Treitschke.

Treitschke, Weber, and the Sociologists of Conflict

Treitschke took Ranke's history chair at Berlin University in 1874. And there for twenty-two years as an

21. Leopold von Ranke, *History of the World,* quoted in Meinecke, *Machiavellism,* p. 384.
22. Leopold von Ranke, *Weltgeschichte,* 9 vols. (Leipzig: Duncker & Humblot, 1881-1888), quoted in Von Laue, *Ranke,* p. 86. It follows that since the state essentially is power, it can be described in these terms: "Instead of the passing conglomerations which the contractual theory of the state creates like cloud formations, I perceive spiritual substances, original creations of the human mind—I might say, thoughts of God." Ranke, "Political Dialogues," Von Laue, *Ranke,* p. 169.

unabashed propagandist for pan-Germanism and anti-Semitism, he excited a complete generation of budding civil servants and military officers with lectures that were later published under the ironically modest title *Politics*.[23] These lectures have been taken by authorities to represent the high point of German realpolitik.[24] Where lesser sorts, such as Hegel and Ranke, would hedge on a particular point, Treitschke would bar no holds. Thus, for example, while Ranke customarily used the word "perhaps" to mitigate his evaluation of the state's relationship to power, Treitschke on the podium was adamant: "In the first place, the second place, and in the third place," he would preach to the thunderous applause of his classroom audience, "the essence of the state is power."[25]

But more important for present purposes is the fact that in Treitschke's notes on "The Rise and Fall of States" is found a much more explicit outline than Ranke's concerning the historical origin of the state out of war. And significantly enough, this hypothesis demonstrates a striking similarity to the sociologies of the origin of the state as developed by Gumplowicz, Ratzenhofer, and Oppenheimer.

23. Heinrich von Treitschke, *Politics,* trans. by Blanche Dugdale and Torben de Bille, ed. and abridged with an intro. by Hans Kohn (New York: Harcourt, Brace & World, Inc., 1963).

24. For example, see Hans Kohn, *Prophets and Peoples: Studies in Nineteenth-Century Nationalism* (New York: Macmillan Co., 1947), pp. 105-30.

25. Heinrich von Treitschke, *Bundestaat und Einheitstaat, Historische Politische Aüfsatze* (Leipzig: S. Hirzel, 1886-1897) quoted in Meinecke, *Machiavellism,* p. 399. Or consider such typical claims as the following: "The state is power precisely in order to assert itself as against other equally independent powers." Treitschke, *Politics,* p. 12.

"The state is public force for Offense and Defense. It is above all power which makes its will to prevail. . . ." Ibid., p. 14.

"The state is not an Academy of arts. If it neglects its strengths in order to promote the idealistic aspirations of man, it repudiates its own nature and perishes." Ibid., p. 15.

There is no evidence to support the proposition that the three sociologists of conflict borrowed their theories directly from the Prussian historians. As was intimated earlier, the available information suggests that the professional relationship between these two groups of scholars was far from amicable. Yet both Gumplowicz's and Oppenheimer's intellectual careers took place in universities such as Krakow, Vienna, Berlin, and Frankfurt, whose social science faculties were dominated by historians of realpolitik persuasion, places where liberal thinking was sanctioned by few appointments and fewer still promotions. To this extent then, it would have been difficult for them not to have come into direct contact with Machiavellianism.

It is not surprising that realpolitik had great appeal to the sociologists of conflict. Take Gumplowicz for example. His espousal of the doctrine of might before right can be interpreted in essentially the same terms as were just applied to Hegel and Ranke. For here apparently is still another story of intellectual disillusionment with sentimental notions of politics in the face of their more sobering realities.

Gumplowicz (1838-1909) was born to a porcelain dealer sometime authority on Jewish scripture and the daughter of a wealthy merchant family in Polish Galicia.[26] Like so many of his generation he too was caught up in the storm of national liberation that was then threatening to rip the Habsburg Empire into a plurality of petty states. Fully committing himself to the cause of Polish nationalism, Gumplowicz used his spacious house in Krakow to shelter his fellow insurgents and his legal expertise as a defense attorney to shorten their jail sentences. He earned quite a reputation both through his scathing pamphlets on the in-

26. Bernhard Zebrowski, *Ludwig Gumplowicz: Eine Bio-Bibliographie* (Berlin: Prager, 1926).

ternal contradictions within the Austro-Hungarian
Empire and his editorship of the official organ for the
dissemination of Polish culture and propaganda, *Kraj*
(The Land).

Yet unfortunately, in spite of the efforts of Gumplowicz and his co-conspirators, the Polish liberation
movement failed miserably. It was brutally suppressed
by Prussia in 1863 and overcome by a systematic policy
of Russification in the Ukraine. *Kraj* fought a hopeless
battle for its existence and went bankrupt in 1874. And
with it died Gumplowicz's dream of an independent
Polish republic with its own national language. It was
in the depths of depression that he wrote of the abor-
tive revolt in the following terms:

> Democratic frankness has not asked afterwards how
> strong the adversary was. There is only the opinion of this
> particular outlawed conscience and his particular view of
> the truth. The half unconscious neophyte's enthusiasm
> expects to subdue and to crush through its sincerity,
> through the foregone conclusion of its assumptions about
> the indifference of the masses, their blindness and un-
> reasonableness. It continues only as overflowing feeling in
> prose and poetry. The valiant, burning year, the year of
> fresh and vigorous thinking and impulse, of the effective
> pathos and of the exciting rhetoric; it is gone and nothing
> is left but a frustrated hull, a broken pen, and an inkwell
> filled with bad temper.[27]

As a result of his experiences, Gumplowicz, who as a
young man had already entitled his first publication
*The Ultimate Will in its Historical and Scientific De-
velopment,* became thoroughly disenchanted with liberal idealism and with Romantic characterizations of
the Polish *Volkgeist.* Instead he began reading the
French and English positivists and materialists St.
Simon, Comte, and Bagehot, and within a short time
discovered the truth contained in the unrelenting polit-

27. Ibid., p. 10.

ical realism of the Prussian historians. And it was directly out of his study of their doctrines that his *Rassenkampftheorie,* the original sociology of conflict, evolved. Ironically, he first presented his portrait of history as a never-ending struggle for power in *Race und Staat,* his inaugural address at Graz University in 1876, the same day on which he renounced forever his political ambitions.

Consider now the case of Oppenheimer (1864-1943), the son of a Jewish Rabbi. Being a member of a religion that throughout Germany and the Slavic East was considered a pariah caste, he was well aware of the resistance he would face if he attempted to become a university professor. Thus like Gumplowicz's brother Maksymilian, he embarked on one of the few careers then available to those of his heritage, medicine. It was only after more than a decade of work as a physician that he finally convinced himself that come what may, his true calling lay in the scholarly life.[28] Oppenheimer returned to graduate school at Kiel University. It was during the course of his reading in political economy that he came upon the political sociology of an obscure professor of jurisprudence at Graz University, Ludwig Gumplowicz. Gumplowicz's austere characterization of social life fascinated Oppenheimer and he began immediately to borrow its basic assumptions to provide the underpinnings for his own philosophy of history.[29]

28. Paul Honigsheim, "The Sociological Doctrines of Franz Oppenheimer: An Agrarian Philosophy of History and Social Reform," *Introduction to the History of Sociology,* ed. by Harry Elmer Barnes (Chicago: University of Chicago Press, 1965).
29. In his classic investigation of the development of the state, Oppenheimer claimed that "the pathfinder, to whom before all others, we are indebted for this line of investigation is Professor Ludwig Gumplowicz of Graz, jurist and sociologist, who crowned a brave life by a brave self-chosen death." Franz Oppenheimer, *The State: Its History and Development Viewed Sociologically,* trans. by John M. Gitterman (New York: Vanguard Press, 1926), p. 20.

This was no doubt in large part occasioned by Oppenheimer's intuitive capacity as a marginal man to see behind the formalistic official facades of law and government to the brutal goings-on underlying and giving rise to them. The owner of impressive educational credentials on the one hand, yet subject like Gumplowicz and Simmel to arbitrary discrimination, he apparently found it easy to identify with Europe's underclasses. Observing the violent historical relation that created the state from beneath as a Jew, it was impossible for him to be misled either by the contract notion of the state's origin or by "the 'nursery tale,' as Marx scornfully called the 'Law of Previous Accumulation.' "[30] He saw in the landed estates of East Germany not a monopoly that had been achieved, as liberalism would have it, through pacific economic competition, but a vestige of feudal privilege that had been forcibly seized from honest tillers of the soil many centuries before.

It should be added that regardless of his revulsion to the aristocracy, Oppenheimer was an outspoken nationalist. Often called a "staunch patriot" for his partisan activities in World War I, from 1914 to 1916 he served with the government as a professional consultant on economic warfare, charged with insuring food supplies and arranging the requisitioning of workers. He was also appointed to head the *Komitee für d. Osten,* which conducted relief activities among East German Jews who had been rendered homeless and uprooted as a result of the war. Following Germany's defeat he enthusiastically joined with those who refused to succumb to the wave of romantic despondency that swept over the population, and helped to form the ill-fated Weimer Republic. He drew up what was later to

30. For an assessment of the importance of being a Jew on sociological thinking, see Franz Oppenheimer, "Tendencies in Recent German Sociology," *The Sociological Review* XXIV (Oct., 1932): 253.

be dubbed the Hindenburg Decree, which provided for the redistribution of land to war veterans. And had it not been sabotaged by jealous opponents, Oppenheimer's lifelong dream for the internal colonization of uncultivated land by propertyless urban dwellers would have become law.

Ratzenhofer's intellectual biography (1842-1904) is similar in significant respects to that of Oppenheimer, for he too did not begin writing sociology until late in his life. And again, Gumplowicz played such a major role in the development of his perspective that most reviewers deem it sufficient in elaborating upon the sociology of the origin of the state out of conflict to describe only the hypotheses of one of the two Austrians.[31] Gumplowicz in turn believed Ratzenhofer to be among the greatest of all social theorists.[32] And he was deeply grieved upon hearing of the unexpected death of his compatriot.[33]

31. For example, see Howard Becker and Leon Smelo, "Conflict Theories of the Origin of the State," *The Sociological Review* XXIII (July, 1931): 65-79.
32. In one of his letters to Lester F. Ward, Gumplowicz said that while he regarded the work of both Schäffle and Lilienfeld as "a small piece of nothing *(Bagatelle)*, Ratzenhofer is far above me. I once had a theory of polygynous herds, eternal fight or war, organization of the state, social fights . . . all in new forms; the whole thing as a necessary process of nature. That is all with me, but Ratzenhofer is a deep philosopher. He spins from his thinking a new systematization of the world, and surrounds all areas of life by explaining all from one principle. . . . He is a **genius**. . . . Ratzenhofer's work is one of the immense **philosophical systems** in existence, much greater than Spencer." Ludwig Gumplowicz, "The Letters of Ludwig Gumplowicz to Lester F. Ward," ed. by Bernhard J. Stern, *Sociologus: Zeitschrift für Volkerpsychologie und Soziologie* (Leipzig: C. L. Hirschfeld Verlag, 1933), August 7, 1902, pp. 10-11.
33. Again, Gumplowicz's letters to his American colleague Ward provide a revealing insight into his relationship with Ratzenhofer: "Your letter of November 8th (the day our unforgettable Ratzenhofer died) has arrived. What you wrote me about the unfortunate Ratzenhofer interested me very much. I was anxiously waiting for his return (he had written to me concerning his impressions of America) [Ratzenhofer had gone to America to present a paper at the 1904 St. Louis Exposition. He died on passage back

There is little question as to why the realpolitik of Gumplowicz made so much sense to Ratzenhofer. The latter was a professional soldier cut in the classic German mold. He was a chivalrous man, in other words, with great courage under fire, who experienced astounding successes in his chosen vocation within a short period of time. As a cadet, Ratzenhofer engaged in the traditional duels over his women and honor, and it was the grievous wounds he received in one of these encounters that eventually led to his death on passage back from the St. Louis Exposition in 1904. He saw action in several military campaigns. Here he distinguished himself, was promoted to Lieutenant, and as a result received an appointment to an Austrian military academy. By the age of thirty he held a position on the General Staff and was put in charge of the Austrian Army Archives. It was then that he began to cultivate an intellectual interest in military strategy. This narrow focus of study expanded to include the political sources of legal rights after he was promoted to Lieutenant Field Marshal and appointed to the presidency of the Supreme Military Court in Vienna.[34]

Like his cohorts, Gumplowicz and Oppenheimer, Ratzenhofer was a nationalist. As we shall see later, he believed the state to be both the ultimate telos of history and the primary means by which morality and culture among human beings is made possible.[35] Indeed, he left his home to join the army at the age of sixteen not only for adventure and his revulsion to the uninspiring life

---

to Europe] and now he is returning as a corpse. I cannot tell you how hard this loss is to take. I had in him a true friend and comrade in arms. What he could have done for our science yet. He would have brought all of these problems into a system. He is an irreplaceable loss." Ibid., Nov. 11, 1904, p. 16.

34. Robert Schmid, "Gustav Ratzenhofer: Sociological Positivism and the Theory of Social Interests," *Introduction to the History of Sociology.*

35. Gumplowicz, *Outlines*, p. 265. See also pp. 252-53.

style of his father, a petit bourgeois watchmaker, but more importantly because of his patriotism.

Now it was precisely in the midst of his military career that the object of Ratzenhofer's fervor, the Austrian Empire, began disintegrating. Beginning with Italian Sardinia expelling Austria from Lombardy, the dismemberment of the Empire continued in 1866 when by force of arms Prussia both excluded the Habsburgs from the newly founded German *Kleindeutsch*, and then liberated Italian Venetia from Austrian rule. Finally, the dissident Magyars seized political sovereignty from Austria in 1867 as Hungary, splitting the original Empire into two nation states linked only by a common foreign policy. One of the major causes of the Habsburg's demise was rampant nationalism. It seems that Austro-Hungary had the unfortunate fate of containing within its borders, a large number of diverse ethnic groups, Germans, Poles, Serbs, Croatians, Slavs, and Jews, each one of which began demanding its political independence after 1850. The national liberation movements might easily have been crushed by the superior military force of the Austrians had not the Habsburgs embarked on what in retrospect was a rather foolish policy of constitutionally promoting the teaching of all the disparate national languages within its schools. While on a short-term basis this had the desired effect of pacifying the insurgents, in the long run it spelled disaster for Austro-Hungary. As Gumplowicz bitterly relates in the following statement, it was the frightful consequence of the Habsburgs putting national rights ahead of their long-range power interests that turned many Austrians, Ratzenhofer included, from advocates of liberalism to apologists for realpolitik:

It is possible that this witches' Sabbath of "national rights," which raged in Austria the same decade that Germany got a taste of the "might before right" theory of the Iron Chancellor, has a share in the Austrians' some-what different standpoint on the question of might and right. The German reacts perhaps unconsciously against the all too powerful imposition of might. The Austrian, because legality has been so emphasized, may have be-come a little anxious for the national might.[36]

In light of these facts, then, it is no mystery why the writings of those who today are known as the sociologists of conflict are imbued with realpolitik; why, in other words, with some reservations, they would agree with Treitschke that "without war no state could be. All those we know of arose through war, and the protection of their members by armed force remains their primary and essential task. War, there-fore, will endure to the end of history, as long as there is a multiplicity of states."[37] Ratzenhofer, for example, in a review of one of Gumplowicz's books, once had oc-casion to derogatorily comment on Kant's proposal for "perpetual peace" in the following terms:

The idea of perpetual peace is a relic of a class of ideas which supposes the state to have arisen through Rousseau's social contract. . . . It is true that the human race may sometime approach the ideal condition of peace. . .but we are still far removed from this stage, and the peace idea propagated by women of both sexes [sic] is fallacious of and injurious to its advocates.[38]

According to Treitschke, all modern states without exception can trace their origins back to intertribal conflict. A plurality of tribes, he begins, each charac-terized by a type of domination and therefore a "petty

36. Ibid., p. 297. See also pp. 235-37.
37. Treitschke, *Politics*, p. 38.
38. Quoted in Ludwig Gumplowicz, *"Soziologie: Positive Lehre von den Wechselbeziehungen* by Gustav Ratzenhofer," review of *Soziologie: Positive Lehre von den Wechselbeziehungen,* by Gustav Ratzenhofer, in *AJS* XIV (July, 1908): 107.

state" in its own right, engage in war. With their superior discipline and unity, certain tribes discover their capacity to conquer and subject to their rule tribes of a more pacific and "womanly" nature.[39] The successful domination of one tribe by another initiates a process whereby small states evolve into larger unities: a process ending, says the Prussian historian, only when the state loses its vigor and is either itself conquered or a delicate balance between its own power and that of neighboring states is reached.[40]

With some additions in detail Gumplowicz and Ratzenhofer generally concur with Treitschke. For instance, Gumplowicz begins his account of the state by focusing on the groups from which it derives, which he calls "races."[41] Each race has an interest in its own biological survival and this transposes into an animosity toward strangers when there arises competition for scarce economic resources. This signals the beginning of war between them.

Instead of races, Ratzenhofer's basic unit of research is the individual, whom, he maintains in a like manner, necessarily has a stake in his own survival at the

39. According to Treitschke: "Political history dawns on a world of petty states. The next step brings us to intertribal conflicts and a combination of larger masses into a common organization. Spoilation and conquest actuated the formation of larger states, which did not arise from the sovereignty of the people, but rather were created against their will. The state being the self-authorized power of the strongest tribe." Treitschke, *Politics*, p. 59.

40. Says the German realist: "States are more often founded by the sword. We observe an unceasing tendency in modern history toward the building of a great national power from a small center, which begins with the mere lust of power and by degrees grows in consciousness, until it draws the strength which unites it from the recognition of its common nationality." Ibid., p. 60.

41. Gumplowicz claims that: "If then, race characteristics are constant and the number of human races or varieties is still undetermined, it follows that when man's existence on earth began and before races had mingled and 'penetrated' there were countless distinct (*heterogen*) human swarms, several representing the various race characteristics which have persisted unchanged in penetration." Gumplowicz, *Outlines,* p. 177.

expense of his fellows. Such a circumstance would compel him to absolutely hate all others with whom he is in contact were it not for the tempering instinct of love for his blood relatives.[42] As a result, the hatred is directed only to nonmembers of the clan, giving rise to a struggle for existence (*Kampf um das Dasein*) between blood relations:

> Although the human being like all other creatures of his kind wants to feed himself and propagate peacefully, the increased propagation and the tightness of food develops the individual interest for an absolute hostility (*absolute Feindseligkeit*) against all people. In so far as the human being is tied by blood propagation and work to a common interest, this hostility is silent. . . .[43]

According to both the Austrians, war in the most primitive case takes the form of the victor simply exterminating the vanquished and seizing the land upon which he lived. Under certain conditions that the authors do not make explicit, however, the conquering race realizes that it is for its own best economic interest to spare the less fortunate opponent and enslave him. Thus is created a political relationship between closed ethnic groups, a higher level of social relationship than that guaranteed exclusively by kinship:

> The meeting of differentiated people leads to flight or fight. The struggle has as its purpose either the killing of the opponent in order to take his food and place of living, or servitude. This servitude is a social compromise be-

---

42. To Ratzenhofer: "Social reciprocation is nothing but the expression of the instinct of preservation (*Brotneid*) and the love instinct (*Blutleibe*). All possible movements of social contact are modifications or developing forms of these natural instincts, which in themselves are conscious tendencies . . . or developing qualities of inborn interests." Gustav Ratzenhofer, *Die Sociologische Erkenntnis* (Leipzig: F.A. Brockhaus, 1898), p. 245. This volume will hereafter be referred to as *Erkenntnis*.
43. Ibid.

tween destruction and culture, and leads therefore to a higher level of the social process, in which the social structure is no longer founded upon blood relations but upon domination relations (*Herrschaftsverhaltus*).[44]

Oppenheimer's description of the evolution of political communities is similar in form to that of Treitschke and the other two sociologists of conflict. But unlike Ratzenhofer and Gumplowicz, he explicitly characterizes the preconditions necessary for warlike contacts between primitive peoples to give rise to states. Oppenheimer claims that neither the huntsman nor the grubber of the soil have the inclination nor the ability to engage in state-building. The peasant is too pacifistic, while the huntsman does not have an economy that is easily adapted to include forced labor.[45] On the other hand, the mounted nomads of the prairies with their superior horsemanship, development of military tactics, and ethic of discipline have a unique capacity

---

44. Ibid., p. 246. In Gumplowicz's words: "Thus nature laid the foundation of ethnically composed states in human necessities and sentiments. Human labor being necessary, sympathy with kindred and tribe and deadly hatred of strangers led to foreign wars. So conquest and the satisfaction of needs through the labor of the conquered, essentially the same though differing in form, is the great theme of human history from prehistoric times to the latest plan for a Congo state." Gumplowicz, *Outlines*, p. 203. See also pp. 199-202.

45. Oppenheimer claims that "the huntsman carries on wars and takes captives. But he does not make them slaves; either he kills them or else adopts them into the tribe. Slaves would be no use to him. The booty of the chase can be stowed away even less then grain can be 'capitalized.' " Oppenheimer, *The State*, p. 37. On the other hand, the author asks for the peasant "what purpose, . . . would a looting expedition effect in a country, which throughout its extent is occupied only by grubbing peasants?" Ibid., pp. 30-31. Such raids would simply entail a loss in labor efficiency and any surplus of food that is seized would spoil (Ibid., pp. 31-32). For a description of the comparative histories of Japan and Europe in terms of conquest and assimilation, see Franz Oppenheimer, "Japan and Western Europe," *The American Journal of Economics and Sociology* III (1943-44): 539-551, IV (1944/45): 53-56, 239-44.

to conquer extensive territory. Furthermore, they have an economic need to capitalize on subjugation. With the small size of his family plus the inefficiency of grazing fields making the further expansion of cattle herds both unwieldy and biologically difficult, the nomad, unlike the huntsman, discovers that if he spares the defeated horticulturalist, he can use him as a shepherd in his pasture or as a farmer to cultivate feed grain.[46]

Of course this realization does not come at once. The first form of interaction between herdsman and peasant "comprises robbery and killings in border fights, endless combats broken neither by peace nor by armistice. It is marked by killings of men, carrying away of children and women, looting of herds and burning of dwellings."[47] However, inevitably there develops a stage in which

the peasant, through thousands of unsuccessful attempts at revolt, has accepted his fate and ceased every resistance. About this time, it begins to dawn on the consciousness of the wild herdsman that a murdered peasant can no longer plow and that a fruit tree hacked down will no longer bear. In his own interest, then, wherever it is possible, he lets the peasant live and the tree stand. The expedition of the herdsman comes just as before, every member bristling with arms, but no longer intending nor expecting war and violent appropriation. The raiders burn and kill only so far as is necessary to enforce a local respect, or break an isolated resistance.[48]

With the introduction of slaves into the economy of the herdsman, the essential condition of statehood,

46. Oppenheimer adds that in order to prevent overgrazing, thefts of whole herds at once, and/or the spreading of plagues among the animals, the rational herdsman will want to divide his cattle over a large territory. But such division necessitates the addition of more shepherds. Ibid., pp. 38-39.
47. Ibid., p. 56. See also pp. 57-64.
48. Ibid., p. 64.

domination, is reached.[49] This political relationship becomes further concretized as the conquerors come to live permanently on the same land as their subjects to "protect" them from other roaming bands of herdsmen, and begin to arbitrate the disputes of the peasants that otherwise would impair their capacity for work.[50]

With adequate nourishment of milk and meat now guaranteed by larger herd sizes, the population of the ruling class grows, necessitating the enslavement of tillers of the soil in still more far-reaching areas. Thus the state expands by conquest, claims Oppenheimer in agreement with Treitschke, into an empire.[51]

Oppenheimer did not deal in any depth with the variables that determine a successful policy of imperialism. However, Gumplowicz and Ratzenhofer together did develop a fairly sophisticated theory of violent expansion. In particular, they both believed that there are essentially two conditions affecting the evolution of states through war: (1) A state will continue to distend its borders to the extent that neighboring states are weaker and can be overrun,[52] (2) but only if the rulers of that state are secure in their positions.[53]

---

49. Compare the following characterization with Treitschke's hypothesis. "The state, completely in its genesis, essentially and almost completely during the first stages of its existence, is a social institution forced by a victorious group of men on a defeated group, with the sole purpose of regulating the dominion of the victorious group over the vanquished, and securing itself against revolt from within and the attacks from abroad." Ibid., p. 15.

50. Ibid., pp. 77-78.

51. In the words of Oppenheimer: ". . .[M]en must soon realize the fact that rental increases with the number of slaves one can settle on the unoccupied lands. Henceforth, the external policy of the feudal state is no longer directed toward the acquisition of land and peasants, but rather of peasants without land, to be carried off home as serfs, and there to be colonized anew." Ibid., p. 178. "The more slaves a noble has, the more rental he can obtain. With this, in turn, he can maintain a warlike following, composed of servants, of lazy freemen, and of refugees. With their help, he can, in turn, drive in so many more slaves to increase his rentals." Ibid., p. 179.

52. Gumplowicz, *Outlines,* p. 232.

53. Ibid., pp. 232-33.

If the conformity of the subjects cannot be counted upon; if, for example, as in Gumplowicz's and Ratzenhofer's Austria, disparate national patriotisms conflict with loyalty to the state, then the central authority cannot successfully embark on a path of foreign conquest. "It is a simple outcome of this law," Gumplowicz tells his readers, "that statesmen have always regarded internal divisions in neighboring states as security against attack upon their own."[54] Furthermore, again suggesting the case of nineteenth-century Austria, it also follows that a state experiencing domestic unrest contains the seeds for its own eventual destruction, not so much because this is necessarily a harbinger of internal revolution, but rather because its resistance to foreign invasion is thereby lowered. "The fall of many a powerful civilized state under the assault of rather small barbarian hordes could not be comprehended," Gumplowicz maintains, "if it were not known that domestic social enemies of the existing order let the secretly glimmering hatred of the propertied and ruling classes burn into flame at the moment of danger."[55]

In consideration of the points brought out in the last paragraphs, those familiar with Max Weber's lectures on imperialism will note their obvious similarity to the views of both Treitschke and the sociologists of conflict. This is certainly understandable in light of the fact that from the time he was a youngster, Weber (1864-1920) had enjoyed a rare opportunity to learn the meaning and significance of German realpolitik first hand from the mouths of its foremost disseminators.[56] Treitschke, Sybel, Dahlmann, and Baumgarten were all at one time or another house guests of his father,

54. Ibid., p. 233.
55. Ibid., pp. 305-6.
56. For example consult: Max Weber, *From Max Weber: Essays in Sociology,* trans., ed. and intro. by Hans H. Gerth and C. Wright Mills (New York:

himself an important political figure in the National Liberal Party. Weber read Machiavelli's *Principe* at thirteen, listened to and recoiled from Treitschke's preachments at Berlin University, and studied under the Nobel prize historian and political realist Theodor Mommsen.[57]

Weber experienced the customary trials and successes of his age group and social class. At Heidelberg he enthusiastically joined a student dueling and drinking corps, received the appropriate scars, and later became a proud if not completely convincing reserve officer in the German Army. Weber conformed to the general tenor of the day by becoming a frank German nationalist. In one of his first pieces of research, a survey of agrarian conditions in East Prussia, he wrote of the German peasantry as representing a "high culture" and the Slavs as a race that cannot understand the true meaning of freedom, those "swarms of nomads from the East," as he called them. Repeatedly in his

Oxford University Press, 1958). Henceforth this volume will be referred to as *Essays*; Paul Honigsheim, *On Max Weber,* trans. by Joan Rytina (New York: Free Press, 1968; Michigan State University, East Lansing, Michigan: Social Science Research Bureau, 1968; J.P. Mayer, *Max Weber and German Politics* (London: Faber and Faber, 1956).

57. For interesting comments on Mommsen's tutelage of his star pupil the young Weber, see Carlo Antoni, *From History to Sociology: The Transition in German Historical Thinking.* Mommsen is famous for his *History of Rome,* which is essentially a military and political history. He traces the party struggles between the oligarchs and populares, the resulting reform movements, revolutions, civil wars, and their influence on law. The notion that the Roman Empire was founded on force is made explicit. Reinhard Bendix, *Max Weber: An Intellectual Portrait,* (Garden City, New York: Doubleday & Co. Inc., 1962) has attempted to point out Weber's theoretical indebtedness to Mommsen. Henceforth this volume is referred to as *Intellectual Portrait.* Says Bendix; "But whereas Mommsen did not hesitate to use the language of nineteenth-century party struggles for his interpretation of Roman history, Weber gradually developed the same perspective into an image of society and a set of sociological categories, which he used in his world-wide comparative studies of religion and political organization." Bendix, *Intellectual Portrait,* p. 9.

articles and speeches, notwithstanding his injunctions to others to refrain from value judgements, he admitted that first, last, and always it is the "power value" of Germany relative to other nation states that was his standard for evaluating the wisdom of policy decisions. Thus in the East Prussian case, he advocated that the borders be shut to Slavic migration and that unused *Junker* land be redistributed to German peasants to induce them from fleeing to the cities for employment. Only in this way, he said, can the Eastern marches be defended against the Russians and German culture be maintained.[58] Weber has often been applauded for his wartime speeches that cautioned against the forcible annexation of any foreign territory. But as J.P. Mayer has pointed out, in these same pronouncements he did support the military occupation of Luxemburg, Poland, Belgium, and the Baltic countries for strategic purposes.[59] After all, as he persuasively told his audience in his 1895 inaugural lecture at Freiburg University:

> We have not to bequeathe to our descendents peace and human happiness, but the eternal struggle for the preservation and up-breeding (*Emporzuchtung*) of our national character. ...[T]he power political interests of the nation are, when they are involved, the final and decisive interests in the service of which its economic policy has to be placed. ...[T]he national state is for us the secular power organization of the nation and the "reason of state" of this nation state is for us the ultimate value and yardstick also in questions of economic policy.[60]

58. See Mayer, *Max Weber and German Politics,* pp. 40-44.
59. Mayer says that "it is open to doubt whether Weber's war aims were *de facto* much different as compared with the war aims of the *Alldeutsche.*" Ibid., p. 75.
60. Max Weber, Inaugural Lecture, Freiburg University, reprinted in *Gesammelte Politische Schriften* (München: 1921), quoted in Hans Kohn, *The Mind of Germany: The Education of a Nation,* p. 282. Compare this translation with that of Gerth and Mills in Weber, *Essays,* p. 35.

Consistent with the teachings of realpolitik, Weber refused to cloak the state in any but the robes of power. The state, he maintained throughout his career, is simply a closed corporation that monopolizes violence over a territory. Accordingly then, the state has evolved out of a struggle between groups for control of violence. Political history, he claimed, dawns upon a plurality of kinship groups overseen, perhaps temporarily, by elders.[61] In time the younger more "warlike members of a group on their own initiative consociate through personal fraternization to organize marauding raids."[62] Cultivating an ethic of military prowess and discipline and living off the booty of successful raids, such warrior communities are able to effectively command the obedience of those living in the territory over which they lay claim.[63] And to this extent a rudimentary form of the state is established.

On the plains, Weber adds, here reminding one of Oppenheimer, the mobility of the nomad warrior on horseback enables him to "pacify" large areas.[64] And almost universally "the land of foreign territories has been politically incorporated in more or less violent fashion" by the mounted Bedouin.[65] It was thus that

61. Max Weber, *Economy and Society*, ed., intro., trans. by Guenther Roth & Claus Wittich, 3 vols. (New York: Bedminster Press, 1968), II. 901-5.

62. Ibid., p. 905.

63. Weber claims that, "Through the cultivation of military prowess and war as a vocation such a structure is able to lay effective and comprehensive claims to obedience. These claims will be directed against the inhabitants of conquered territories as well as against the military unfit members of the territorial community from which the warrior's fraternity has emerged. The bearer of arms acknowledges only those capable of bearing arms as political equals. . . ." Ibid., p. 906.

64. "The 'empire' of the Mongols, however, certainly did not rest on any extensive trade in goods. There, the mobility of the ruling stratum of horsemen made up for the lack of material means of communication and made centralized administration possible." Weber, *Essays*, pp. 163-64. Cf. *Economy and Society*, II, 914-15.

65. Weber, *Economy and Society*, II, 916.

the Persian, Chinese, Egyptian, Mesopotamian, and Mongolian empires grew from small bands of close-knit herdsmen led by charismatic leaders into states comprising vast distances. Again in concurrence with Oppenheimer, Weber argues that except in the rare cases where the peasant population was simply exterminated and its land seized, the native in conquered territories was given life in exchange for his obedience, and his labor capitalized upon, thus developing the opportunity for tremendous profit:

> As Franz Oppenheimer again and again has rightly emphasized, ground rent is frequently the product of violent political subjection. Given a subsistence economy and a feudal structure this subjection means, of course, that the peasantry of the incorporated area will not be wiped out but rather will be spared and made tributary to the conqueror, who becomes the landlord.[66]

Despite these enumerated similarities, the accounts of Weber and Oppenheimer are not identical. For example, Oppenheimer devotes significant space to what he calls the "maritime city-state." These too, like the empires of the plains, were established primarily through conquest, but this time by "sea nomads." Originally on the Baltic, Caspian, and Mediterranean Seas and later on ocean coasts, the Phonecians and Moors, the Normans, Dutch, and Portuguese forcibly seized harbors to serve as fortified ports to enable them to engage in further piracy, to collect protection payments from passing merchants, and to oversee and tax inland markets.[67] It was thus that Corinth, Carthage, Hong Kong, and Shanghai were established to increase the profitability of the economic exploitation of the native. It was in such places that the cultivation of extensive

66. Weber, *Essays*, pp. 165-66.
67. See Oppenheimer, *The State*, pp. 137-55 for a discussion of the evolution of city states.

trade relations by the rulers led to the invention of money, and the measurement of wealth not in terms of land, as in the plains states, but rather in terms of movable property.[68] This was a development that was to have important consequences for the future of both types of states and will be commented upon in the next chapter.[69]

Conclusion

To go further would belabor a point that by now should be obvious; namely, that when the sociologists of conflict theorized about politics, they spoke in a manner almost indistinguishable from Heinrich von Treitschke on the one hand and Max Weber on the other. Neither Weber nor Treitschke, contrary to a long tradition of liberal thinking on the subject, believed that war was a destructive historical event. And Gumplowicz, Ratzenhofer, and Oppenheimer agreed with them: There are no political formations that are not formations of violence. War not only extends peace over larger and larger territories as one group conquers and subjects the people of other groups, but it increases the shared interests between those facing a common enemy. It is the unity of the small nomad clan developing through a long history of constant war that gives it the capacity to defeat numerically larger foes. And once the state is founded, further war helps give rise to that psychological unity between

68. For the distinction between these two types of property, see Ibid., pp. 158-62.
69. The use of slave labor lowers the overhead of production for rich slave owners, permitting them to undersell their poorer competitors. In time wealth becomes concentrated in fewer hands and previously free men flee as paupers to the city, there as "jobless scavangers" to participate in the mob politics that sounds the death knell for the city state. Ibid., pp. 169-73.

master and subject called "nationalism." "We learn from history that nothing unites a nation more closely than war," Treitschke told his students at Berlin. "It makes it worthy of the name *Nation* as nothing else can."[70] Or as Max Weber said in his customarily more restrained manner: ". . .[I]n the great moments, in case of war, the significance of national power strikes their [the masses] soul—then they realize that the national state rests on genuine (*urwuechsigen*) psychological foundations. . . ."[71]

In saying this much, can we go still further? In other words, is it possible that the sociologists of conflict, like Treitschke, were legitimizers of German and Austrian imperialism and contributors to a state of mind congenial to the use of war to solve problems in foreign affairs? For Harry Elmer Barnes there was no doubt about this. He was moved to say about Gumplowicz that

He was the most eminent and productive sociologist who has written in the German tongue and his complicity in producing the military obsession of 1914 cannot be doubted. He was the most extreme advocate among sociologists of any standing, of the unqualified applicability of a misconstrued and perverted Darwinian biology to the support of political fatalism. . . . His representation of war as the sole agency in political development and the only reliable arbiter of the superiority of national *Kultur* was eagerly pounced upon by militarists . . . such as Moltke and Bernhardi in Germany . . . to furnish a plausible pseudo-scientific cloak for the advancement of their class and party interests. . . . Further, his frequent asser-

70. Treitschke, *Politics*, p. 59. Or again consider the following: "When we pursue this thought further, we see how war, with all its brutality and sterness, weaves a bond of love between man and man, linking them together to face death, and causing all class distinctions to disappear." Ibid., p. 245.
71. Weber, Inaugural Lecture, quoted in Mayer, *Max Weber and German Politics*, p. 42. In more subdued language, Oppenheimer essentially agrees with this when he claims that the peasant comes to look upon his one-time conquerors, the nomads, as saviors when the latter begin to protect them

tion that the state was above all consideration and obliga-
tions of morality . . . was a congenial doctrine expanded by
Nietzsche, Treitschke. . . .[72]

However, perhaps we should be more careful than
Barnes in assessing the relation between Treitschke
and the sociologists. In the first place, it must be recognized that after all, Treitschke was an explicit advocate of war, maintaining that as an ethical force, and
indeed as "the objectively revealed will of God,"[73] the
state has a moral obligation to uphold its power and to
extend it through conquest, a position in which it
would be unfair to put the sociologists. Gumplowicz,
Oppenheimer, Weber, and Ratzenhofer all cautioned
their readers not to surround the state and politics
with notions of morality and God on pain of confusing
truth with propaganda. On the other hand, even
though he predicted that a European war with America
on the side of France would be a disaster for Germany,
Weber was certainly not above advocating the use of
international violence if it were practical. If, in other
words, it would augment Germany's "power value"
vis-à-vis England, France, and Russia. Furthermore, at
least Gumplowicz took the position that war and imperialism, being derivatives of natural laws, are in-

from outside aggressors. "Here," he says, "is one of the principle forces of
that 'integration,' whereby in the further development, those originally not
of the same blood, and often enough of different groups speaking different
languages will in the end be welded together into one people, with one
speech, and one feeling of nationality." Oppenheimer, *The State*, p. 69. See
also p. 70.

72. Harry Elmer Barnes, "The Struggle of Races and Social Groups as a
Factor in the Development of Political and Social Institutions: An Exposition and Critique of the Sociological System of Ludwig Gumplowicz,"
Journal of Race Development IX (April, 1919): 415-16. This article is hereafter referred to as "The Struggle of Races."

73. Treitschke, *Politics*, p. 8. "The subjection of politics to the universally
prevailing moral law is recognized in practice," says Treitschke. Thus, "we
must admit the validity of the moral law in regard to the state." Ibid., p. 51.

evitable social phenomena.[74] Thus the reasonable man
who acts on the basis of necessity, will submit himself
to this truth and instead of futilely attempting to hit
his head against the stone wall of reality, will hero-
ically but passively accept the horror of it.[75] But in this
sense, Gumplowicz's ethics were certainly compatible
with those of Treitschke. For it was the latter's belief
that it is exactly when a man (or a state) is acting
most in obedience to the necessity of his own nature
that he is most fully exercising his capacity for freedom. In conclusion then, there is probably more truth
in Barnes' evaluation of the early sociologists' role in
producing a moral climate conducive to war than their
contemporary followers would care to admit.

But, we might ask, what is the chief moral demand made of this person,
the state? "When we apply this standard of deeper and truly Christian
ethics to the state, and remember that its very personality is power, we see
that its highest moral duty is to uphold that power." Ibid., p. 52. "The in-
junction to assert itself remains always absolute." Ibid.

74. War and imperialism are both consequences of natural laws; namely,
"solicitude for the means of subsistence (*Lebensfürsoge*) forces each social
aggregate to try to make every other social aggregate coming within its
reach serve that supreme end," and thus are both inevitable. Gumplowicz,
Outlines, p. 184.

75. According to the Austrian pessimist, "human action is reasonable when
[it] . . . correspond[s] to natural tendencies and complement[s] them; and un-
reasonable if it mistake[s] these tendencies and oppose[s] them." Ibid., p.
259. "Whatever is natural is moral. Therein lies the eternal, fixed and un-
changeable basis of all ethics and morals." Ibid. See also pp. 259-80.

3

The Sociologists of Conflict on Conflict within the State

Sociology and National Liberalism

Heinrich von Treitschke shared with Max Weber and the sociologists of conflict a Machiavellian concept of the state and a positive attitude toward international violence. But this is not to suggest that there were no important differences in the substantive content of the research carried out under the auspices of nineteenth-century German historiography and sociology. One divergence that stands out as particularly impressive is that in contrast to the sociologists, scholars like Ranke and Treitschke devoted much of their efforts to international affairs, describing, for example, the crucial decisions made by such outstanding individual statesmen as Charlemagne, Frederick the Great, Napoleon, and Bismarck. While the sociologists also wrote about war and imperialism, their attention was generally limited to the relationships between groups such as ethnic minorities, classes, and parties within the state. In addition to this, the historians' characteristic interest in

61

the uniquely prophetic qualities of individual political leaders was replaced altogether by Oppenheimer, Gumplowicz, and Ratzenhofer, with an uncompromising desire to reduce all individual action to its presumable group basis.[1]

Several persons have sought to describe how this shift in focus from the unusual individual to the ordinary group member was inspired by a larger intellectual movement led by reform-minded German economists and jurists of the late eighteen hundreds.[2] While it is clearly beyond the scope of our immediate interest to discuss this movement in any depth, it is absolutely essential for a full understanding of the German sociologies of conflict that it be briefly touched upon.

Domestic ferment posed grave dangers to the corporate existence of both Germany and Austria after 1860. In Austria it was the national liberation movements that threatened to destroy the Empire. In Germany it was socialism—the revolutionary new religion of the proletariat—that preoccupied the minds of middle-class liberals and landed oligarchs. As we have seen, the danger that radical nationalism comprised for the

1. In the following quotation Gumplowicz gives clear expression to the proposal that sociologists study group life. "On the altar of her method of study, sociology sacrifices man. He is the lord of creation, the author of historical events as historians think, he who as monarch or as minister guides according to his will the destiny of people . . . sinks away, in sociology, to a meaningless *cipher*. In complete contradiction to the portrays of the historians, even the statesman is for the point of view of the sociologists only a blind tool in the invisible but all-powerful hand of his social group, which itself in turn only follows an irresistable law of nature." Ludwig Gumplowicz, *Soziologie und Politik* (Leipzig: 1892), p. 54, quoted in Barnes, "The Struggle of Races," pp. 402-3, Contrast this statement with the position of Ranke in his "Political Dialogues," Von Laue, *Ranke,* p. 157.
2. The following account is indebted to Eugen von Philippovich, "The Infusion of Socio-Political Ideas into the Literature of German Politics," *AJS* XVIII (Sept., 1912): 145-99. Small, *Origins of Sociology,* pp. 132-314. Franz Oppenheimer, "Tendencies in Recent German Sociology," *The Sociological Review* XXIV (Jan., 1932): 1-13; (April-July, 1932): 125-37.

Habsburg Dynasty was not simply an illusion of Gump-lowiczian prophets of doom. It took only a few decades for the once awe-inspiring Austrian Empire to disintegrate into a number of independent states once the fever of nationalism had infected it. Now whereas the Austrian response to nationalism was to constitutionally guarantee the liberal idea of the equality of all national languages within its borders, Bismarck's reaction to the increasingly vocal demands of the Social Democratic Party was, beginning in 1878, to suppress its meetings, confiscate its presses, and imprison its leaders. And yet within a short fifteen years the S.D.P. was the second most powerful political party in Germany, as indicated by the number of seats it held in the *Reichstag*. Clearly Bismarck's answer to "*the* social question," as it was called, was no more correct than the Austrian government's solution to the "racial problem." Merely to repress discontent and then ignore it, was apparently no more effective than to appease it and then try to forget it.

It would not be farfetched to suggest that in a large measure the German and Austrian sociologies evolved out of attempts by individuals to address in a detached scientific way the very social conflicts that were threatening to tear their countries apart—social conflicts that, in their minds, were being ignored by aloof university professors like Treitschke. Thus, in part, it was his awareness of the danger that a militant labor movement presented to the future strength of Germany that motivated Oppenheimer to advocate the state expropriation of landed estates and their redistribution back to their "rightful owners," the peasantry.[3] And as

3. For two of his many works on this subject, see: Franz Oppenheimer, "Farm Communities in Eastern Prussia," *Proceedings of the Institute of Public Affairs: Bulletin of the University of Georgia* XXXVI (1936): 121-33; Franz Oppenheimer, "Principles of Farm Community Organization," *Proceedings of the Institute of Public Affairs: Bulletin of the University of Georgia* XXXVI (1936): 108-120.

was indicated earlier, Gumplowicz's interest in the democratic reforms of racial integration and compulsory language education arose out of his judgement that the Habsburg's domestic policy of promoting ethnic pluralism was foolishly nearsighted. Lastly, Ratzenhofer's applause of what he took to be the present political trend toward increasing control of individual selfishness, can be explained by his fear that rampant individualism would undermine the social order and with it nullify the only possibility for a civilized culture. "Individualism itself in the maturity of sociological wisdom," he warned his readers, "is now teaching us at the last hour to recognize the necessity of speedily contemplating the organization of society before the lower interests of the rising masses and their parasites shall swallow up those personalities who have saved the higher interests. . . ."[4]

In this same respect too, Weber, Gustav Schmoller, and Adolph Wagner, among the most noteworthy spokesmen for the *Verein für Sozialpolitik* (The Union for Social Policy, founded in 1873), modern history's best example of an effective lobby of reformist university professors, supported the institution of workman's insurance, unemployment compensation, and old age pension, primarily to mollify the strident demands of the proletariat for full citizenship.[5] But inspite of their

4. Quoted in Ludwig Gumplowicz, *"Soziologie: Positive Lehre von den Menschlichen Wechselbeziehungen* by Gustav Ratzenhofer," review of *Soziologie: Positive Lehre von den Menschlichen Wechselbeziehungen* by Gustav Ratzenhofer, *AJS* XIV (July, 1908): 104. This review contains a description of Ratzenhofer's social policy including attacks both on the Jews for their "atavistic cults" and "senseless prescriptive rites" and the nobility for their being "opponents of the state." Ibid., p. 109. In regard to such enemies of the people, he advocated a "sound policy of force." "The capacity for the energetic application of force to the moral basis of character which rules undaunted over life and death and shrinks from no act necessary to the common good," he argued, "is a fundamental demand of civilization." Ibid., p. 107.

5. For Weber's political position on domestic social issues, the reader is

advocacy of welfare programs and bitter denunciations of Prussian landlords, no more than the sociologists of conflict, can they be considered revolutionaries or even liberals in the strict sense. The *Verein für Sozialpolitik* was basically nationalistic in orientation, giving loud vocal defense to prewar German plans for foreign conquest. Its members opposed the reactionary social and economic policies of persons like Treitschke not because they intrinsically valued Western ideas of liberal democracy, but because they believed that aristocratic conservatism merely aggravated dissent and thus indirectly decreased the power of the German state.[6]

again referred to Honigsheim, *On Max Weber,* and Weber, *Essays,* pp. 32-44. Bendix, *Intellectual Portrait* contains selections from and analyses of Weber's position papers spelling out the *Junker* responsibility for the agricultural problems east of the Elbe River, which were presented to the *Verein für Sozialpolitik*. Ibid., pp. 13-47. These studies result in conclusions that are quite similar to those of Oppenheimer. Small, *Origins of Sociology,* pp. 234-94, has presented a detailed account of the *Verein für Sozialpolitik* including excerpts from its manifesto, a description of Schmoller's fellow "socialist of the chair," Adolph Wagner's opposition to the conservatism of the *Junker* Estate, and lastly, extensive translations from papers making up the Schmoller-Treitschke controversy. The latter, like Ranke and in fact most historians in Germany at this time, was a conservative in the classical sense.

6. Small's comments on the founding of the *Verein für Sozialpolitik* are particularly revealing in this regard: "The conception of the state as an organic unity was the point of departure in their formulation. In their conception it was the duty of the state, whether acting as government or as a voluntary society forming a common opinion, to act always with a view to realizing the unity of all the members of the state." Small, *Origins of Sociology,* p. 237. The author maintains that this doctrine was not new to Germany: "If there is one thing more certain than all else about German civilization, it is that the Germans always believe in the right and the duty of society, and particularly of society in the form of the state, to preside over the destiny of individuals. The Germans were, are, and are likely to remain collectivists. They do not believe that the best results for all concerned are to be gained under a regime in which each individual is the sole judge of what is good for himself and the world. . . . The Germans believed that the best results are obtained for all the members of a nation, when there is a machinery for ascertaining and forcing the collective will against each and every individual who may have an insubordinate will." Ibid., p. 238. See also pp. 239-40.

For this reason, then, we propose to classify Weber, the supporters of the *Verein für Sozialpolitik*, and the sociologists of conflict all as national liberals. By "national liberalism" I am referring not to the short-lived party of that name, but to a mind set that measures all proposed domestic reforms in terms of the degree to which they will increase social order, social control, and thus the state's "power value." Grouping Weber, Schmoller, and the sociologists of conflict under a single label is not to deny that their outlooks were not in some ways significantly different from one another. Oppenheimer, for example, was much more concerned with the welfare of the individual than the others. Weber was perhaps the most nationalistic and Schmoller the most conservative. Gumplowicz was more withdrawn from politics, and Ratzenhofer less pessimistic and more liberal. But to exclusively emphasize these dissimilarities overlooks the fact that they did after all share the same basic political perspective, of neither Treitschkean nationalism nor Marxist socialism, but a mixture of the two that I choose to call national liberalism.

Nineteenth-century German national liberalism found expression in the theorizing of all of the above mentioned social scientists in their cultivation of what for German literati was a relatively new object of research—society. "Society," as they came to understand it, was to refer neither to the classical economists' abstract individuals who mechanically behave only in such a way as to maximize their material profit, nor to the *Volkgeist*, which the conservative legalists Savigny and Eichorn imputed to explain the evolution of customs and rights. The national liberals felt, in the words of Eugon von Philippovich, that if Smithian economics "confines itself to the selfish endeavors of men in industry, so that it becomes a science of greed,"[7] and thus cannot resolve the social problem of the inequitable distribution of wealth, the existence of which it legitimizes; the romantic jurists cannot account for the fact that "the very social movement itself [i.e. the labor movement] showed that in the larger part of the *Volk* existing right was felt to be wrong."[8] Consequently, in what Oppenheimer has interpreted as a synthesis of the two approaches, liberal economics and conservative jurisprudence, the national liberals subordinated the egoistic individual to the moral expectations of the *Volk*, or better yet the group, and derived the "person," the conscious social actor imbued with intentions and a will. On the basis either of conflicting or shared purposes with others, such persons would, they argued, freely act respectively, either in conflict or concert with them in a process of interaction or "becoming," designated by the term "society."[9]

7. Philippovich, "The Infusion of Socio-Political Ideas into the Literature of German Politics," p. 173.
8. Ibid., pp. 160-61. It was, according to Philippovich logically impossible for jurors to confront this issue because of the peculiar meaning of the word designating the object of their study, *"Recht."* It implies both "right" or morality as well as "legality." Thus, it is impossible for the law to be inconsistent with the *Volk* because it is the moral expression of the *Volk*.
9. In the words of the reformist German sociologist: "Such was the situation from which the new science of sociology took its rise. The Enlightenment was the thesis, the intellectual counter-revolution [as it found expression in the work of e.g. Savigny] was the anti-thesis, and sociology is the attempt at a synthesis." Oppenheimer, "Tendencies in Recent German Sociology," p. 6. Gumplowicz's interpretation of his own method of approach to the study of history concurs with that of his German pupil, Oppenheimer: "All the differences and disputes in the domain of social science turn upon the antithesis between 'mankind' and the individual. There was no third standpoint, no middle way known to theorists. If we prefix to each the adjective 'social,' giving it the meaning not of the abstract whole but of the limited social circle, like the syngenetic group, we shall have found the middle way which social philosophy has here-to-fore missed." Gumplowicz, *Outlines*, p. 238. See also pp. 240-51.

With this synthesis established, the national liberals were justified in generalizing the notions of realpolitik from the persons and processes of interaction that had so far monopolized the attention of German scholarship (namely, states and their foreign affairs) to the society of lesser corporations or persons such as parties, classes, races, or even individual humans. "The same tendency which animates the state as a whole," it could now be submitted as it was by Gumplowicz, "animates each social division within it."[10]

Class and Class Conflict

In their theorizing, the term "class" plays a crucial role for the sociologists of conflict. Yet, unfortunately they use the term without ever explicitly characterizing what they mean by it. From the context of the statements in which the word is used, however, it is not difficult to see that the class position of a particular professional group, race, or occupation is equivalent to its ability to appropriate the surplus economic production of society; its ability, in other words, to seize a specific amount of the national wealth.[11] But to the extent that this in turn is indicative of the degree of power that a guild, a profession, or a race has relative to other groups, then classes, say the sociologists of conflict, have the same source as all domination rela

10. Gumplowicz, *Outlines*, p. 208.
11. "All classes whatever have the same goal; viz. the total result of the productive labor of all denizens of a given state," says Oppenheimer. Every class attempts to obtain as large a share as possible of the national production." Oppenheimer, *The State*, p. 261. According to Gumplowicz, "the motive of each [class within the state] is essentially the same as that which animates the state as a whole. . . . In particular, the superior class seeks to make the most productive use of the subject classes. As a rule this leads to oppression and can always be considered exploitation. The subject classes drive for greater powers of resistance to lessen their dependence." Gumplowicz, *Outlines*, p. 199.

tions; namely, social conflict. They would dispute the claim that differences in wealth and status among men can be explained by what Oppenheimer, after Marx, often called the "nursery tale" of previous accumulation. According to this theory, men in their "natural state" are free and equal. Some being more clever, thrifty, and lucky than their fellows, there evolves through peaceful competitive collaboration, a division of labor and a hierarchy of classes. In Oppenheimer's view, "all orthodox sociology begins with the struggle against this supposed law of class formation. . . .[E]very step of progress made in the various fields of the sciences of sociology has been made by tearing up, one by one, the innumerable and far spreading roots which have proceeded from this axiom."[12]

On the contrary, Oppenheimer argued, ultimately all class stratification can be traced back to the violent subjugation of one race by another. "The historical origin of social classes," he agreed with Schmoller, "is force, and that not so much of the force of individuals as of whole clans and stocks, of whole classes and peoples. The one stock enslaves another. Thus arrives inequality of possession, and what is of more importance . . . inequality of culture."[13] Even with the

12. Oppenheimer, *The State*, p. vii.
13. Gustav Friedrich von Schmoller, "The Social Question and the Prussian State," quoted in Small, *Origins of Sociology*, p. 249. Schmoller goes on to say that,

"the guilt and the wrong with which the beginnings were made do not cease. Force merely becomes more refined. It is converted into fraud, into shrewd overreaching, into unjust exploitation of political power. Up to the present day there is no distribution of property and income in any people which is entirely free from this—so to speak—tragic guilt" Ibid. Oppenheimer agrees that "a sound sociology has to recall the fact that class formation in historic times did not take place through gradual differentiation in pacific economic competition, but was the result of violent conquest and subjugation." Oppenheimer, *The State*, p. vii.

Ratzenhofer tells us that "subjugation by the rulers is the start of all social stratification and the beginning of all statehood (*Staatswesen*)." Ratzenhofer, *Erkenntnis*, p. 246.

advent of extensive trade relationships, Oppenheimer continues, the "tragic guilt" of nomadic warriors setting themselves up as a ruling class over the peasantry does not disappear. In fact the introduction of a money economy merely alters the position of the one-time warrior from that of feudal magnate directly consuming the goods produced by his manorial tenants, to capitalist speculator competing for profits in the market. In this second case, the desire to increase his competitive advantage drives him to lower the overhead of agricultural production by hiring cheap day labor and by discharging his serfs from feudal bondage. He starts to mechanize production and turns his land to more practical use, such as grazing or the cultivation of a single crop. Land holdings inevitably become concentrated into fewer and fewer hands, as less enterprising farmers are run out of business and forced to liquidate their estates to pay off mortgages incurred in the process of competition. Pauperized, these originally free farmers, along with newly liberated peasants who are unwilling to work for low farm wages, migrate to the cities. This has the effect of increasing competition for scarce industrial jobs, lowering wages for those who do find work, and inflating prices on consumer goods. The final consequence of the original violent seizure of the land of the tillers of the soil by the nomad, then, is the unintended creation of an impoverished urban proletariat.[14]

While consenting with Oppenheimer that some class relationships have had their origin in warlike contacts between different ethnic groups, Ratzenhofer and Gumplowicz also explicitly recognized that conflicts within the already existing state can have the same result. Thus as Gumplowicz saw it, there is in historical

14. For example, see Oppenheimer, "Tendencies in Recent German Sociology," pp. 254-56 and "Wages and Trade Unions," *American Journal of Economics and Sociology* I (1941-1942): 45-82.

fact a "twofold origin of classes." "Some classes, the ruling, the peasant, and the merchant classes for instance, arose from the union of different (*heterogen*) ethnological elements. . . . But there are others which arise from the others by a process of differentiation."[15]

It is through a more or less peaceful process of differentiation following economic progress that gives rise to such diverse groups as priests, scholars, and skilled laborers. Almost universally when these groups become conscious of their contributions to the society, they begin to demand what they believe is "their just share" of its surplus production. Such claims naturally run counter to the vested interests of the ruling class and also to the material interests of other closed groups. Inevitably then, these interest groups find themselves engaged in a struggle for power with each other. As Gumplowicz describes it:

> In the modern civilized state large industries are opposed to the small, the laboring class to the capitalist and the undertaking classes to the agricultural classes, agriculture to manufacture, and so forth. Each has its own interest which it represents, its own power which it strives to increase, and each bears down upon the others according to its strength and their resistance.[16]

Those groups that already hold dominant class positions use any available means to overpower those who threaten their monopoly of the national wealth. They attempt to see that legislation is framed in their own interest and whenever possible they employ the state's administrative machinery, most importantly the army and police, to quell dissent. They organize to restrict connubial rights, seek to exclude their opponents both from landed wealth and political office by making them

---

15. Gumplowicz, *Outlines,* p. 216. See also pp. 210-15. It is obvious upon reading Oppenheimer that he implicitly appreciated this same point.
16. Ibid., p. 215.

hereditary, and even declare it illegal for others to organize against them politically. Oppenheimer has painted the following portrait of the strategies used by the ruling class in class conflict:

> In the first place, it reserves to its adherents all prominent places and all offices of influence and of profit, in the army, in the superior branches of government service, and in places on the bench; and secondly, by these very agencies, it directs the entire policy of the state, causes its class politics to bring about commercial wars, colonial policies, protective tariffs. . . .[17]

On the other hand, those groups originally out of power such as lawyers, priests, and finally common laborers will each in turn attempt to breakdown these restrictions by demonstrating the ruler's dependency upon their specialized talents for the realization of his goals. The threat to withold their services in all manner of striking, work slow downs, and sabotage has historically been the most effective tactic that those with little formal influence can adopt for this purpose.

However, it is not so much the type of strategy that is used by an enemy that will determine the outcome of these sorts of conflicts. Other things being equal, in domestic power struggles as it is in war, that combatant who is united and disciplined has always persevered over his less well-organized opponent. This is the reason why, although the ruling class is substantially

---

17. Oppenheimer, *The State,* pp. 263-64. Cf. this statement with that of Gumplowicz, *Outlines,* p. 208 and with the following claim of Schmoller, "All class conflict appears to be the consequence of that which we are accustomed to call 'class dominance'. . . . [In other words] that dependence of the weak class upon the strong which comes about from the fact that the latter influences and controls the civic power, that the strong class exploits not only its economic superiority, but the political power, the sovereign rights of the state, the machinery of government . . . for its economic advantage." Gustav Friedrich von Schmoller, "Schmoller on Class Conflicts in General," trans. by Albion W. Small, *AJS* XX [July, 1915]: p. 509.

smaller than its foe, it generally is able to summarily defeat him. According to Gumplowicz, whose position in this regard was later to influence the political thinking of Gaetano Mosca:

> It has already been pointed out that it is not the size of the social group which determines its power. The lords were always in a minority and in modern states with millions of inhabitants power rests with the "upper crust." The intimacy of the union and resultant organization and discipline, together with mental superiority, complement numerical inferiority giving the minority preponderance. The minority applies the strategic maxim: "march as individuals, strike as one."[18]

In the long run, merchants, artisans, and laborers have all applied Gumplowicz's tactical dictum to win certain concessions from their rulers. And without exception, as they have victoriously won the right to appropriate a specified amount of the social wealth, to hold office, and/or to govern their own affairs, successful interest groups have turned against their one-time allies to exclude them from the same benefits. As Oppenheimer describes it,

> The capitalist demands equal rights with the formerly privileged orders, and finally obtains them by revolutionizing the plebs. In this attack on the sacredly established order of things, the capitalists unite with the "plebs" naturally under the banner of "natural law." But as soon as the victory has been achieved, the class based on movable wealth, the so-called middle-class, turns its

18. Gumplowicz, *Outlines,* p. 225. It is because of a more or less vague appreciation of this basic rule that when engaged in a struggle for power, classes generally organize themselves into parties. "Historically this class contest is shown to be a party fight. A party is originally and in its essence nothing save an organized representation of a class," says Oppenheimer. *The State,* p. 261. Thus, he goes on, "all party policy can have but one meaning, viz. to procure for the class represented as great a share as is possible of the total national production." Ibid., p. 262.

arms on the lower class, makes peace with its former opponents, and invokes its reactionary rights on the pro-
letarians, its late allies, . . .[19]

Class Conflict and the Legal Order

The sociologists of conflict realized that if class relations were originally established on the basis of violent
coercion, this alone has never been sufficient to
guarantee their stability over long periods of time. It is
necessary for the inequitable distribution of power and
wealth to be given an appearance of rightfulness and
reasonableness so that even those in the lower classes
will feel a moral compulsion to submit themselves to it.
Consequently, then, the final goal toward which each
interest group within the state struggles, is "to confirm
by right the commanding position which has been acquired or striven for."[20] Custom and tradition have
often times lent an aura of morality to what were at
one time merely situations of brute force. But in modern states the formal declaration of some domination
relations as legally rightful is more commonly used to
justify them.

Interestingly enough, the formal institutionalization
of power relations as legally binding rights not only
secures the conformity of those subject to them, but it
also unintentionally creates a pacifying matrix within
which conflicts in modern states can be fought. Since
laws are normally the product of a closely regulated
legislative process, "then it is clear that the society
[social group] which has acquired the right of legislation in the state occupies the most powerful position,
and it is the aim of every other society to participate in

19. Oppenheimer, *The State,* p. 256.. See also p. 253, 257.
20. Gumplowicz, *Outlines,* p. 228.

the same right."[21] But to the degree that such groups successfully win the right to directly participate in the affairs of legislature, then the types of strategies that they will employ in their struggles to legally protect their interests, will be severely circumscribed. Instead of using physical violence against their opponents, they will find it more realistic to compete with them through debate for votes in houses of parliament. Thus, Gumplowicz concludes, while classes within the modern state, like hordes without it, know no standard of conduct but their own success, conflict between them inevitably evolves into a situation where it "is confined by established political relations to a struggle for control by peaceful means."[22]

Even if law serves to guarantee cooperation in a society and promotes peace between groups with conflicting interests, as implied in the previous paragraph, the sociologists would claim along with Rudolph von Ihering that "the means to that end is war."[23] Just as the struggle between a plurality of ethnic groups and then states spreads the peace of political domination over larger and larger territories, the fights between parties within each state turn what was once a tenuous rela-

---

21. Ibid. "It is well known that the history of European politics generally turns upon the struggle of the lower classes for participation in legislation, that it has been partially successful and that it is still in progress." Ibid.
22. Ibid.
23. Rudolph von Ihering, *The Struggle for Law,* trans. and intro. by John J. Lalor (Chicago: Callaghan & Co., 1915), p. 1. Understandably, Ihering is considered the father of German legal realism for such statements as the following: "All the law in the world has been obtained by strife. Every principle of law which obtains had first to be wrung by force from those who denied it." Ibid. His position was diametrically opposed to that of the conservative jurists like Savigny, who maintained that law was simply the unconscious unfolding of a *Volkgeist.* On this point, see Fritz Berolzheimer, *The World's Legal Philosophies,* trans. by Rachel Szold Jastrow (New York: Macmillan Co., 1924), pp. 338-51.

tion of master and slave into a complex and thus more stable legal order.

Classical liberal thinking, of course, holds that law has its origin in the inalienable "rights" of each individual. Calling this doctrine of natural rights mere "insipience" that derives from an unjustified overassessment of the value of the individual, Gumplowicz and Oppenheimer both agree that it is simply a myth perpetrated by those who are struggling for their own emancipation from feudal prerogatives. Instead of being products of divine forces, "rights are a social creation." Not just any type of social creation, but "a form of communal life produced by the conflict (*Zusamenstosis*) of unlike social groups with unequal power; such unlikeness and inequality is the necessary precondition of all rights."[24] "The hostile contact of different social elements of unlike strength is the first condition for the creation of rights," says Gumplowicz, "the conditions established by force and accepted in weakness, if peacefully continued, become rightful."[25]

The conflict between opposing parties each seeking to establish its interests as rightful in the face of resistance is adjudicated, not on the basis of abstract reason, but by their respective powers. Ihering expresses this notion in the following terms:

> Hence every such attempt [to institute a new law] in natural obedience to the law of self preservation, calls forth the most violent opposition of the imperiled in-

24. Gumplowicz, *Outlines,* p. 261. To Ihering, "But in all such cases, wherever the existing law is backed by interests, the new has to force its way into the world—a struggle which not infrequently lasts over a whole century. Here we find two parties opposed to each other, each of which takes as its device the sacredness of law, the one that of historical law, the law of the past; the other that of law which is ever coming into being, ever renewing its youth, the eternal primordial law of mankind." Ihering, *The Struggle for Law,* pp. 11-12.
25. Gumplowicz, *Outlines,* p. 203.

terests, and with it, a struggle in which, as in every struggle, the issue is decided not by the weight of reason, but by the relative strength of opposing forces. . . . Only thus does it become intelligible that institutions on which public opinion has long since passed a sentence of death continue to enjoy life for a great length of time.[26]

Oppenheimer and Gumplowicz both devote considerable space in their work to descriptions of the evolution of various legal rights through this mechanism. From Gumplowicz's provocative theory of the origin of rights of private property in land and women,[27] to Oppenheimer's study of the granting of city charters and his analysis of the development of manorial rights which abolished slavery in Europe and obligated the tenant to pay only a fixed rent to his landlord,[28] both scholars provide substantial confirmation for the hypothesis that law derives not from liberalism's inherent individual "rights," but from struggles for power.

26. Ihering, *The Struggle for Law*, p. 11.
27. According to Gumplowicz, "property" implies the use of an object not enjoyed by all. Thus as land was in the past collectively worked and used it was not property. "Passing from the use of land in common, we first recognize the beginnings of separate immobvable property when one herd has overpowered another and uses its labor force. As soon as there are subjects who are excluded from the enjoyment of goods which their own labor contributed to produce, in favor of the ruling class . . . then there arises separate or private property in immovable goods." Gumplowicz, *Outlines*, p. 198.
28. The lord, says Oppenheimer, desires to secure a permanent source of tax revenue, while his vassals have relatively short-range goals. Thus, while the latter will persist in forcing tribute through the arbitrary technique of sudden raid and robbery, the lord will attempt to institute a milder form of levying taxes. Because of this, when the lord is victorious in his struggles against his vassals, he also wins as future allies the peasants on their farms: "Laboring humanity, heretofore only an object of the law, for the first time becomes an entity capable of enjoying rights. The labor motor, without rights, belonging to his master, and without effective guarantees of life and limb has now become the taxpaying subject of some prince." Oppenheimer, *The State*, p. 235.

Class Conflict and Bureaucracy

In spite of the generally unifying consequences of social conflict through the development of a common body of legal regulations, Ratzenhofer, Gumplowicz, and Oppenheimer were all appreciative of the potential danger that internal friction held for the state's corporate existence. Thus, in the words of Ratzenhofer, the actual history of any political community is a story of the "individualizing" forces constantly threatening to destroy the state and the "socializing" tendency of the state that guides the energies of individuals into directions consistent with the commonweal of the whole.[29]

With the possible exception of Gumplowicz, who was never inclined to make predictions for mankind as a whole, the sociologists forecasted that present political developments favor the cause of social unity, rather than "anarchy" or revolution. For example, Ratzenhofer believed that the conquest state (*Frobererstaat*) will eventually evolve into a culture state (*Kulturstaat*), which is characterized by relative social equality and domestic peace.[30] Oppenheimer, on

29. To the Austrian sociologist, "The social process is a continual change of the individualizing of the newly built social structures from those existing, . . . and the social structures which have become socialized. . . . Differentiation has its limit in the number of individuals, that is, differentiation can spread up to the atomization of society. . . . Socialization (or zeal for socialization) has its limit in humanity." Ratzenhofer, *Erkenntnis,* pp. 246-47. Schmoller claims in agreement that, "every great society exhibits historically a picture of a social differentiation process. A counter-balancing process also goes on by virtue of the force of common heredity, common language, common religion; in short the aggregate of cultural factors, and finally, the unity of law, of institutions, of the civic power. Every actual situation is a diagonal of these two opposing series of factors." Schmoller, "Schmoller on Class Conflicts in General," p. 504. See also Oppenheimer, *The State,* pp. 104-5.

30. Ratzenhofer describes how with each new conquest, the variability of

the other hand, in a manner consistent with the founding members of the *Verein für Sozialpolitik*, hopefully anticipated the creation of a thoroughly bureaucratic state, the administrators of which, while pledging their loyalty to the constitution, would stand above partisan class interests and promote justice and unity. As he viewed it,

> as a matter of principle, the state officials, paid from the funds of the state, are removed from the economic fights of conflicting interests. . . . Were it possible ever to thoroughly realize this principle . . . one would find in officialdom that moderating and order making force, removed from the conflict of class interests, whereby the state might be led toward its new goal. It would become

social structures within the state increases. As this occurs, each structure becomes more and more dependent upon the others for its well being: "Just as variation leads to a limited fulfillment and complication of the organisms so social differentiation causes a higher developed and complicated aggregation of superior, equal and subordinate social structures. Because of their interest and life interests, they stand in a reciprocal dependence which goes as far as social contact between them is possible." Ratzenhofer, *Erkenntnis,* p. 248. With increasing interdependence among the parts, it becomes easier to disrupt the enterprise of society as a whole. Thus there arises coterminously, a demand for increasing control of individual deviation: "By increasing the net of social contacts the violent disturbances of social conditions diminish, since each disturbance in this complicated build-up of reciprocally dependent social structures finds many opponents on each side. Just as with a thin distribution of people the superior power *(Übermacht)* wants to bring about the order of the social enterprise, . . . so in this the latest society the superior power wants to bring about order . . . by compromise of the conflicting interests." Ibid. Furthermore, besides lowering the possibility of violent conflict, "to the extent that the culture state replaces the conquest state, the differences in the interest satisfaction of the individual persons are equalized; the political, social and economic inequality of the people is reformed back to the equality of shared gratification of the primitive tribe. It is therefore justified to assume as the finish of development, a situation in which despite the diversity of the professed individualities, a cultural, political, and social equality of people under the leadership of the most intellectually and morally perfect individuals." Ibid., pp. 249-50.

the fulcrum of Archimedes whence the world of the state might be moved.[31]

Although Oppenheimer was equivocal on the following point, it is clear that bureaucratic state administration, no matter how obediently its clerks impersonally enforce the law of the land, is really a means through which many of the domination relations of a society can find efficient expression. If this is the case, then it should be expected that the source of bureaucracy would be traced by Oppenheimer back to social conflict, the mother, he claims, of all class stratification. And indeed, according to the one-time Frankfurt professor of economics, while bureaucratization of the state maintains social order in the face of domestic unrest, like law itself it has its origin in power struggles. And in this regard, his theory of the bureaucratic state is virtually identical to that of Weber's. To illustrate this fact, the following paragraphs will contain a detailed comparison of their accounts of the rise of bureaucratization.

Mention was made in the second chapter, of the states of the plains, the foreign policies of which were historically directed to the acquisition of land, the peasant populations of which could then be exploited for the material benefit of their nomadic rulers. Ac-

31. Oppenheimer, *The State,* pp. 267-68. He goes on to say that "they [bureaucratic officials] do ameliorate the bitterness of the struggle, by opposing extremists in either camp, and by advocating adjustments to existing law. . . ." Ibid., p. 270. Somewhat like Gumplowicz, Schmoller sees that the fate of the conquest state is a vicious cyclical process. Warriors conquer subjects, who are slowly admitted into full citizenship through a struggle for emancipation. "If the movement goes too far, if political incompetents gain too great an influence, if the democratic masses acquire merely momentary advantage and profit, there follows, instead of the older aristocratic class control, the still worse democratic class control." Schmoller, "Schmoller on Class Conflicts in General," p. 511. In this situation a dictator appears as a savior to the people, and he attempts to forcibly establish social order in the midst of anarchy, thus starting the whole process anew. Ibid., p. 510. "This

cording to both Oppneheimer and Weber, the success of such pursuits necessitated the delegation of authority from the lord to his vassals on the empire's borders, both to insure internal peace and to maintain a vigilant defense against intruders. But because wealth in these nomadic states was usually measured in land and not in movable commodities or money, the lord always found that he had to pay his vassals in land fiefs in exchange for their military services. Among other things, this meant that he had to grant his vassals the complete freedom to use the land and the peasantry over which they exercised authority in any manner they saw fit. Naturally, to effectively execute their charge, such vassals had to cultivate their own loyal guards and administrators and develop extensive stores of personal military equipment. Wherever this condition has been fully obtained, vassals have become cognizant both of the lord's dependency upon them for the maintenance of his own position and the security of their own status from royal threats. And almost universally this realization has been historically followed by their banding together and demanding further concessions from the throne. Politically, the most significant demand that one-time loyal vassals have made upon their lord is that the fiefs that were originally

can be prevented only if improvement and strengthening of the civic apparatus keeps pace in the free states with the increasing influences of egoistic class interests. It is necessary also that the civic power shall remain in clean hands and shall continue to be stronger than the power and influence of the classes. This is possible only through progressive development of a more and more precise and just constitutional and administrative law, by the education of civic officials of a nonpartisan type in positions superior to class control, and who from highest to lowest govern state and society in harmonious cooperation." Ibid., p. 511. "These groups are the bearers of an ideal conception of the state and its economics. Even so far as they are of feudal aristocratic or of bourgeois origin, their horizon is no longer that of their economic class. . . . Together with the lawyers, physicians, artists, journalists, they constitute a sort of neutral one in contrast with the really struggling classes." Ibid., p. 514.

given them only in exchange for direct services, be
made their own private property; that they be given
the legal right to hereditarily pass them on to their
sons with no absolute guarantee that they will obey
the royal summons to war, and to capitalize on them
for other goods or services. To the extent that their
struggle to appropriate land fiefs has been successful,
there has evolved in place of a unified empire, a feudal
territory of independent private landholdings. It was in
this way, both Weber and Oppenheimer agree, that the
Japanese, Hungarian, Bohemian, Polish, German,
Spanish, Italian, French, Persian, Mesopotamian, and
Egyptian empires all disintegrated into a plurality of
feuding principalities.[32]

Furthermore, both men maintain that a condition
that is necessary for the prevention of this otherwise
inevitable course of events is the lord's centralization of
control over the means of administration, especially of
military violence, in the territory over which he claims

32. For Weber's classic analysis of the struggle for power between the lord
and his vassals, see *Economy and Society,* III, 1082-88. See Bendix,
Intellectual Portrait, pp. 362-81 for a summary of Weber's theory. Oppenheimer says that, "the more the state expands, the more must official
power be delegated by the central government to its representatives on the
borders and marches, who are constantly threatened by wars and insurrec-
tionary outbreaks." Oppenheimer, *The State,* p. 192. "Such an official, then,
receives the dues of the subjects, determines when and where forced labor is
to be rendered, receives the deobands, fees and penalties payable, and in
consideration of these must maintain the armed force, place definite numbers of armed men at the disposal of the central government, build and
maintain highways and bridges, feed and stable the ruler and his following,
or his 'royal messengers', and finally furnish a definite 'sergentry' consisting
of highly valuable goods, easily transported to the court, such as horses, cattle, slaves, precious metal, wines, etc." Ibid., pp. 193-94. "By all these
means, the powerful frontier wardens gradually attain an even greater, and
finally a complete, *de facto* independence, even though the formal bond of
feudal suzerainty may for a long time apparently keep together the newly
developed principalities." Ibid., 197. See also pp. 198-201. Although there
are other similarities in the views of Oppenheimer and Weber, the latter

sovereignty. It was his recognition of this that motivated the Pharaoh to create armies of slaves in Egypt. And the conscription of serfs in Rome, Hegas, and the Ottoman Empire demonstrate that this was not a historically unique discovery.[33] In all of these cases and many more, "the hiring of men whose position is indissolubly bound up with his [the lord's] own, and who would be ruined by his fall,"[34] is the explanation for the recruitment of the dregs of society into positions of great military responsibility.

But of all the various techniques that have in the past been used to consolidate the king's power, from the employment of "king's eyes" in Assyria and Persia to Sargon's attempt to eat daily with his soldiers,[35] bureaucratization of the royal army stands out as

goes further than Oppenheimer with his explicit distinction between partrimonial and feudal domination. Although both are fated with the "extension-unstability" paradox, patrimonialism historically begins, not with independent warrior-knights actually contracting with their lord to whom they now owe feality, but rather involves the delegation of authority through leases, loans, etc. to the originally dependent retainer. See Weber, *Economy and Society,* III, 1027-64 for a detailed picture of the struggle for power between the lord and his retainers in England, France, and China. For a summarized description of this fight, see Bendix, *Intellectual Portrait,* pp. 346-60.

33. Weber, *Economy and Society,* III, 968; 1015-20; 1043-44.

34. Oppenheimer, *The State,* p. 216. See also pp. 213-21.

35. In the patrimonial state, Weber talks about the attempt to recruit into the lord's administration celibate clerics in France and Italy to prevent the hereditary appropriation of their positions of trust. Weber, *Economy and Society,* III, 1034-37. He also speaks of the futile effort in China to force potential officials to take competitive examinations for their seats. Ibid., pp. 1048-49. In England, the king sought to prevent the appropriation of benifices by hiring without any pay whatsoever, wealthy and loyal landlords to serve as justices of the peace. Ibid., pp. 1059-64. Both the German authors talk about the situation where, topography permitting, the monarch seeks to equip his military forces from central stores. In Egypt, for example, where the placid Nile River gave quick access to the far reaches of the Empire, this strategy was used. Ibid., pp. 1044-47; Oppenheimer, *The State,* pp. 249-51.

preeminent in importance. This is because bureaucratization presupposes the use of money and not merely
in-kind payments to remunerate administrative officials for services rendered. And only if his warriors are
paid in money can the monarch prevent them from
successfully appropriating royal land and turning it
into private property:

> The infinite increase in the power of the crown is then
> enhanced by a second creation of the system of payment
> in money, by officialdom. We have told in detail of the vi-
> cious circle which forced the feudal state into a cul-de-sac
> between agglomeration and dissolution, as long as its
> bailiffs had to be paid with "lands and peasants" and
> thereby were nursed into potential rivals of their creator.
> With the advent of payments in money, the vicious circle
> is broken, henceforth the central government carries on
> its functions through paid employees, permanently depen-
> dent on their paymaster.[36]

The throne originally used money to engage "condot-
tieri," who as private entrepreneurs raised mercenary
armies for hire. Soon, however, it was discovered that
only the crown itself had a treasury that could bear the
expense of outfitting sizable numbers of troops with
modern weapons. But whether they were paid money
from the profits of a private general or from the king
himself, unlike the feudal vassal these soldiers were

36. Oppenheimer, *The State,* pp. 248-49. Weber agrees with this saying
that, "According to historical experience, without a money economy the
bureaucratic structure can hardly avoid undergoing substantial internal
changes, or indeed transformation into another structure. The allocation of
fixed income-in-kind from the magazines of the lords or from his current
intake—which has been the rule in Egypt and China and for millennia has
played an important part in the later Roman monarchy—easily means a
first step toward appropriation of the sources of taxation by the official and
their exploitation as private property." Weber, *Economy and Society,* III,
964. It thus follows that "the development of the money economy, in so far
as pecuniary compensation of the officials is concerned is a presupposition of
bureaucracy. Today it not only prevails but is predominant." Weber, *Essays,*
p. 104.

completely dependent for their war-making capacity upon some central authority, and thus they were necessarily obedient and well disciplined. Consequently, although relatively small in size, these armies easily outshone their feudal opponents. Tightly organized into ranks armed with pike or gun, they would calmly fire or thrust, while their chivalrous foe, the vassal, would gallop in disarray into the battle, engaging in individual and generally ineffective combat.[37] Oppenheimer says that,

> the system of money payment strengthened the central power so mightily and immediately, that even without the interposition of the agrarian upheaval, any resistance of the landed nobility would have been senseless. As is shown in the history of antiquity, the army of a central government, financially strong, is superior to feudal levies. Money permits the armament of peasant sons, and the drilling of them into professional soldiers, whose solid organization is always superior to the loose confederation of an armed mass of knights.[38]

In concurring again with Oppenheimer, Weber goes on to say that within the newly established bureaucratic state, parties have continued to form on the basis of class as well as status interests, seeking by means of any available techniques to have them protected by the legal violence of the state. The propertyless and bourgeosie parties attempt to destroy all vestiges of traditional discretion in domination and seek to increase the extent of universalism in the government's rule, while liturgical groups, estates, and others with

37. Weber, *Economy and Society,* III, 969-70.
38. Oppenheimer, *The State,* pp. 246-47. Weber makes similar observations concerning the importance of money salaries in cultivating military discipline. Weber, *Essays,* 255-61. In another place, he says that "only the bureaucratic army structure allows for the development of the professional standing armies which are necessary for the constant pacification of large territories as well as for warfare against distant enemies, especially overseas enemies." Weber, *Economy and Society,* III, 981.

particularistic privileges resist such efforts.[39] Particularly in the Occident, the outcome of these conflicts, says Weber, has been "democracy by leveling," or the increasing equality of all citizens before the law, regardless of their unique ethnic, class, or status group attachments.[40]

Just as the first incipient movements toward bureaucratization by an enlightened despot turned what were once independent feudal vassals into obedient officials, thus assuring the unity of the modern state, then too these latest struggles between commoners and their "natural superiors" have served to further cement the population into a single whole. Indeed, as Weber argues, "where the bureaucratization of administration has been completely carried through, a form of power relation is established that is practically unshatterable."[41] And since this is true, then "such a machine makes 'revolution' in the sense of the forceful creation of entirely new formations of authority, technically more and more impossible."[42] Since bureaucracy is the most practical way to organize corporate affairs, even groups with purportedly revolutionary goals will of necessity have to so organize if they are to have any hope of defeating the state. But such a move will inevitably entail a sacrifice of the end of revolution itself.

As indicated earlier, both Oppenheimer and Schmoller were lavish in their praise of the unification and rationalization of control by bureaucratization, because

39. For Weber's description of the resistance of German and English lawyers to the institution of rational Roman Law, see *Economy and Society*, III, 976-78; 1028-31. For a briefer account of the struggle of the French *parlements* against encroachment of their privileges, see Ibid., p. 1040. See Oppenheimer, *The State*, pp. 239-41 for his analysis of the efforts of merchants and craftsmen to obtain charters giving freedom from feudal domination to citizens of the city. For the attempt by propertyless workers to realize the same goals, see Oppenheimer, *The State*, pp. 265-67.
40. Weber, *Economy and Society*, II, 695-700.
41. Weber, *Essays*, p. 228.
42. Ibid., p. 230.

they saw it as signifying the finish of economic exploitation of one class by another and a move in the direction of what the former called a "Freeman's Citizenship." Thus in a summary of his book, *The State*, Oppenheimer concluded that "this has been the path of suffering and of salvation of humanity, its Golgotha and its resurrection into an eternal kingdom—from war to peace, from the hostile splitting up of the hordes to the peaceful unity of mankind, from brutality to humanity, from the exploiting state to the Freeman's Citizenship."[43]

Weber, on the other hand, approached this latest state of history with no little remorse. For he believed that increasing bureaucratization entailed the danger of turning the grandeur of the political struggle into the sedentary routine of administration under the "dictatorship of the official" and the doing away of the "political leader." In other words, he realized that not only has traditional domination its own "built-in" paradoxes, but so too does bureaucratic authority. Created in part out of the efforts of the lower classes for freedom from capricious and arbitrary rule, it may result in a more oppressive type of domination than ever. For Weber then, there is no way to escape from the *karma*, the vocation of politics. Political action logically can never result in the Kingdom of God on earth, but only in power relations. "I repeat," he told an audience after the First World War, "he lets himself in for the diabolical forces lurking in all violence.... He who seeks the salvation of the soul of his own and of others, should not seek it along the avenue of politics, for the quite different tasks of politics can only be solved by violence."[44]

---

43. Oppenheimer, *The State,* p. 290.
44. Weber, *Essays,* pp. 125-26.

4

German Intellectual Sources in American Social Science

How is it that the German realpolitik described in the previous chapters came to be assimilated into the thinking of Ward, Small, Park, and Bentley? Why weren't these men, all of whom had outstanding liberal credentials, abhored and revolted by a Machiavellian *Weltanschauung* that praises both war and domestic strife as progressive phenomena? There are many ways to answer these questions, so perhaps we should discuss each in turn, beginning in this chapter with the simplest.

During the time that Ward, Small, Park, and Bentley were embarking on their careers, it was the general expectation that all budding scholars not only read German literature and history, but if at all possible, they further their education in Germany itself. These four men conformed to this custom with a passion. And well they might, for it had a great historical precedent, going back to at least 1812.

Friederich List and Francis Lieber

In the decades following the Revolution when adolescent America was attempting to convince itself that it had a national identity, a cultural uniqueness apart from Mother England, several writers came upon the storehouse of German higher learning, and began translating it for consumption back home. The first academic field to experience the inspiration of German historiography was economics, when the writings of Friederich List were presented to American literati through his close friends Matthew and his son Henry Carey.[1]

List was one of the founders of German national economics, a specialty that among other things, sought to understand the relations of production in a country by submitting them to the methodology of historicism. "Historicism," it will be remembered, refers to the analytical procedure of interpreting historical phenomena as derivations from the will or from intentions instead of as instances of abstract deterministic laws. In place of the attempt to explain the division of labor and the distribution of wealth by reference to a presumably universal theory of economics a la Adam Smith and the school of classical economics, List and his colleagues sought to trace these same things back to their particular *Volkgeist*. They argued, like the conservative German jurists did for the law, that each separate nations' system of economics has unconsciously evolved from its unique spiritual essence.

List believed that one particular nation could borrow from another its economic policy only on pain of doing grave injury to its peculiar historical destiny. In the

1. For example, see Merle Curti, *The Growth of American Thought* (New York: Harper & Bros. Pub., 1943), pp. 247-53. Ralph H. Gabriel, *The Course of American Democratic Thought* (New York: Ronald Press, 1940).

case of America, this meant that a theory of economics more appropriate to American national character than the British notion of *laissez faire* should be adopted by its governmental leaders. In particular, List advocated that the government actively intervene in the economy by instituting protective tariffs for the benefit of American businessmen. Such taxes on British imports would, he claimed, free them from having to compete from a disadvantageous position with regard to English merchants and eventually pave the way for complete American national independence.

Not only economics but also American political thought began to be converted to the world view of the German historical school during the eighteen hundreds. Several persons[2] have brought attention to the fact that prior to the Civil War, both Calhoun and Webster in their famous debates concerning the right of states to secede from the Union, appealed to the wording of the Constitution to justify their arguments. But if the essence of constitutionalism is the belief in the official, who, restrained by an abstract set of formal rules, thus finds his sphere of authority carefully delimited, then the War between the States saw constitutionalism temporarily suspended for the sake of military expediency. In order to defeat the South and preserve the Union, the North had found it necessary in several cases to develop the actual powers of the Federal Government far beyond their normal peacetime constitutional limits. This deferment of an abstract set of rules to the ideal of solidarity, plus the fact that blood and iron and not rational debate was the final arbiter in the controversy, threw doubt both upon the efficacy of the contract notion of the origin of

2. For example, see Charles E. Merriam, *A History of American Political Theories* (New York: Macmillan Co., 1910), esp. the chapter entitled "Political Theory in Relation to the Nature of the Union."

the state and the belief that a formal constitution could be used to express national concord in the minds of many Americans. This induced them to embark on a search for a vocabulary that could more convincingly give vent to their public spirit than the "empty" categories comprising the content of statute books.

According to most commentators, it would be difficult to overestimate the role that recently arrived German immigrants played in helping American nationalists provide written expression for their new-found patriotism.[3] Carl Schurz, Charles Follen, Carl Beck, Karl Heinzen, and finally Francis Lieber, all of whom fled to this country during the political repression following the failure of the 1848 "Revolution," were only the most well-known of the lot. The intellectual inspiration of Lieber, for example, a one-time friend of Niebuhr, who himself was a progenitor of the German historical school, has been discovered in the writings of Elisha Mulford, John Jameson, Theodore Woolsey, Westel Willoughby, and John Burgess, five of the fathers of modern political science in America.[4] In fact, Albion Small, who also fell under the influence of Lieber, felt that "in political science the work of Fran-

3. In contrast to those from eastern Europe and the Mediterranean, the German immigrants arriving in America after 1848 were highly educated and thus made immediate substantial contributions to American cultural life. Charles Franklin Thwing, *The American and the German University* (New York: Macmillan Co., 1928) has described the place of Francis Lieber, Charles Follen, Germann von Holst, Philip Schiff, Albert Michelson, and Kuno Francke in American thinking. This book is hereafter referred to as *The University*. Curti, *The Growth of American Thought* discusses the German immigrants' donations to American fine arts, pharmacy, medicine, and the manufacture of scientific instruments. Ibid., pp. 313-15.
4. For an excellent study of the German intellectual influence on these persons, see Charles B. Robson, "The Influence of German Thought on Political Theory in the United States in the Nineteenth Century: An Introductory Study," (unpublished Ph.D. dissertation, University of North Carolina, 1930). The following account is indebted primarily to Robson's analysis.

cis Lieber at Columbia stands out before our present
retrospect as far and away more notable than any
other factor in this field."[5]

It was in part Lieber who first showed Americans
how to become more than mere interpreters of the law;
how to examine the religious, social, and economic
forces that make laws and which constitute the real
"life spirit of the state." To him and his students go the
credit not only for distinguishing between the nation
and its government, but also for detailing exactly how
the latter arises out of involuntary coercion and not exclusively from rational debate. It was not until American social scientists fully appreciated this idea, that
they could even understand, much less sympathize
with what German professors had for so long taken as
an axiom of political life; that the essence of the state
is complete sovereignty, with unlimited power over its
subjects.

Lieber also attacked the conventional social thought
of his American pupils by proposing that the state
enter into the social affairs of society, not just to protect private property, but also to guarantee the complete equality of all its citizens. The state, as he saw it,
was the basic and most effective instrument that a society could employ for its own moral and social uplift.
The state's ultimate end was to be none other than the
perfection of humanity and the civilization of the
world.

German Intellectuals and the
Progressive Movement

Lieber's theory of positive state intervention in the

---

5. Albion W. Small, "Fifty Years of Sociology in the United States," *AJS*
XXI (May, 1916): 727. This article is hereafter referred to as "Fifty Years."

goings-on of society, especially when apparently confirmed by the example of Germany's successful institution of social welfare programs, was not lost on sensitive American minds. The *Sozialpolitik* of the Iron Chancellor, Bismarck, which had unquestionably improved the common man's lot, did not, as deToqueville might have feared, increase his revolutionary propensities, but actually heightened his affection for the Fatherland. What had recently been intense strife between classes began to give way to the determination of all strata, in spite of their domestic differences, to unite behind the German Empire in its efforts to gain prestige in the world community.

This observation impressed many American reformists, who by the end of the nineteenth century were increasingly apprehensive lest their beloved Union, which had lately cost so much in blood and treasure to secure, would be torn assunder by class conflict. Their concern for social order found partial expression in what is now known as the Progressive movement, a political revolt of the old middle class in which many of the early American sociologists including Ward, Small, Park, and Bentley played significant parts. Because their involvement in this movement had such a great impact on their sociologies of conflict, a few points should be made about the sources of middle-class discontent following the Civil War.

Richard Hofstadter[6] has attempted to show how the intelligentsia of the Progressive movement were in many cases members of what will hereinafter be called "local society."[7] They were the lawyers, small indepen-

6. Richard Hofstadter, *The Age of Reform: From Bryan to F. D. R.* (New York: Alfred A. Knopf, 1955).
7. This term is taken from C. Wright Mills, *Power Elite* (New York: Oxford University Press, 1959), pp. 30-46. See also C. Wright Mills, *Sociology and Pragmatism: The Higher Learning in America,* ed. by Irving Louis Horowitz (New York: Oxford University Press, 1966), pp. 325-37.

dent merchants and bankers, teachers, clergymen, and physicians who had come to monopolize prestige and political influence in the relatively isolated rural communities of what was once the American frontier.[8] Relative to the fortunes that the Rockefellers, Carnegies, and the Morgans built after 1865, members of local society had only moderate economic means. Yet they dominated affairs in the towns in which they lived, both through their ownership of the local newspaper and the influence they could wield at the town hall. The families of local society had generally lived in the same region for several generations, sent their offspring to the nearby private college, and had then induced them to return, marry others of their type, settle in the area, and perpetuate the family line and its position. In the decades following the Civil War, during which a primarily agrarian American economy evolved into an industrial empire, local society, as so understood, found its tenuous hold on power and repute threatened at an accelerating rate. Besieging them from one side were the money grubbing and vulgarly ostentatious "robber barons" who were monopolizing control over the national economy by running local merchants, farmers, and factory owners out of business. From the other side, working in the factories of the captains of industry, toiling in their mines, or on their railroads, were the hundreds of thousands of proletarian immigrants with their equally alien style of life.[9]

Hofstadter has documented in some detail how local society's fear of losing its power and esteem vented itself in the diversity of grievances issued by the intelligentsia who were attached to the Progressive move-

8. Hofstadter, *The Age of Reform,* pp. 135-36.
9. For example, see Hofstadter's intriguing chapter entitled "The Status Revolution and Progressive Leaders," Ibid., pp. 131-72.

ment. Bossism, urban machine politics, the corruption of government officials, the concentration of wealth into the hands of a few, and the increasing violence used by both capital and labor to defend their selfish claims, all were called to task by those accustomed to the more genteel life of the rural community. They hoped that by engaging in concerted political action they would once again reestablish "honesty and virtue" in government, economic competition between small entrepreneurs, and peace, unity, and harmony for all.

There will be much more to say about this later. At present it is sufficient to note that not a few of the most important ideologists in the forefront of this campaign against both corporate capitalism and organized labor, borrowed directly from the German social sciences many of their arguments. At least a partial explanation for this seems to lie in the fact that since 1812, beginning with Joseph Coswell, George Ticknor, Edward Everett, and George Bancroft, the sons of local society had been sent in ever increasing numbers to study in Germany.[10] And many of these fledgling American scholars found in the theorizing of those such as Gustav Schmoller and Adolph Wagner, an apt vernacular with which to express their anxieties about what they believed was an impending revolution. Consequently, they came to advocate essentially the same programs for the solution of this social problem as had earlier been proposed by these particular German national liberals. For instance, like their German teachers, they suggested that the American government extensively involve itself in the nation's economic affairs both to "curb the greed of the capitalist, and the shortsightedness of the laborer." Some of them even returned from Europe with the aim of making American

10. Thwing, *The University,* pp. 12-39 gives a well-documented description of the experiences of these four persons while in Germany.

colleges over into centers for the training of civil servants and the scientific gathering of information relevant to the determination and evaluation of public policy.[11] However, the most radical of the Germanophiles claimed that truly melioristic state interference would entail not only the training of experts and bureaucratic officials to *administer* the law, but more importantly the active participation of the social science professions in the *politics* of determining the law to be enforced.

The American Economic Association out of which the American Sociological Society was later to grow, is one of the best examples of this last point. This organization was explicitly modeled in 1885 by Richard T. Ely, E. R. A. Seligman, Henry Carter Adams, and others after the *Verein für Sozialpolitik*, that German social science lobby in which Schmoller, Wagner, and Weber had played such influential roles. Many years later Ely was able to recount a moving conversation he once had with Dr. Johannes Conrad of Halle during a seminar on this very subject which, he says, was the basic reason for his attempting to establish in America a group analogous to the *Verein für Sozialpolitik*.

> I remember very distinctly Conrad's speaking to us Americans who were in his seminary one evening, urging us to organize a similar association in the United States upon our return, emphasizing the fact that the times were changing. The old order was passing away, and if economic students were to have any influence whatever upon the course of practical politics it would be necessary to take a new attitude toward the whole subject of social legislation; and if the United States were to have any particular influence in the great social legislation and the great readjustment of our society on its legal side which

11. For an excellent discussion of this development, see Jurgen Herbst, *The German Historical School in American Scholarship* (Ithaca, New York: Cornell University Press, 1965).

seemed to be coming, an association of this sort would have very real value.[12]

The Americans in Germany

The idea of the *Wanderjahr* on the European continent increased tremendously in popularity among American college students during the course of the nineteenth century; so much so, in fact, that by 1900 close to 10,000 of them had registered for at least one semester of study in Germany:

In the first half of the century, apparently less than two hundred were matriculated in all the German universities, of which fifty-four are found at Berlin between 1826 and 1850, two at Leipzig, between 1828 and 1846, and sixteen at Halle between 1826 and 1849. In the fifth decade, the number came to exceed one hundred, and the sixth increased at least three-fold. In the seventh, American students again increased three-fold, passing beyond a thousand. In the eighth, they enlarged by a small proportion above the one thousand of the preceeding period. In the ninth decade, they touched the highest mark, exceeding two thousand, in which Berlin is to be credited with

12. Richard T. Ely, *Ground Under Our Feet* (New York: Macmillan Co., 1938), p. 134. See also pp. 132-49. Quotations from the statements issued at the first meeting of the A. E. A. reveal the sway that the *Verein für Sozialpolitik* held over the thinking of the early American economists:

1. We regard the state as an agency whose positive assistance is one of the indispensible conditions of human progress. . . .

2. We believe that political economy is still in an early stage of development . . . and we look, not so much to speculation as to historical and statistical study of actual conditions of economic life for the satisfactory accomplishment of the study.

3. We hold that the conflict of labor and capital has brought into prominence a vast number of social problems, whose solution requires the united efforts, each in its own sphere, of the church, of the state and of science.

4. . . .[W]e believe in the progressive development of economic conditions, which must be met by a corresponding development of legislative policy." Ibid., p. 140.

thirteen hundred and forty-five, Leipzig with three hundred and forty-five, Heidelberg with two hundred and fifty-three, Halle with almost one hundred. In the tenth and last period of the century, the decline begins a declination which continues until the war period opens, when an almost vanishing point is reached.[13]

It is fortunate that the reminiscences of several of these persons concerning their adventures while in Germany have been preserved.[14] Through their diaries, one can almost relive the startling discoveries they made in what was then the center of Western intellectual culture.

Most of the American students had been born and raised as God-fearing Protestants in small towns like Virden, Illinois; Davenport, Iowa; Ashfield, Massachusetts; and Grass Valley, California. They had been taught the unassuming populist life style that commentators often associate with life in rural farm communities, and had become accustomed to the uncultured, "crass materialistic," demeanor of its citizens. Not surprisingly then, accounts of their study in Germany are filled with contrasts between the old and the new world.

One of the first things to catch their attention was the premier place that the life of culture and refinement seemed to hold among Germans of all social strata. Unlike the situation in America in the late

---

13. Thwing, *The University,* pp. 42-43.

14. With no attempt to be exhaustive, I have drawn from the following autobiographies: Ely, *Ground Under Our Feet.* John W. Burgess, *Reminiscences of An American Scholar* (New York: AMS Press, 1966). Henry Adams, *The Education of Henry Adams* (New York: Modern Library, 1931); Hutchins Hapgood, *A Victorian in the Modern World* (New York: Harcourt, Brace & World, 1939); Edward A. Ross, *Seventy Years of It* (New York: D. Appleton-Century Co., 1936); Nicholas Murray Butler, *Across the Busy Years: Recollections and Reflections,* vol. I (New York: Charles Scribner's Sons, 1934); G. Stanley Hall, *Life and Confessions of a Psychologist* (New York: D. Appleton & Co., 1927).

eighteen hundreds, virtually every German town had its own museums, weekend plays, concerts, and operas. And more than one of the American students was moved to comment that more Shakesperean plays were conducted in a single week in Germany than were held in all of the English-speaking countries in a year. Furthermore, at least according to their reports, these events were not understood by the theatergoers to be mere distractions from the more important practical things in life, but as means to the attainment of a well-rounded education. Some of the young men, such as G. Stanley Hall, who was later to become one of the first American psychologists, went even further. He spoke of how the Germanic emphasis on culture was simply a smaller aspect of the general awe and reverence that all Germans held for creations of the spirit and of the emotions. This capacity, he said, to sentimentalize, to display exuberance of affection, to be receptive to the manic-depressive extremes of both pain and joy, was something that most Americans with their rigid Puritanical backgrounds find difficult to understand. But not Hall. Although he admitted that it drove him to drinking to lift his spirits, he found this ability to surrender oneself to feelings so unique and refreshing that he longed never to return to his homeland:

I sometimes wondered if I had become so ardent a Teutonophile by way of atavistic regression, although this would be a far cry. Perhaps, on the contrary, it was because beyond the Rhine I found, so highly developed, qualities that I lacked but admired; namely a capacity for sentiment, *gemut* or the power of abandonment to the moods, feelings, ideas, and companions of the present moment. At any rate, I longed to spend the rest of my life in that country and planned several quite unpractical ways of doing so. Crude as some, at least, of my friends both in and out of the university thought me and only partially *verdeutsch* as I was, when I came home I felt the whole atmosphere of this country, and especially that of staid old New England most oppressive. . . .[15]

Germany appeared as a living contradiction to many of the American students. For wrapped in a curious combination with the emphasis on spiritual and cultural freedom was a pervasive sense of order, officialdom, and government control. Berlin might be taken as a good example. Here was a city that like Chicago had gained over two million inhabitants during the nineteenth century, but that seemed to be free of the concomitant frontier roughness, noise, dirt, and general anarchy. Not only was it impeccably clean and well lighted at night by the *public* utilities, a far cry from the analogous situation in a Chicago or St. Louis, but its streets were systematically laid out and actually paved! In Berlin of the nineties, the period of the biggest influx of American students, everything from the slaughterhouses, water works, canal and dock companies, street and railway companies, the post office, and even the pawnshops were staffed by civil servants, whose appointments were the result of their scores on rigorous competitive examinations. This no doubt impressed the Americans who were familiar with the political machinations and bribery that seemed to characterize the typical American municipal government of the day.

Of all the bureaucratization of public affairs, however, it was the militarization of German life that most stuck in the minds of the Americans. Some had observed the parades, operas, and art shows that exalted German military might, or the gruesome photographs of the victory over France in 1870 that hung in the halls of the *Volkschulen*.[16] Several of them, like John

15. Hall, *Life and Confessions of a Psychologist,* p. 223.
16. For typical impressions of German militarism, see for example Ely, *Ground Under Our Feet,* pp. 33-38, 45-46; Butler, *Across the Busy Years,* p. 117; Ross, *Seventy Years of It,* p. 31; Hall, *Life and Confessions of a Psychologist,* p. 195.

Burgess, were even present during the return of the Prussian Army from its celebrated battle with the French at Sedan in 1871. Burgess, who was later to found Columbia's School of Political Science, was reading public law at the time at Berlin University. With his roomate, the future Secretary of State Elihu Root, he was fortunate enough to have attended the parade that glorified the recently demonstrated military superiority of Germany over France. He described his impressions of the observance in the following way:

> It was more to us to see the power of the new Germany make its triumphant entrance into the new imperial capital than to have heard a few lectures which we would only have partially understood. It gave us a more correct conception of the new Germany than we could have obtained from the reading of books or the hearing of lectures. It was the most magnificent manifestation of power that the world has ever furnished.[17]

Life in the university itself also shocked the Americans as being foreign to what they had come to expect while at home. First, in contrast to America's long-standing reputation as a center for anti-intellectualism, there was the simple fact that the German universities housed what were then the most eminent scholars in the western world. "I had never before been offered so rich a choice of subjects or such an array of illustrious teachers," Burgess wrote many years following matriculation at Leipzig and Berlin. Indeed, in his opinion, "Mommsen," his chief professor, "was Nietschze's conception of a superman. . . ."[18] Nicholas Murray Butler, who took Burgess' advice to study politics directly at the feet of the masters, also went to Berlin and came to the same conclusion regarding the quality of its faculty. There is little reason to believe that the thrill that he experienced when he first entered the gates of

17. Burgess, *Reminiscences of An American Scholar,* p. 96.
18. Ibid., p. 124.

the University was atypical for the American graduate student of this period:

> In and out of its door and across this court had walked for seventy-five years some of the great men of the world. . . . It was a great occasion for the young American when he first put his foot inside that academic building. Every hallway and every lectureroom seemed to echo with the footsteps and with the voices of great scholars who had shaken or molded the world of thought.[19]

Almost to a man the Americans reported substantial intellectual growth during their sojourn in Germany, this "Land of Damned Professors," as at least one of them called it.[20] "Germany almost remade me," Hall could remember several decades later, "especially the trienium there. It gave me a new attitude toward life. . . . I fairly reveled in a freedom unknown before."[21] Butler entitled his account of his stay overseas "A Voyage of Discovery," and claimed in conclusion that "surely this was a real voyage of discovery, and the discoverer often staggered under the load that he was called upon to carry. Indeed it took the better part of a subsequent generation to enable him to digest and to assimilate it all."[22] Even Edward A. Ross, a charter member of the American Sociological Society, who otherwise was quite critical of German culture, felt compelled to admit that "Soon after matriculating [at Berlin] I went through a period of 'storm and stress,' during which I grew so fast intellectually that often on Sunday I found strange, even incomprehensible, the views I had entered in my diary the previous Sunday."[23]

19. Butler, *Across the Busy Years,* p. 118.
20. Price Collier, *Germany and the Germans From an American Point of View* (New York: Charles Scribner's Sons, 1914), pp. 276-334.
21. Hall, *Life and Confessions of A Psychologist,* p. 219. See also pp. 219-22.
22. Butler, *Across the Busy Years,* p. 129.
23. Ross, *Seventy Years Of It,* pp. 26-27.

As to the reasons for their almost unanimous experience of intellectual development, there was little agreement among the Americans. For some it was the lectures of those like Mommsen and Curtius at Berlin that were said by Burgess to be "solemn ceremonies," public events at which were presented "finished orations that would have been a credit to Demosthenes himself."[24] Consider for example, the addresses of Treitschke, which were a "must" for the Berlin student body after 1874. His explicit advocacy of war as "part of the divinely appointed order," his debunking of the idea of "perpetual peace," and his bitter attacks on the Jews for their being "sub-German" of course attracted a great deal of attention in educational circles. But it was not simply the content of his speeches, but the theatrical form of giving them that drew the crowds. The auditorium was always filled long before the appointed hour with students from all departments, public officials, and military figures. Occupying the rows of benches on the basis of seniority, the audience would collectively stamp its feet in impatient anticipation of Treitschke's arrival. The master himself would sweep onto the stage in the company of several attendents, who escorted him like an honor guard to the podium, and then sat in special chairs on either side. Treitschke was not the only person at Berlin to employ dramatic props to flavor his lectures. Perhaps even more well known was the systematic sociologist Georg Simmel, whose presentations attracted just as large and diverse a crowd. As was the case for Treitschke, it was not just what Simmel *said* that mesmerized the audience, but the manner in which he expressed it. Paul Fechter has described it in the following way:

One could observe how the process of thought took possession of the whole man, how the haggard figure on the lec-

24. Burgess, *Reminiscences of An American Scholar,* p. 122.

ture platform became the medium of an intellectual process the passion of which was expressed not in words only
but also in gestures, movements, actions. When Simmel
wanted to convey to the audience the core of an idea, he
not only formulated it, he so-to-speak picked it up with
his hands, his fingers opening and closing; his whole body
turned and vibrated under the raised hand. . . . His intensity of speech indicated a supreme tension of thought; he
talked abstractly, but his abstract thought sprang from
live concern, so that it came to life in the listener.[25]

Not all of the Americans thought as highly as
Burgess and Butler did about the university lecture
system. Henry Adams, for example, the future historian and philosopher, and great grandson of John
Quincy Adams, said that though while in England he
believed he had stepped back into the seventeenth and
eighteenth centuries, in Germany he "felt his middle
ages and sixteenth century come alive."[26] Arriving in
Berlin in 1858 with the intention of studying civil law,
he attended his first lecture, and "his first was his
last."

He had thought Harvard College a torpid school, but it
was instinct with life compared with all that he could see
at Berlin. The German students were strange animals,
but their professors were beyond pay. What sort of instruction prevailed in other branches, or in science,
Adams had no occasion to ask, but in Civil Law he found
only the lecture system in its deadliest form as it
flourished in the thirteenth century.[27]

More common, however, were the experiences of
those like Ross who registered at Berlin University to

25. Paul Fechter, *Menschen und Zeiten* (Gütersloh: Berdelsmann, 1948),
52-56, quoted in Lewis Coser, *Masters of Sociological Thought: Ideas in Historical and Social Context* (New York: Harcourt Brace Jovanovich, Inc.,
1971), p. 211.
26. Adams, *The Education of Henry Adams,* p. 74.
27. Ibid., p. 75. See his biting remarks interspersed throughout the chapter
on "Berlin (1858-1859)."

read comparative philology and law. He listened to the lectures of Wagner, Zeller, and Frederick Paulsen, who later put Robert Park on the trail of Ferdinand Tönnies' study of community and society. According to Ross, the speeches of "Paulsen so impressed me that I caught up even his mannerisms. For years after, when I was about to make a particularly good point in lecturing, I brought up my right forefingfer just as he did."[28]

Even more than the impressiveness of their professor's lectures, it was the Germanic notion of intellectual craftsmanship, the idea of the intellectual life as something of a quasi-religious vocation that held sway over the minds of the young Americans.[29] It was in the German university where they became exposed for the first time in their lives to the belief in the possibility of personal enrichment through an uncompromising commitment to the individual quest for objective historical truth. Independent graduate study and research, the rigorous standards of historiography, including the techniques of document collection and the testing and criticism of data, were completely novel institutions to the Americans. They were equally unfamiliar with the paraphernalia of professional social inquiry, such as the specialized library, the research seminar, the research monograph, and the learned periodical. Indeed, the typical American college where they had completed their undergraduate study, more closely resembled the German *Gymnasium* than it did the university. Neither were understood to be places for the conducting of nor the training in research. In both cases, their curricula were comprised mainly of drilling in Latin and Greek, the memorization and recitation of passages from the classics, and some history and moral dogmatics.

28. Ross, *Seventy Years of It,* p. 27.
29. For a classic statement of this position, see Max Weber, "Science As a Vocation," *Essays,* pp. 129-59.

It is not difficult to understand, then, why almost immediately upon their return from overseas, the Americans embarked on a concerted campaign to establish the German ideal of the university in the structure of American higher learning. Graduate fellowships and Ph.D. degrees were granted in America for the first time in 1879. Johns Hopkins University was founded in 1867, primarily as a graduate school and as a center for the conducting of research in both medicine and academics. Charles Thwing claims that almost all of the original fifty-three faculty members of Johns Hopkins had previously studied in Germany, where thirteen of them had received the *Dr. Phil.* degree.[30] In similar veins graduate education in political science was instituted at Columbia University under the leadership of John Burgess[31] and later at Clark University by G. Stanley Hall.[32] The graduate research centers at Harvard, Cornell, Michigan, Wisconsin, and California were established on similar principles following the initial successes of these schools. Further testimony to the Germanic influence on American higher education can be seen in the increasing specialization and nationalization of academic professional organizations and in the proliferation of scholarly journals after 1870.[33]

30. Thwing, *The University,* p. 43.
31. Burgess, *Reminiscences of an American Scholar,* pp. 190-210.
32. Hall, *Life and Confessions of A Psychologist,* pp. 258-353.
33. From the original American Social Science Society developed The American Philological Association in 1869, The Archeological Institute of America in 1879, The Modern Language Association in 1883, The American Historical Association in 1884, The American Economic Association in 1884, The American Psychological Association in 1892, and The American Sociological Society in 1901. According to Merle Curti, at least 79 local and national learned societies were formed in the 1870s, 121 in the 1880s, and 45 in the 1890s. Curti, *The Growth of American Thought,* p. 585. For a discussion of the expanding use of professional periodicals during this period, see Bernard Berelson, *Graduate Education in the United States* (New York· McGraw-Hill Book Co., Inc., 1960).

The dangers that these "newfangled" pedagogical notions presented to the pietistic oriented American colleges of this period, is symptomized by the vigorous resistance put up by their predominantly ministerial faculties to the "bumptious innovators and educational swashbucklers" newly arrived from their stay in Germany, imbued with attitudes "of intellectual conceit and moral lawlessness."[34] Colleges like Amherst, Brown, and Knox had traditionally been places for training in moral discipline and explicitly not for research. Research implies doubt, but the Protestant colleges already had a monopoly of absolute Truth in the Bible.

Ross, Burgess, and Butler had as a result of their instruction under the students of Ranke, come to believe, however, that truth, like history itself, is a constant process of becoming. "Speaking for myself—and I believe for most of us—" said Ely reflecting on his study with Conrad, Wagner, and Knies, "I may say that the idea of relativity as opposed to absolutism and the insistence upon exact and positive knowledge produced a profound influence upon my thought."[35] The present body of scientifically established "truth," they felt, should not be treated as dogma, but merely as a tentative achievement, being open to both further elaboration and rigorous criticism in light of new evidence. One of the "arrogant young scholars," John Burgess, described it this way:

> The first principle of the system of education which the faculty of Political Science [at Columbia University] followed in all its work was free and untrammeled individual research and complete freedom of instruction in imparting the results of such research. Their attitude towards what was considered established truth was one of

34. It was under such categories that Burgess found himself classified. For example, see Burgess, *Reminiscences of an American Scholar,* p. 204.
35. Ely, *Ground Under Our Feet,* p. 146.

question, if not of distrust, as being something produced by the thought of man, and needing continual reexamination and adjustment under purer light and changing conditions. The progressive development of truth, instead of the monotonous maintenance of so-called established truth, was our principle.[36]

It would be a mistake to give the impression that persons like Butler, Hall, and Ely were simply passive recipients of and disseminators for German *Sozialwissenschaft*. After all, theorists of cultural diffusion have long been able to show the various subtler forms of resistance to those alien artifacts that the host society can not readily assimilate into its own cultural system. The cultural contacts between Germany and America of the late nineteenth century afford an excellent illustration of this process.

In most cases the American intellectual immigrants had an unshakeable faith in the possibility of both individual and social progress that was probably reinforced by their own biographical experiences in a land of expanding opportunities. Consequently, one cultural difference between the two countries, Germany and America, that unfavorably impressed them related to the overriding pessimism that seemed to permeate much of the German scholarship of the day. There will be several occasions in later chapters to make reference to this characteristic old-world *Weltschmerz*, but perhaps the subject should be briefly introduced at present. At the possible expense of oversimplifying the situation, suffice it to say that during this time it was a source of some prestige for German literati if they could elaborate in morbid detail on the finitude of human existence. Not only to describe as Schopenhauer. Nietzsche, and Eduard von Hartmann did, the irrational subconscious passions that motivate individual behavior, e.g. "the will to power;" but also like Gumplowicz, to stoically live by the adage

36. Burgess, *Reminiscences of an American Scholar,* p. 203.

that freedom of choice is but a cruel illusion, these were means to admiration by one's fellow writers. It is understandable, then, that existentialist philosophy that finds its basic premise in the uncompromising recognition of the limits of man's reason and capacities should first be cultivated in German scholarly circles. And it is also easy to see why such somber preoccupations naturally went against the grain of the scions of American local society.

Edward Ross provides an interesting example of this. First as an undergraduate at Coe College and later as a teacher at Fort Dodge College in Iowa, he read nothing but "Rank corn and cotton optimism," as he called it. Upon his arrival at Berlin he was introduced to Hegel. He would likely have found in the *Phenomenology* a philosophy compatible with his own hopeful outlook were it not for the fact that after several hours of attempting to wade through Hegel's turgid style, he concluded that his metaphysics were "pure nonsense." It was for this reason that he turned to the writings of Hegel's literary arch-rival Arthur Schopenhauer. His negative reaction to Schopenhauer's attack on the catagory of reason and his effort to reduce the cosmos to the will was soon revealed in a letter sent home in which he said,

> I will be happy in spite of *vanitas vanitatum* but I must get out of this despairing atmosphere soon. Poor Europe is like a charnel-house with an air that is heavy with death and decay. My heart keeps crying "back to America" the land of optimism, of progress, of freedom of will and of wealth! Back to the beautiful bubble! Back to the people still left in the sweet illusion of hope! Home or die.[37]

37. Edward A. Ross, Correspondence of Ross to Mrs. Beach, Jan. 10, 1889, Ross Papers, State Historical Society of Wisconsin, Madison, quoted in R. Jackson Wilson, *In Quest of Community: Social Philosophy in the United States, 1860-1920* (New York: Oxford University Press, 1970), p. 96. Cf. Ross, *Seventy Years of It,* p. 31. Observe as well Ross' negative reaction to German despondency in Edward A. Ross, "Turning Towards Nirvana," *Arena* IV (Nov., 1891): 736-43.

Conclusion

However vehemently American graduate students like Ross declared their final allegiance to American values or even Protestantism, they were generally viewed with distrust by the faculties of the denominational colleges where after their return from Germany, they sought employment. Albion Small, for instance, related an incident that should not necessarily be considered peculiar for this period, of how the staff of Colby College unjustifiably accused him of agnosticism because of his devotion to skeptical empirical inquiry, and thus successfully prevented him from teaching certain undergraduate courses in moral science. Ironically, with excess time on his hands, he now had the long-awaited opportunity to pursue even more insistently the research out of which evolved the first textbook in American sociology.

If sociology was originally accused of being foreign, "un-American," or possibly even socialistic by its critics, perhaps in some ways they were more correct in their assessment of its actual roots than are some of the professions' contemporary historians. For often, sociology has been spoken of as a uniquely American cultural product. More commonly, when its ties to foreign scholarship are admitted, emphasis is placed upon its French or English heritage. But the fact is that nearly all of the early founders of the profession of American sociology were at least in part intellectually tied to the German historical school. With no attempt to be exhaustive, the names of Cooley, Ross, Mead, Dewey, Ellwood, Thomas, and Veblen provide instances confirming this hypothesis. But not since Small's classic study of the origins of sociology in Germany has an attempt been made to demonstrate in a detailed way the interrelationship that exists between American and German sociology. In the following chapters, I will seek to partially correct this oversight by analyzing the lives and work of four early American sociologists, Ward, Small, Park, and Bentley, who were typical in regard to the prominent place that German learning held in their social theorizing.

5

The Early Life and Careers of Ward, Small, Park, and Bentley

The early lives and careers of Ward, Small, Park, and Bentley can all with little effort be placed in the midst of the pattern of cultural diffusion just described. In fact, the biographies of Small, Park, and Bentley are so strikingly similar to each other, that they can be discussed virtually as one.

Small, Park, and Bentley

To begin with, it can be said about this last trio that like Ely, Ross, and Hall, who were spoken about in the previous chapter, they were all descendents of what has herein been designated by the term "local society." They were, in other words, all raised in small towns on what was then the disappearing rural frontier of an expanding America by families of at least local prominence. Apparently it was during this time that they were successfully socialized into the American cultural ethic of optimism that was later to color the lenses through which they were to view social life.

Albion Woodbury Small's (1854-1926) ancestors in

America go back several hundred years and were at one time wealthy farmers, having title to the northern half of York County in Maine.[1] Born in Bucksfield, Massachusetts, raised in Bangor, and a graduate of a Portland high school, Small was the son of a prestigious and later well-to-do Baptist minister, who was known in some circles as the "St. Chrysostom of the Maine pulpit."[2] Like G. Stanley Hall, the young Small was brought up in a rigid Puritan atmosphere including hard work during the week with Sunday set aside as a day of silence, prayer, and fasting. However, while Hall reacted to this overbearing quasi-monasticism with revulsion, Small became so impressed with the religious life that upon graduation from Colby College he spent three years from 1876-1879 at Newton Theological Seminary, thereafter receiving several calls to the pulpit.

Arthur Fisher Bentley (1870-1957) was born in Freeport, Illinois, but graduated from a Grand Island, Nebraska high school where his father owned and operated a bank.[3] He was, like Small's father, successful enough in this enterprise to guarantee his son the best educational advantages. And although the young Bent-

1. For the following biographical account of Small, I am indebted to Thomas W. Goodspeed, "Albion Small," *AJS* XXXII (July, 1926): 1-14 and his "Albion W. Small," *University Record* XII (n.s., 1926): 240-65. The reader is also directed to the autobiographical notes interspersed in Small, "Fifty Years," and in Herbst, *The German Historical School in American Scholarship,* pp. 154-60.

2. Goodspeed, "Albion W. Small," p. 242.

3. For the following biographical account of Bentley, I am indebted to the articles by Sidney Ratner: "Arthur F. Bentley, 1879-1957," *Journal of Philosophy* LV (July, 1958): 573-78; "Introduction," *John Dewey and Arthur F. Bentley: A Philosophical Correspondence,* ed. by Sidney Ratner and Jules Altman (New Brunswick, New Jersey: Rutgers University Press, 1964); "A. F. Bentley's Inquiries into the Behavioral Sciences and Theory of Scientific Inquiry," *Life, Language, Law: Essays in Honor of Arthur F. Bentley,* ed. by Richard W. Taylor (Yellow Springs, Ohio: Antioch Press, 1957); Arthur F. Bentley, "Epilogue," *Life, Language, Law.*

ley had to be called back prematurely from his *Wanderjahr* in Germany because of his father's financial problems during the depression of 1893, he was able to retire from worldly pursuits in his early forties on the basis of a sizeable inheritance in Paoli, Indiana in 1911.

Robert Ezra Park's (1864-1944) birthplace was in the rural community of Harveyville, Pennsylvania. But following the example of his two predecessors Small and Bentley, he too was eventually raised and attended school away from this location in Red Wing, Indiana.[4] Like Small's family, Park's ancestors also were early settlers in the Massachusetts Bay area and they included in their number several doctors. Park's father met the basic criterion for membership in local society by working as an independent wholesaler of groceries. While his business suffered during the depression of the nineties, it subsequently recovered and became so successful that when he died he was able to leave his son a significant legacy which he used to finance his education and worldwide travels.

Besides the fact that Small, Park, and Bentley were all nurtured in relatively identical circumstances, at least in regard to the social class of their parents, there were other biographical parallels in their lives that are worth mentioning. In the first place, all three of them first came upon the works of German scholarship while studying in American colleges. And partly on the basis of their reading of Kant, Hegel, and Ranke, and their interpreters Holst, Lieber, and List, they became moti-

4. For the following biographical account of Park, I am indebted to: Robert E. Park, "An Autobiographical Note," *Race and Culture,* in *The Collected Papers of Robert Ezra Park,* ed. by Everett C. Hughes, et al., I (Glencoe, Illinois: Free Press, 1950); Helen MacGill Hughes, "Park, Robert E.," *International Encyclopedia of the Social Sciences* XI: 416-19; There is little biographical material now published on Park. I wish to thank Everett C. Hughes for his personal note, however, and Ms. Winifred Raushenbush, Park's personal secretary, for some points on Park's early life.

vated to seek a graduate education in the German universities.

Albion Small affords the best example of this process. As was the case for John Burgess several years earlier, Small's initial awareness of the rich intellectual resources in German social science came through his reading of Francis Lieber at Colby College. This occurred during his senior year (1875-1876) while taking, of all things, a course on mental and moral philosophy. As was typically the situation for a good Protestant college in those days, there was nothhing in the curriculum that covered the subject of political economy. Thus when Small's instructor, then president of the school, Dr. Henry E. Robbins, began "smuggling" Wayland and Bagehot into his lectures as his main references, he "nearly precipitated a revolution in the faculty." As Small describes it:

> Dr. Robbins put me on the track of Lieber's two major works. They were to me oases in the desert. They helped me to consciousness of my intellectual interests. They were distinct among the impulses that sent me to Germany three years later, and I have frequently recurred to them meanwhile as samples of the spirit in which social problems should be studied, rather than as direct sources of social doctrine.[5]

Lieber's inspiration was apparently not to be denied, although it was ignored for three years while at Newton Theological, Small attempted to convince himself that he was cut out for the life of a preacher. In 1879, however, he and his close friend, one Charles R. Brown, finally gave into worldly temptations and traveled to Germany to study together. Small himself planned a three-year course in political economy and history, and with Brown matriculated at Leipzig in 1879-1880 and sat in the lectures of Schmoller and

5. Small, "Fifty Years," pp. 728-29.

Wagner at Berlin in 1880-1881. His indebtedness to Germany is indicated by the fact that he
brought back to America not only abstract knowledge,
but also the daughter of a General von Massow of
Weimer. Like Ross and Ely, Small was probably impressed by the stilted atmosphere in late nineteenth-
century Germany, inasmuch as Fraulein Massow's
marriage to an American commoner was considered a
disgrace to her family, whose pastor refused to officiate
at the wedding.

Consider now the instance of Arthur Bentley. Following short stays at York College and the University of
Denver, he spent the years from 1890-1892 at Johns
Hopkins, where he received his bachelor's degree. Mention was made in the previous chapter about the attempt by its founders to establish this institution on
the basis of the same principles as the German university. Apparently the effort was successful, because even
by 1890 the Baltimore research center and faculty had
gained quite a reputation in American higher education, and students clamored for the right to listen to
the lectures of Herbert Adams, Charles Freeman, and
Richard Ely. The competition for the relatively few
graduate fellowships was even more keen, and thus the
selection committee for the University was in an excellent position to choose its clientele on the basis of very
rigorous standards. Indeed, one of the disappointed ap-
plicants for a fellowship in history and politics in 1879
was none other than Albion Small. He later confessed
that the reason for his failure to obtain a grant was
that even with a bachelor's degree from Colby College,
his undergraduate training qualified him only for entrance in the first and second courses in history and
economics in the undergraduate sequence. Frustrated
in his attempt to gain admission into the only graduate
school in America during that time, he had of necessity
to sail to Germany if he was to receive any graduate

education at all. At any rate, in light of the increasing demand for graduate training in a situation of scarce opportunities, it is no wonder that the list of alumni of Johns Hopkins comprises a virtual Social Register for early American social science. Besides Bentley, Ross, and eventually even Small, it also included in its number John Freeman, Woodrow Wilson, Thorstein Veblen, C. M. Andrews, Amos Warner, F. J. Turner, Franklin Blackmar, and J. M. Vincent.

Out of all the faculty recently returned from Germany and commited to the ideal of *Sozialwissenschaft*, Bentley mentions Ely as having the most influence upon his own thinking.[6] Thus soon after Ely left Hopkins to teach at Wisconsin in 1892, Bentley, feeling little inclination to further his education there, got passage on a ship to Germany. There is some evidence to suggest that Ross, just arrived from overseas and apparently affected by what he considered to be his own intellectual growth, helped persuade Bentley in this decision. But according to his own account, although he "fell short of actual contact" with him, it was the Austrian economist Karl Menger, whose behavioristic and utilitarian economics he had read under Ely, who ultimately drew him to Europe.

On board ship Bentley struck an acquaintance with Hutchins Hapgood, the future muckraker and literary critic, who many years later was able to provide the following glimpse of Bentley, and the serious intent with which he planned to pursue his graduate study:

A few days after the departure of the ship, I met on deck a strangely vivid young man, Arthur F. Bentley. He was passionately determined to solve the mystery of society. . . . His state of mind was in striking contrast to

6. "I went to Johns Hopkins University," Bentley once said, "because Richart T. Ely was there, my goal being economics." Bentley, "Epilogue," pp. 210-11.

mine . . . perhaps unconsciously I knew I was going on a romantic quest. I had been set free, and many colored adventures lay before my mind's eye. But Bentley was realistically passionate, with a serious purpose of learning everything known about sociology and with a determination to add to that knowledge and solve the puzzle of human society.[7]

In Berlin, Hapgood lived with Bentley and the soon-to-be French scholar Celeste Bouglé. He had little trouble adjusting to his new environment, and within a short time was consciously exploiting the many opportunities to carouse, drink, travel, and engage in sexual explorations. This was not the case with Bentley, however. According to Hapgood, "Bentley's passionate desire to discover the sociological ultimate revealed an infinite mental turmoil. He was an unhappy, restless soul, bitterly critical of himself and his inability to reach the heights."[8] While the others in the American colony spent their time "loafing and inviting the soul," Bentley threw himself into his work, systematically reading and learning the language. "He was controlled only by his own demands on himself. Bentley made these demands on himself with great intensity, and worked very hard, but on the whole unhappily. Sometime later, when he was in London, I got an eloquent letter from him about his passionate disappointment in not being able to solve the mystery of sociology."[9]

Bentley studied under both Wagner and Schmoller, but he was not as satisfied as Small appears to have been with their efforts to characterize the "sociological ultimate." Besides Wilhelm Dilthey, in whom he seems to have found some intellectual stimulation, he also listened to Simmel's lectures. As will be seen later, Simmel made a great impression on Bentley, who many

7. Hapgood, *A Victorian in the Modern World,* p. 84.
8. Ibid., p. 99.
9. Ibid., p. 112.

years after his return from Germany called him "the keenest and most searching investigator society has yet had, undoubtedly the one with the greatest yield of permanently applicable knowledge."[10]

This assessment was not unique for its time. While just a *Privatdozent* supporting himself exclusively on the basis of direct remuneration from his pupils, Simmel was one of the most popular instructors at Berlin. There was an ongoing competition for the scarce number of seats in his lecture room, and Hapgood wrote of a humorous incident that arose from this fact when he arrived an hour early one day to obtain a front row seat. Several minutes after his arrival when the other spectators were piling in he found himself confronted by an upperclassman member of a dueling corps, who demanded his seat on grounds of seniority. Being a good American democrat he naturally refused to comply with the demand, whereupon he was immediately challenged to a duel. This he was able to avoid only after some debate by pleading ignorance of the prestige hierarchy in the University.

The story of Robert Park's educational career is similar in several respects to those of Small and Bentley. After spending one year at the University of Minnesota, he registered at the University of Michigan, which, under the leadership of President Angell, like California and Wisconsin was one of the recently created centers for the teaching of German social and academic ideas. It was fortunate for Park that his interest lay in philosophy because John Dewey had just been named to chair that department when he arrived. Dewey was another of the typically outstanding products of Johns Hopkins, having studied there under G. Stanley Hall and George Morris and taken his Ph.D. in 1884. The young Dewey at Michigan was, during

10. Quoted in Ratner, "A. F. Bentley's Inquiries into the Behavioral Sciences and Theory of Scientific Inquiry," p. 29.

Park's attendance there, still intellectually beholden to the idealistic Morris, who had received Hegel directly from his followers while studying in Germany. What most appealed to Dewey was the Hegelian notion that cultural institutions are instances of the "objective mind," upon which each individual is dependent for his psychical life. On the basis of a short biographical note attached to his dissertation where Park mentions Dewey as the only academic figure whom he remembers at Michigan, Lewis Coser has concluded that it was here that he was first introduced to pragmatism and progressive reformism.[11] Such an inference is generally unjustified in light of the fact that the Dewey of the 1880s had not yet developed pragmatism, still being an explicit Hegelian. Furthermore, it was not until his marriage to Alice Chipman in 1886 that he even began to turn his attention from the realm of transcendent spiritualism to the more worldly area of social reform.[12] On the other hand, Dewey's notion of the source of the personality in culture is on a parallel with the doctrines of Cooley, Mead, James, and Royce, all of whom came to hold important positions in Park's sociology. Possibly then, it is more correct to say that Park first received an inkling of the modern theory of socialization from Dewey, than any well-developed idea of meliorism or clearly defined pragmatism.

Park came into contact with Josiah Royce and William James when after twelve years of work as a newspaperman following his graduation from Michigan, he returned to the academic life as a graduate student in philosophy at Harvard in 1899. As the continuity of Royce's philosophical psychology with Dewey's Germanic idealism suggests, Park's graduate school experience probably further impressed upon his

11. Coser, *Masters of Sociological Thought: Ideas in Historical and Social Context,* p. 373.
12. On this point, see Mills, *Sociology and Pragmatism,* pp. 287-95.

mind the theoretical significance of the subordination
of the individual to the group for his moral capability.
The Roycean-Dewey viewpoint was certainly not con-
tradicted by Hugo Münsterberg, a graduate (like G.
Stanley Hall) of Wilhelm Wündt's psychological
laboratory, who, while at Harvard as a visiting professor, was said by Park to also have affected his thinking.

It is difficult to say exactly what impelled Park to
continue his education in Germany, although it is very
unlikely that either Münsterberg or Royce, who himself had spent a year at Leipzig and Göttingen, would
have discouraged him from doing so. But for whatever
the reason, soon after taking his master's degree from
Harvard, he followed what was by then the diminishing American flock of students to Berlin. There, like
Bentley before him, he sought out one of the scarce
seats in Simmel's classroom. "I intended to stay abroad
for a year," he said some decades later, "but I remained
for years. There listening to the lectures of Georg
Simmel at Berlin, I received my only formal instruction
in sociology."[13]

While at Berlin, he read a treatise by the Russian
sociologist Bogdan Kistiakowski, who at one time had
been a student of the neo-Kantian philosopher Wilhelm
Windelband. Apparently he was so impressed with this
book that he moved to Strasbourg to read under Windelband, and later to Heidelberg where he eventually
earned his *Dr. Phil.* Thus, Park was the only one of the
four sociologists whose work is being analyzed herein
who completed his formal education in Europe. Both
Small and Bentley returned to Johns Hopkins after
their overseas jaunts where their names were added to
the list of eminent recipients of the doctorate from this
university.

13. Park, "An Autobiographical Note," p. vi.

This does not complete the story of the place held by German scholarship in the minds of the three Americans Small, Bentley, and Park. In the first place, all of them remained in close touch with German erudition following their careers as graduate students. For example, Bentley pursued an extended eleven-year correspondence with Simmel's protégé Leopold von Wiese.[14] These letters are technical in nature and provide an excellent means of tracing the divergent paths taken by two men, one a German and the other an American, from the same intellectual source, their major instructor Georg Simmel.

Small also corresponded with some German professors, although it appears as if no records of these exchanges were preserved. Fortunately for the future of the discipline of sociology, however, his scholarly excursions back to Germany were not kept to himself. He published scores of painstaking translations of the writings of Schmoller, Schäffle, Simmel, Ratzenhofer, Philippovich and others in the early numbers of the *American Journal of Sociology,* and for this reason has been called the "foremost disseminator" of German higher learning to America.

Like Small, Park too, later in his career, was a dispenser of German sociological literature to American audiences, primarily through his *Introduction to the Science of Sociology,* which he edited with Ernest Burgess.[15] Moreover, it was partially through Park's mediation that a book that he came upon while at Berlin University, Ferdinand Tönnies' *Gemeinschaft und*

14. The correspondence runs from July 1, 1926 to Jan. 28, 1938. It is at Indiana University, Lilly Library, Bentley Papers, Arthur F. Bentley-Leopold von Wiese Correspondence.

15. Robert E. Park and Ernest W. Burgess, ed., *Introduction to the Science of Sociology* (Chicago: University of Chicago Press, 1921). Park was the senior editor of this text.

Gesellschaft, received a favorable reception in America. It was from his father-in-law Park, that Robert Redfield first learned of the distinctions originally promulgated by Tönnies, which he was later to use in his classic studies of folk society.

Brief mention should also be made of the fact that Small, Bentley, and Park were involved not only in close interchanges with German literati, but with each other, as well as with many of their similarly educated colleagues. This is most clearly illustrated in the case of Small. He wrote to both Ward and Ross (as did Ward and his nephew Ross with each other), but was also an intimate friend of William I. Thomas at the University of Chicago, where for several years they comprised two of the three members of the faculty of sociology. Thomas had followed the example of thousands of his predecessors by treking to both Berlin and Göttingen, where he was taught the *Volkerpsychologie* of Wündt and Lazarus, after which he returned to earn his Ph.D. in sociology at Chicago.

The lakeside university during the period of Thomas' and Small's stay unabashedly emulated the scholarly activities of Johns Hopkins, and it was not only sociology that ultimately became professionalized as a result. Perhaps Chicago's most prestigious department at this time was philosophy, which could boast of the likes of Dewey, Mead, and James Tufts on its staff. The diplomatic Small did not hesitate to capitalize on the proximity of these now famous academicians and cultivated a relationship to which even to this day the field of social psychology is indebted.

Just before the war when Thomas replaced Small as the dominant figure in the department, Park was induced to return to university life and lecture on the subject of race relations. What was intended as a temporary appointment became permanent, and over the next several years Park became intimate friends with Small, later serving as a pall bearer at his funeral in 1926.[16]

Even Bentley who lived and wrote but a brief time in formal academia, spent it at Chicago from 1895-1896, lecturing on French and German sociology. According to his biographer, Sidney Ratner, "owing to the ambitiousness and difficulty of the subjects proposed by Bentley for study by the group, they and Bentley quietly agreed to discontinue their meetings after some five sessions."[17] Some years thereafter, following work as a reporter for several newspapers in Chicago, the disillusioned teacher retired to his apple orchard in Paoli, Indiana, there to quietly pursue a very productive scholarly life writing in sociology and philosophy. But even here, Bentley kept somewhat abreast of changes in both fields, especially through a vast exchange of letters with Dewey.

A Biographical Appendix on Ward

It is appropriate now to consider the case of Lester F. Ward (1841-1913), for his life might be taken as an exception to the patterns of intellectual development just observed. In the first place, he apparently was not born into what I have called "local society."[18] While he claimed at least that he could trace his ancestry back to English nobility and was, like his three contem-

16. For the standard history of the department of sociology at Chicago, see Robert E. L. Faris, *Chicago Sociology, 1920-1932* (San Francisco: Chandler, 1967).

17. Ratner, "Introduction," p. 27.

18. For the following biographical account of Ward, I am indebted to: Samuel Chugerman, *Lester F. Ward: The American Aristotle* (Durham, North Carolina: Duke University Press, 1939); Commager, *Lester Ward and the Welfare State;* John C. Burnham, *Lester Frank Ward in American Thought* (Washington D. C.: Public Affairs Press, 1956).

poraries, raised on the rural frontier, his father was an itinerant mechanic and jack-of-all-trades and his mother a poor clergyman's daughter. Ward was one of ten children who lived a materially and culturally impoverished life. Born in Joliet, Illinois, he began working as a common laborer for local farms and factories at a young age, and it was not until he was sixteen that he embarked on a long journey of self education. In 1865, following service in the Civil War, during which he was seriously wounded, he obtained the position of a minor clerk in the Treasury Department. Finally when he was twenty-six years old he received his first opportunity to attend college, the night sessions at Columbian (now George Washington) University. Ward had a voracious appetite for learning, taking academic degrees in law and medicine and even a Master of Arts degree all within the next five years.

Robert K. Merton and others have proposed to explain cases similar to Ward's by invoking reference group theory. According to this notion, it is often easier to forecast the behavior of persons by locating the groups with which they seem to psychologically identify, their "reference groups," rather than by classifying them into aggregations with which they share some objective attribute such as amount of wealth or skin color. And indeed without claiming to be too precise, there is substantial evidence to support the hypothesis that although Ward was born into what might be considered the proletariat, he clearly identified with those whose style of life was similar to the educated members of local society.

Let us be more specific. As I have used the term, "local society" refers to the families that occupied the top circles in each of the small American towns in the last half of the nineteenth century. As every sensitive analyst from Lloyd Warner to Robert Lynd has shown, by no means was membership in local society open to everyone with a given amount of money. In other words, local society was always much more than simply a social class in the Weberian sense. In the first place, one's money had to be made in a respectable manner; either through direct inheritance, taking over the family business, or as a doctor, lawyer, professor, or clergyman. In addition to this, a claimant to local society also had to be a "one hundred percent native American," which meant that his family ties in that region had to go back at least one generation. Lastly, he had to be "appreciative of culture." That is to say, he had to have attended college, know a little Greek and Latin, and struggled with the Classics. Without question Small, Park, and Bentley all met these several requisites. All three of them were from long-standing white Anglo-Saxon families, the bread winners of which were successful bankers, merchants, or clergymen, and above all, they had the proper education. At no little expense to their families they attended the best universities in the world, which at that time were in Germany. And all engaged in literary occupational pursuits as scholars, journalists, and secretaries, etc.

But what about Ward, can the same be said of him? It is true that Ward was poor. But that's beside the point. For he spent the major part of his life struggling to pass the three major tests for entrance into local society: appropriate type of money, the correct color of blood, and the proper culture. Whenever possible, he pointed out to his readers and listeners that despite his temporary financial straits, he was one of a long line of early American settlers and English noblemen. After many disappointing years, he finally succeeded in making his money in the "correct" way, as a college professor at Brown. And perhaps most importantly, he vigorously sought to attain the most visible accoutrement of local society, its "culture."

It has been argued that Ward "knew the plain people. . . , those who rode the coaches instead of Pullman palace cars, workingmen, privates in the army, the humblest civil servants of Washington, the immigrants, the poor, the denizens of the slums, whom he thought were potentially the equals of the rich and privileged."[19] But even granting the truth of this observation, he did not empathize with the lowly masses to the extent that he wished to emulate them. He moved just as easily with the highly prestigious scientists of the Smithsonian Institute, the Bureau of Statistics, and the U. S. Geological Survey such as Major John Powell, Clarence King, and Ferdinand Hayden, as he ever did with lower-class persons. That he preferred the company of trained biologists and paleontologists over that of "immigrants, the poor, and the denizens of the slums," was unambiguously demonstrated by his emphasis upon education as "the great panacea;" that is, his belief that a formal education is absolutely necessary for a happy, fulfilled, and progressive life of achievement. Samuel Chugerman has suggested that this proposed cure-all for the world's problems was in large measure a product of Ward's lonely struggle, in the face of odds that would have shattered men with less determination, to *rid* himself of what he took to be the most characteristic encumbrance of the masses —their ignorance.[20] Ward thought it was their stupidity that disposed the poor to engage in what he considered to be the "utopian" and "irrational" fancies of the Greenbacks, Populists, grangers, and socialists move-

---

19. Commager, *Lester Ward and the Welfare State,* p. xxvii.
20. Chugerman, *Lester F. Ward: The American Aristotle,* p. 26. Cf. Hofstadter, *Darwinism in American Thought,* p. 76.

ments of his day, none of which he felt any compulsion to join.[21]

In addition, it is significant in this regard that Ward sought not to receive training in a practical field as a lower class person might do, but rather for the liberal education that was, during this time, one criterion of membership in local society. He mastered Latin, French, and later German. He attempted to learn Greek, and read widely in philosophy from Mill and Locke, to Hegel and Schopenhauer. This plus his gaining of medicine and law degrees and the passing of the Supreme Court bar examination, are all symptomatic of pursuits of those who feel some harmony with local society.

A note might be added here concerning Ward's well-known vanity. As will be seen later, he had a certain fondness for "pompous Latin and Greek derivatives," and often interspersed the meat of his sociological messages with terms like "synergy," "social karyokinesis," "tocogenesis," "anthropoteology," and "telesis." This propensity to introduce technical sounding jargon has been interpreted as a "salve for his acute sensitivity about his humble origins."[22] This unconscious need to compensate for the miserable circumstances in which he was raised may also have been the motive behind his original plan to include twelve volumes in his autobiography, entitled *Glimpses of the*

21. Soon after entering the government as a clerk, Ward founded the National Liberal Reform League, which, with its journal the *Iconoclast*, was concerned with such "non-proletarian" matters as "uniting upon the cardinal principles of hostility to the leading doctrinal teachings of the so-called Catholic and evangelical Protestant churches, and of zeal for the triumph of reason and science over faith and theology." Lester F. Ward, *Young Ward's Diary*, ed. by Bernhard J. Stern (New York: G. P. Putnam's Sons, 1935), quoted in Gabriel, *The Course of American Democratic Thought*, p. 206.

22. For example, see Hofstadter, *Darwinism in American Thought*, p. 69. Burnham's *Lester Frank Ward in American Thought* contains a scathing critique of Ward's vanity.

Cosmos. The publisher finally persuaded him to reduce his life story plus "glimpses" to a more wieldy and less expensive six volumes. But when compared to the relative paucity of autobiographical material written by Bentley, Park, and Small, this suggests that like any nouveau riche, he needed conspicuously to demonstrate to his reference group, local society, that he had indeed finally arrived. The others had less reason to go to such obtrusive lengths to prove their membership in a group into which, after all, they had been born.

While Ward had no chance to study in Germany, once he became established as an eminent scholar in several fields he began reading German sociology and corresponding with many persons, including Simmel, Ratzenhofer, and Gumplowicz.[23] Thus in time he too was able indirectly to exploit some of the same cultural opportunities afforded in Europe as his more fortunate American colleagues. The content of Ward's correspondence will be considered in the next chapter, but suffice it to say at present that of the exchange between him and Gumplowicz, its editor, Bernhard J. Stern, was moved to comment that

the intimacy of the letters of Ludwig Gumplowicz to Lester F. Ward could be anticipated by those aware of the close intellectual sympathy of these pioneers in sociology. Ward was one of the most active proponents of Gumplowicz' views in the United States; Gumplowicz sought to popularize Ward's views in Europe. They might well be described as collaborators.[24]

23. The letters from Simmel and Ratzenhofer may be found at Brown University Library, Providence, Rhode Island, Lester F. Ward Papers.
24. Gumplowicz, "The Letters of Ludwig Gumplowicz to Lester F. Ward," p. 3.

6

Lester F. Ward's Sociology of Conflict

Isaiah Berlin, the prominent English historian and philosopher, once proposed to divide all men of learning into two types, distinguished by the demon that drives them. There is, he said, the hedgehog, the cosmologist who seeks to explain all things by means of a single principle. Then there is the fox, corresponding to today's research scientist, who in ignoring the big picture finds satisfaction in honing to a still finer edge the formulations defining his narrow specialty.

Lester F. Ward was one of the last of a vanishing if not entirely extinct breed of American hedgehogs. He was one of the few American scholars who could ever justifiably claim, as in his vanity he did more than once, that he knew every fact worthwhile knowing. Formally educated during a period before the philosophical unity of the American college disintegrated with the advance of professionalism into a plurality of warring departmental fiefdoms, he found it easy to dabble in widely diverse fields from which he acquired a surprisingly broad fund of information. But Ward's intellectual energy was by no means exhausted in the mere accumulation of college degrees. He was also driven by a need to synthesize all that he knew into a unified system, to reduce it all to a primary overarching law. This he finally succeeded in doing in his first book *Dynamic Sociology*,[1] which was published at the age of 42 in 1883.

In this treatise Ward employed cosmic principles to explain in turn the creation of progressively more complex organizations of energy, first the solar system, then plant and animal communities, and finally human society. In those days apparently few persons had the impulse to pick up a book written by an obscure, self educated government bureaucrat—especially a book in which the author, displaying few inhibitions against parading his expertise on all subjects, put his readers through several hundred tortuous pages of physics and chemistry, before even mentioning the title subject. And, understandably, the final destination of a substantial portion of the original edition was not a college library shelf, but Ward's own basement.

Ward was rescued from a certain fate as a forever misunderstood genius by Albion Small, an aspiring political economist recently returned from Germany, who was then making his first tentative excursions into this new area called "sociology." It was he who introduced *Dynamic Sociology* to respectable circles in a chapter in America's original sociology textbook at Colby College. For the young Small, *Dynamic Sociology* said it all. It was the "catalyst" that precipitated into an expressible form the vague ideas in his own mind, the "philosopher's stone" that finally put his own notions on a solid scientific footing.[2]

When Ward embarked on the research that eventually culminated in *Dynamic Sociology*, he was completely ignorant of the vast European and especially

1. Lester F. Ward, *Dynamic Sociology*, 2 vols. (New York: D. Appleton & Co., 1920).
2. Albion W. Small, "Lester Frank Ward," *AJS* XIX (July, 1913): 76.

German literature on similar subjects. Except for a cursory appreciation of the standard English and French liberal thinkers Hobbes, Locke, Voltaire, and Mill, his most intimate associations up to 1883 had been with physical scientists. Naturally then, he viewed himself as "a voice crying in the wilderness" and his work as "putting new landmarks on the map." But as he soon discovered, there were indeed well-developed anticipations of his own perspective, particularly in the publications of a one-time revolutionary, now aging professor of jurisprudence in Graz, Austria, Ludwig Gumplowicz. *Race und Staat,* a well-documented attempt to reduce Eastern European history to the theme of racial conflict and conquest, was the first of Gumplowicz's pamphlets to fall into Ward's hands. It made an immediate and favorable impression on him. The result was a correspondence between the two men that, beginning in 1897, lasted a decade up to the time of Gumplowicz's self-inflicted death.

The exchange of letters reveals that Gumplowicz played an important role in the presentation of Ward's *Pure Sociology* and his article entitled "Contemporary Sociology" to the German-reading public. As we shall see, both publications contain adulations of Gumplowicz, which gives one an idea as to why, generally rebuked by his fellow colleagues, he might have expended such great effort to get them published in German. In return for these services, Ward apparently undertook to have both Gumplowicz's *Rassenkampf* and *Race und Staat* sold in English translations. In spite of his failure to do so, Gumplowicz expressed his gratitude to Ward often and at length. The following excerpt from one of his letters to Ward provides a glimpse of the high esteem which Gumplowicz held for him:

3. For example, see Small, "Fifty Years," p. 749.

I cannot find words to thank you for your support. What you say there is fully the truth. If I did not write to such indirect attacks and *Ignorierungen,* I did this because of a belief that the truth would come through if only after my death, for the realities are still obtainable—or can be touched. My *Race and State* exists, in spite of all, in the library. I was therefore silent. Now my dear friend you have done while I was living, what I thought would only be done after my death. You have given me contentment during my life, which commonly people who have something new to say rarely experience in their life. I no longer need to wait for a defender after my death. I found him during my life. That is rare luck.[4]

Reflecting on Ward's contributions to American sociology near the end of his own career, Albion Small came to the judgement that Ward's later theorizing added nothing of significance to the pronouncements contained in his original book, *Dynamic Sociology.*[5] But to me it would certainly seem odd if a person like Ward were to avidly read the work of another, lavishly praise it, maintain an extended correspondence with its author, and then fail to take it into consideration in the reformulation of his own hypotheses. It is my belief that at least in the context of his notion of the rise of the state and the nature of dynamics within it, Ward's views can be shown to have been substantially altered in time to accord with those of Gumplowicz.[6] In fact, Ward himself had occasion to admit as much in several places:

4. Gumplowicz, "The Letters of Ludwig Gumplowicz to Lester F. Ward," Aug. 13, 1907, pp. 25-26.
5. Small says that "although Ward afterward wrote three major works besides two minor ones and numerous monographs in exposition of his views, I have never discovered that in any essential particular, they added to or subtracted from the system contained in *Dynamic Sociology.*" Small, "Fifty Years," p. 752. Cf. Small, "Lester Frank Ward," p. 77.
6. This assessment agrees with that of Harry Elmer Barnes, "Two Representative Contributions of Sociology to Political Theory: The Doctrines of William Graham Sumner and Lester Frank Ward," *AJS* XXV (Sept., 1919).

Some of the theories put forth to explain the origin of the state may contain germs of truth, but the greater part of them are utterly worthless, as embodying no principle capable of understanding anything. Each writer imagined himself competent to formulate a theory of the state. I made bold to enter the lists in my initial work which appeared in 1883. I was culpably ignorant of Morgan's great work published five years earlier and Gumplowicz's *Rassenkampf* appeared the same year as my own book. Of course I knew nothing of his pamphlet *Race und Staat,* 1875, which contains a clear statement of the principle. My guess was as good as the average, but was wide of the mark, and in light of the great Austrian theory and of ethnological proofs I do not hesitate to repudiate it to the same limbo as all the rest.[7]

To see just how extensively and in what ways Ward changed his political sociology to conform to that of Gumplowicz's, it is necessary to examine it in detail both prior to and following his contact with Gumplowicz. For this purpose I will compare Ward's theory of the rise of the state as presented in *Dynamic Sociology* with that in *Pure Sociology,* a monograph prepared some years following the initiation of Ward's correspondence with Gumplowicz.

Ward's Original Notion of the Rise of the State

To begin with, Ward's hypothesis concerning the origin of the state as presented in *Dynamic Sociology* is, in the words of Harry Elmer Barnes, "exceedingly archaic."[8] The story begins with a description of humanity in its presumably "original" Hobbesian-like state of nature. Here is man as *"homo homini lupus*

7. Lester F. Ward, "Sociology and the State," *AJS* XV (March, 1910).
8. Barnes, "Two Representative Contributions of Sociology to Political Theory," p. 159

... the worst enemy of man,"[9] each individual flee-ing out of fear of violence from his closest neighbor. This not only renders primitive man a solitary being, but leads him eventually to "diffuse the race over the globe."[10] However, there soon follows a time of "con-strained association" when the distribution of the popu-lation becomes so dense as to make the desire for an isolated existence an impossible dream.[11] Now with no opportunity to otherwise escape his terrifying situation, there arises in the mind of each individual, at least an unconscious craving for some sort of social order.

According to the contract theory of the genesis of the state, men living in an anarchic situation, being ra-tional, will agree to limit their own action in order to overcome the imposition and abuse of their fellows. But Ward explicitly rejects this notion even in his earliest publication:

> It is from some such idea of the origin of government that has been derived the theory of a "social compact" and the implied "contract" into which writers are so fond of saying that each member of society has entered; voluntarily con-senting to give up a certain number of his rights to the state and pay into its treasury a certain sum for the ben-efit of others, and for his own protection. But it is worthy of serious inquiry whether the very foundation of this doc-trine be not false, and the doctrine itself unsound.[12]

Ward argues that those *few* who are of superior intel-ligence, motivated by nothing more than the wish to increase their own fame and fortune, unilaterally come to occupy positions of control over their less well-

9. Ward, *Dynamic Sociology,* I, 453.
10. Ibid., p. 464.
11. Says Ward: "In this state the individual was free, but he was utterly insecure. There reigned the ulmost liberty and the ulmost license. ... Intel-lect was the servant of selfish passion, alone, and all forms of abuse were of constant occurrence." Ibid., p. 465. Cf. Ibid., II, 215-21.
12. Ibid., II, 222.

endowed subjects. Using their minds in a cunning manner, they offer protection to their fellows from each other, with the promise to regulate their economic and sexual affairs, while demanding in return complete submission to their rule.

> Government must, therefore, be regarded as an invention of the human mind, the result of an extraordinary exercise of the rational, or thinking faculty. As such, it could not have been the simultaneous conception of a whole community or any large number of people. It must have been the emanation of a single brain or of a few concerting minds, the special exercise of a particular kind of cunning, or sagacity, whereby certain individuals, intent on securing the gratification of the special passion known as the love of power, devised a plan, or scheme, of government.[13]

After the establishment of government, men enter the last step in the genesis of social forms, called by Ward national "politarchism." Here, the anarchic strife between individuals, now silenced, is transferred to that between independent sovereign communities.

It is perhaps significant that attatched to this protrayal of the evolution of government are what appear to be implicit disclaimers. This seems to suggest that Ward was really quite skeptical about the validity of his account. The original state of man, he says upon reflection, is "represented by the genus of true animals which Haekel has called *Pithecanthropus* and is equally hypothetical with that now extinct genus."[14] And "the second stage [the actual rise of the government] embodies none of the elements of permanency and can not be expected to be found extensively prevailing at *any* age of the world. It is essentially a transition stage, and like transition forms in biology, is

13. Ibid., p. 224.
14. Ibid., I, 467.

characterized by an ephemeral duration."[15] On the other hand, "to the third state, . . . belong not only all the savage tribes at all advanced and possessing any settled habits or forms of government, but also all barbarians, semi-civilized races, and races and nations calling themselves civilized and enlightened."[16]

But if this is true, then only his analysis of the last evolutionary step seems to be scientifically testable. In other words, if the first stage is no longer in existence, and the second can never be observed, then neither are logically subject to confirmation nor disconfirmation. Ward himself may have had an inkling of this when in his *Outlines of Sociology,* published in 1897, but probably written prior to that time, he called this particular three-stage treatment of the state's genesis merely "hypothetical."[17] It is entirely possible that he never really intended his story to be anything more than an ethical judgement, to emphasize the point that the state is a product of man's rational capacity and therefore resides on a higher ethical level than individual anarchy.

When he first came upon it at about the age of fifty, Ward found himself very receptive to Gumplowicz's *Staatstheorie* with its "ethnological proofs" as he called them. But it was not just the scientific evidence that Gumplowicz had painstakingly collected to verify his hypotheses that attracted Ward to his work. Even in *Dynamic Sociology* Ward evinces an unmistakeable attitude of realism, a mind set for seeing in political affairs the darker side of life, which would very likely have predisposed him to sympathize with Gumplowicz's realpolitik regardless of the evidence to support it. For

15. Ibid.
16. Ibid.
17. Lester F. Ward, *Outlines of Sociology* (New York: Macmillan Co., 1913), p. 232.

example, his denial that governments are the products of voluntary contracts between subjects and rulers is certainly consistent with a point Gumplowicz repeatedly made. And his dispute with "idealistic philanthropists" that laws dealing with social welfare result frm the altruistic sentiments of politicians would have received warm applause from Gumplowicz. In a style that reminds one of Gumplowicz at his best, Ward tells his readers that such laws are the exclusive result of intellectual force that "constitute[s] the method which mind was compelled to adopt in order to thwart mind."[18] Thus it follows that,

> no matter how grievous the wrongs suffered, or how loud the protestations of philanthropists, it will all avail nothing until the victim class is represented and its voice is heard. What is the meaning of this fact? What is it to be represented? It is to be clothed with power. This shows that rights can only be obtained by force, that the only limit to man's efforts to acquire is his power to succeed, that the only way to secure justice is to enforce it, and that human right and natural right are essentially one.[19]

Gumplowicz's Influence on Ward's Notion of Conflict

Ward minced no words when in his second notable publication, *Pure Sociology,* he acknowledged Gumplowicz's decisive theoretical advance over his own work:

> Gumplowicz and Ratzenhofer have abundantly and admirably proved that the genesis of society as we see it and

18. Ward, *Dynamic Sociology,* I, 514.
19. Ibid., p. 518. "Under the normal operation of the psychic and social forces," Ward argues, "the weaker yield to the stronger as certainly as that in physics motion will take place in the direction in which the stronger force acts." Ibid., p. 503.

know it has been through the struggle of races. I do not
hope to add anything to their masterly presentation of
this truth, which is without question the most important
contribution thus far made to the science of sociology. We
at last have a true key to the solution of the question of
the origin of society. It is not all but it is the foundation of
the whole, and while the edifice of sociology must be built
upon it, its full recognition and comprehension will de-
molish all the cheap and worthless rookeries that have occupied the same ground. It is the only scientific explanation that has been offered of the facts and phenomena of
human history. It proceeds from a true natural principle
which is applicable to man everywhere, which is in harmony with all the facts of ethnology and anthropology.[20]

Pure Sociology is divided into two basic sections: "social statics"—an analysis of the preconditions of social
order and unity and "social dynamics"—a description of
the conditions causing social change.[21] Furthermore,
Ward crosscuts this division by distinguishing between
the passive *genesis* of statics and dynamics resulting
from the relatively "blind" control of social forces by
each other in social conflict, and the active *telesis* of
statics and dynamics resulting from the conscious control of social energy.[22] Now it is in the context of his
discussion of the *genesis* of social forms and their
change through time that Ward developed some of his
most suggestive ideas concerning the cosmic principle
of "synergy," and it is here that Gumplowicz's influence
on his theorizing is most readily observable. Since
synergy is generally spoken of by Ward as a situation
of conflict, the following presentation of Gumplowicz's
inspiration will be divided into two parts: the static

20. Lester F. Ward, *Pure Sociology* (New York: Macmillan Co., 1914), p.
204. Cf. Lester F. Ward, "Contemporary Sociology," *AJS* VII (May, 1902):
759-62.
21. See Ward, *Pure Sociology,* pp. 182-85 and pp. 221-22.
22. For this distinction, see Ibid., pp. 463-66.

consequences of conflict and the dynamic consequences of conflict.

Static Consequences of Conflict

In Ward's cosmology all existing psychical, biological, and social structures are the products of conflict between simpler bodies moving with particular momentums. Forces traveling in opposite directions mutually obstruct one another creating more complex syntheses of energy. It is in this way that not only moral law, but also plant and animal species, as well as the planets have come into being. "They are all the result of some form of struggle among . . . forces whereby the centrifugal and destructive character of each force acting alone is neutralized and is made to contribute to the constructive work of [evolution]."[23]

Without the resistance of one force to another, energy would merely become catabolic, breaking down previously existing structures.[24] As applied to social life, this means that if order is to be preserved, then there must be factors that prevent the complete annihi-

23. Ibid., p. 193. Or saying it in another way: "Synergy is primarily and essentially . . . a process of equilibration, i.e. several forces are first brought into a stage of partial equilibrium. It begins in collision, conflict, antagonism, and opposition, but as no motion can be lost it is transformed, and we have the milder phases of antithesis, competition, and interaction passing next into a *modus vivendi* or compromise, and ending in collaboration and cooperation." Ibid., p. 175.
24. In Ward's terms: "We shall find that [the social world] is also a theater of intense activity, and that competing and antagonistic agencies are fiercely contending for mastery. The complete domination of any one set of these forces would prevent the formation of society. If such a hegemony were to supervene in any given stage it would sweep society out of existence. Only through the joint action of many forces, each striving for mastery but checked and constrained by the rest and forced to yield its share in conforming to the general principle can any structure result." Ibid. Cf. Ibid., p. 169.

lation of even deadly enemies by each other. For with the extermination of one opponent and the unilateral omnipotence of the other, there would naturally be nothing to constrain or balance the force of the victor. At the level of human existence, the main condition guaranteeing what Ward calls the "equilibration" of forces is intelligence.

"Intelligence" is probably the most important category in Ward's social theory. But since it is introduced in so many different settings, it is difficult to characterize its meaning in any single way. For our purposes, however, it seems possible to distinguish between the intelligence that Ward says appears in the genesis of social structures, from that which he calls "telic" reasoning. As compared to the latter, which will be elaborated upon in more detail below, genetic thinking does not enable its holder to control his original desires. Although it does give man the capacity to weigh different actions in terms of their practicality to achieve individual desires, it is sort of an unconscious appendage to the will. Or in more colorful language, it

has been an "accident" that came into the world at a late and comparatively modern date, was not welcomed, and for the greater part of its career held the position of vassal to the feudal lord, the will, which it not only served in abject submission, but ... did not hesitate to stoop to acts of the meanest class and do the henchman's work of dark deeds and sinister practices.[25]

Let us see, as described in Ward's *Pure Sociology,* the part that man's rudimentary ability to judge the different utilities of proposed ways of acting has played in political development. It will be remembered that in *Dynamic Sociology,* Ward introduced his discussion of this subject by hypothesizing the existence of a "natural state," a situation where individuals are un-

25. Ibid., p. 467. Cf. Ibid., pp. 486-88.

willingly locked in "constrained association." In *Pure Sociology,* however, following Gumplowicz's direction, he speaks of the initial phase in political history as comprised of a plurality of highly antagonistic *hordes,* each attempting to exterminate those with which it comes into contact, in order to insure its own survival in a situation of economic scarcity.

> Regarding one another as so many totally different orders of beings, every race became the bitter enemy of every other, and therefore on the approach of one race toward another there was no course but that of war. The proximity of hostile races was a powerful spur to invention, attention being chiefly turned to the production of the means of offense and defense.[26]

In time, through natural selection, a "semisubconscious" genetic intelligence evolves to temper the natural fear and emnity that the members of hordes have to strange outgroups. And as a fox uses the ruse to trap his unwitting victim, the idea begins to develop of coercing weaker hordes into submission in order to exploit their labor for long-range economic purposes.

> The idea of making some economic use of such proximity was not slow to rise in the mind of those groups that proved themselves superior. The use of the bodies of the weaker races for food was of course the simplest form of exploitation to suggest itself. But this stage was succeeded by that of social assimilation through conquest and subjugation, where the conquered race became something more than a factor in subsistence. Still the conquered race remained an economic element, and the conquering race soon learned to utilize it to far greater advantage than cannibalism could yield. The profound inequality produced by subjugation was turned to account through other forms of exploitation.[27]

26. Ibid., p. 203.
27. Ibid., p. 267. Thus in slavery, "the aim of the conquering race was to gain the maximum advantage from the conquest. The conquered race pos-

Reason dictates the practical necessity of sparing the conquered race, and directing it to permanently slave for its rulers. On the other hand, those who are vanquished come to realize that while further resistance will only be accompanied by violent death, submission to the commands of their conquerors will assure them at least temporary survival. Thus genetic intelligence on both sides allows the two opposing forces to balance one another, leading to the first political relations, and social order.

It is obvious how this theory, borrowed virtually word for word from Gumplowicz, is different from the narrative presented in *Dynamic Sociology*. While it is true that even in his earlier account Ward verbally discounted the classic liberal mechanism of a voluntary contract between rulers and subjects, he did speak of an agreement of sorts. Specifically, a brilliant few come up with a scheme to offer police protection in exchange for tax monies and obedience. In *Pure Sociology,* however, it is a foreign horde, an alien race that on pain of death, compels the members of another group to slave for it. Needless to say, after his reading of Gumplowicz's *Race und Staat,* Ward came to see that the terms of the "agreement" between masters and subjects are much more severe than he had previously assumed.

The history of the state is not completed with the mere establishment of the domination of some races over others. Again, in agreement with his mentor Gumplowicz, Ward claims that the most brutal forms of economic exploitation, such as slavery, are still charac-

---

sessed little that could be seized as booty. This would be soon consumed and gone. The only thing the conquered race possessed that had permanent or continual value was its power of serving the conqueror." Ibid., p. 271. In another place Ward says that "the enslavement of the captured which gradually succeeded and ultimately supplanted cannibalism, was a matter of policy and rational calculation of the greatest gain." Ibid., p. 556.

terized by a mutual terror and hatred of races for one another. "The conquering race looks down with contempt upon the conquered race and compels it to serve it in various ways. The conquered race maintains its race hatred while sullenly submitting to the inevitable, refuses to recognize anything but the superiority of brute force."[28] But the unremitting exercise of military power over all the acts of their slaves becomes increasingly costly to the master race. Thus in the second phase of political evolution, they begin to concede to their subjects rights and duties under a formal system of law. In exchange for these concessions the conquered peoples willingly accept their rulers' claim of the right to hold sway over them, for they believe such an accommodation to be consistent with their own selfish interests. Under law, they are at least protected from the more irrational and distasteful features of tax collection, such as the burning of huts and the raping of their women. And under certain circumstances this is even accompanied by the promise that they can keep some of their surplus agricultural production.

> In a word, the conquering race needs the assistance of the conquered race in framing and carrying out measures of public policy. This is difficult to secure. . . . The only basis of such order is the creation of correlative rights and duties under the law. This can only be secured through concessions on the part of the master race to the subject race and the establishment of the best elements of the latter in the work of social reorganization. . . . Experience alone will dictate a milder policy in its own interest and the basis of compromise will at last be reached.[29]

Both in the original act of subjugation and then in the adoption of a more legal style of rule, man's capacity to think has entered the social process to mitigate the wills of foes to such an extent that "however bitter

28. Ibid., p. 207.
29. Ibid., p. 208. Cf. Ibid., p. 549.

their animosities may have once been, each discovers that he needs the help of the rest. Every man is an aid to every other. . . ."[30] This development is accelerated, says Ward after Gumplowicz, when outside invaders threaten to overrun the recently founded state.

> At such times the more numerous subject class becomes the main dependence and to it the new state usually owes its preservation. When this is the case two other unifying sentiments arise—a dim sense of gratitude on the part of the ruling class and a lively sense of pride on the part of the subject race.[31]

Now the last step in the synergic process is begun, as a shared national sentiment unifies those who not long before looked upon each other as different species of life, and the nation state is created.[32] "It means the end of the prolonged race struggle. . . . The antagonistic forces have spent themselves, social equilibrium is restored, and one more finished product of social synergy is presented to the world."[33]

Even if the state has its origin in violent coercion rather than in good will, this is not a sufficient basis, says Ward, for morally condemning it. This is because in spite of the fact that its founders never act except in their own immediate interests, the unintentional end of the state's apparatus is the quashing of the otherwise

30. Ibid., p. 209.

31. Ibid., p. 210.

32. Ward describes the process as follows: "There begins to be formed a national sentiment . . . a deep seated affection grows up for both the people and the territory. . . . The sentiment that it inspires receives a name derived from the same root and is called patriotism." Ibid., p. 211. Mention should be made of the role that the "systematic appropriation" by the men of the conquering race of the women of the conquered race and its consequent miscegenation plays in the creation of a new nation. "A people is a synthetic creation, . . . It is a new product evolved out of these elements through precisely the same process that goes on at every stage in cosmic evolution. . . ." Ibid., p. 208.

33. Ibid., p. 212.

completely selfish actions of its subjects. And without such a powerful mechanism of social control, man would be destined to live in a condition of perpetual anarchy.

> [The state] in the last analysis, is the result of a social necessity for checking this individualism and of holding the social forces within a certain orbit where they could interact without injury and where they could do constructive work. Without such restraint the competition in society knows no bounds. It is the law of the strongest and would ultimately restrict the human race to limited areas and conditions.[34]

By demanding the obedience of the naturally self-seeking individual to orders issued for the good of the whole society, the state in fact has become an instrument of morality, welfare, liberation, and finally even culture. For what is morality, asks Ward, but the subordination of a person's egoistic desires to the expectations of society? And is this really a type of enslavement, or is it rather emancipation from the bondage to one's animalistic passions, and the means by which men can attest to their uniqueness apart from lower beasts? Ward's responses to such queries are virtually identical to the positions of the most articulate nineteenth-century apologists for the state and debunkers of liberal individualism, the German national liberals. Indeed, were the reader not forewarned, he might believe himself to be reading in the following quotation an excerpt from Ratzenhofer's or Hegel's writings, rather than a statement from the father of American sociology:

34. Ibid., p. 551. Ward continues: "Just as one strong plant or weed may invade a virgin flora and drive out every indigenous plant, converting vast tracts to the exclusion of everything else, so in society without a regulative apparatus, only the strong will remain, and all the more delicate elements that give variety to existence and render culture, art, and science possible will be ruthlessly crushed out." Ibid.

We thus see that the state, though genetic in origin, is telic in method; that it has but one purpose, function or mission, that of securing the welfare of society; that its mode of operation is that of preventing the anti-social actions of individuals; that in doing so it increases the freedom of human action so long as it is not anti-social; that the state is therefore essentially moral or ethical; that being a natural product it must in a large sense be representative; that in point of fact it is always as good as society will permit it to be; that while thus far in the history of society the state has rarely performed acts that tend to advance mankind, it has been the condition to all achievement, making possible all the social, artistic, literary, and scientific activities that go on within the state and under its protection.[35]

Dynamic Consequences of Conflict

Once social structures such as nation states are constructed as the equilibrated products of racial conflict, then they are susceptible to progressive change. And as is the case for the development of social order in the first place, struggles for power are one of the most important motors of social progress. In a manner that again suggests the influence of Gumplowicz and Ratzenhofer on his reasoning, Ward attacks the sentimentally inclined "missionaries of peace" who fail to appreciate this fact:

In making this objective inquiry it [sociology] finds that, as a matter of fact, war has been the chief and leading condition of human progress. This is perfectly obvious to anyone who understands the meaning of the struggle of

35. Ibid., p. 555. Ward in fact approvingly quotes Ratzenhofer, Gumplowicz, and Simmel in this context (pp. 552-55) so the similarity of this excerpt to the notions of Hegel and Treitschke should not be too surprising. It is questionable, however, whether Ward himself would approve of our attempt to associate his concept of "state" with that of Hegel. For his explicit denunciations of Hegel, see Barnes, "Two Representative Contributions of Sociology to Political Theory," p. 157, n. 5.

the races. When races stop struggling, progress ceases. They want no progress and they have none. For all primitive and early, underdeveloped races, certainly, the condition of peace is a condition of social stagnation. . . . The greater part of the peace agitation is characterized by total blindness to all these broader cosmic facts and principles and this explains its complete impotence. . . . It is a mark of an effete mind to exaggerate small things while ignoring great things. Maudlin sentimentality and inconsistent sympathy, thinking on problems of the world without discrimination or perspective, incapacity to scent the drift of events or weigh the relative gravity of heterogeneous and unequal facts, are qualities that dominate certain minds which, from culture and advantages, gain credit of constituting the cream of the most advanced intelligence. Far safer guides are the crude instincts of the general public in the same communities. If the peace missionaries could have their counsel prevail there might have been universal peace, nay general contentment, but there would have been no progress.[36]

According to Ward, war always causes progress because instead of destroying the opponents, it results in their assimilation into a single more complex unit. And it does this "by preserving all that is best in the different structures thus blended, and creating a new structure which is different from and superior to any prior structures."[37] Thus it follows that nation states can be ranked in terms of their cultural achievement on the basis of the number of violent assimilations that they have undergone. During each forced intermixture of foreign cultures through war, the less competitive elements are strained out leaving a residue increasingly more capable of advancement. "Through this continuity of the germ plasm, accompanied by repeated crossing of

36. Ward, *Pure Sociology,* pp. 239-40. For similar remarks, the reader is directed to Lester F. Ward, "Social and Biological Struggles," *AJS* XIII (Nov., 1907): 294-99.
37. Ward, *Pure Sociology,* p. 247.

the highest strains, the maximum achievements are secured."[38]

But for this same reason, conflict *internal* to the state, particularly that which portends of revolution is actually nonprogressive. For in Ward's view, a successful revolution carried out by one party, inasmuch as it entails the possibility of all opposition being done away with, would in effect destroy the necessary and sufficient condition of synergy; namely, a force strong enough to balance and equilibrate the power of the victor. Thus while giving an appearance of improvement and advancement in the human condition, revolution in fact simply dissolves the previously existing order and replaces it with an empty vacuum.[39]

38. Ibid., p. 214. In the course of his correspondence with Ward, Ratzenhofer had occasion to criticize this prediction that war will eventually result in the assimilation of all peoples into a "universal race" that will be a synthesis of the best qualities of each separate race. Said Ratzenhofer: "I doubt that. This universal race can also express the nastiness and ugliness of all races. The realities teach the latter. Perhaps civilization is able to cleanse humanity through education and laws; but the mixing brings only the worsening of the best races. The differentiation has caused the values of the races, on the one hand the Papuas and on the other hand, the Germans. By intermingling fewer become Germans, since the black race is the original one; that is, the more powerful. . . . Thus a moment of devaluation for the most noble race will follow when she wanders. In short, I come to the conclusion—stop the intermingling of people and care for racial purity." Letter, Gustav Ratzenhofer to Lester F. Ward, July 7, 1903, Brown University Library, Providence, Rhode Island, Lester F. Ward Papers.

39. In Ward's terms: "This differential process is what characterizes evolution, and the contrast so often popularly made between evolution and revolution is the contrast between a truly dynamic process and a merely kinetic process which breaks up and destroys existing structures in order to make new ones. The structures destroyed by revolution are organic, i.e. genetic through the secular process of social assimilation. . . . It is impossible to reproduce them, and after the frenzy is over it is soon seen that humanity is inadequate artificially to replace time honored institutions which it has required ages to create, and a reaction usually sets in resulting in a return, temporarily at least, to the conditions as near as possible to those that existed before the revolution." Ibid., pp. 222-23.

Of course this does not mean that all forms of domestic conflict are destructive. There are those that actually preserve the system of order in which they are fought. While maintaining the equilibrium of society, such struggles guide it to a further elaboration and more efficient expression of its basic character. In this case, "the parties that think they are opposing each other are simply working together for the accomplishment of an end of which they are unconscious. They are acting in exactly the same way that hostile races act in the process of social assimilation."[40] But this point aside, the fact remains that Ward's assent to the necessity of war for social betterment and his simultaneous criticism of revolution indicate once again the striking similarity of his views to the *Weltanschauung* of German national liberalism. Let us go into this in a little more depth.

German National Liberalism and American Progressivism

To neither Ward nor the German reformists of associations like the *Verein für Sozialpolitik* was war conceived as necessarily a national calamity. On the contrary, recent experience apparently demonstrated to them that in fact war was a vehicle of public advance. The Prussian victory over the French Army at Sedan in 1870, culminating in a national solidarity that fifty years of legislative debate had failed to realize, might be considered analogous to the use of armed combat in America to attain the same

40. Lester F. Ward, "The Sociology of Political Parties," *AJS* XIII (Jan., 1908): 439.

goal in 1865. Ward in particular, and many of those for whom he wrote, had fought in the very struggles against Britain, Mexico, Spain, and the American Indian that were confirming the United States' claim that its manifest destiny was to rule the new world. Which of those who were also true patriots could fail to understand the broader "sociological significance" of international violence?

This interpretation of Ward's writings will probably touch a sensitive nerve in those accustomed to associating Ward and American sociology with nineteenth-century Progressivism. They picture Ward as the original advocate of the American welfare state, a staunch defender of the little man against the incursions of the conscienceless plutocrat. A man, in other words, who wrote in the finest Progressive tradition, and not a Treitschke-Ratzenhoferian defender of military conquest. But what these persons are apt either to forget or overlook altogether is that American Progressivism borrowed much of its ideological impetus and conceptual baggage directly from Berlin and Göttingen. And it would be odd if American Progressives such as Ward were to adopt one plank from the platform of German national liberalism, the doctrine of the positive state, and completely ignore another; specifically, the maxim of foreign imperialism.

The conventional image of American Progressivism sees it as fighting for domestic reforms at home while brandishing a big stick at foreign militarists abroad. Yet historical evidence clearly shows that such philosophically sophisticated Progressives as Herbert Croly, who himself was a product of the German universities, and Theodore Roosevelt, John Burgess' most eminent student, explicitly equated the struggle for federal meat inspection, federal control of railroads, and the eight-hour day with an imperialistic mission to spread the blessings of democracy overseas.[41] It was the Progressive senators and not the conservative Republicans, who advocated a peacetime draft in the name of national order, patriotism, and equality. And it was they and not the Mugwumps, who repeatedly voted for large naval appropriations and supported in turn American Marines' educative efforts in behalf of the Chinese, Santo Domingoans, Nicaraguans, and Philippinos. And lastly, it was the Progressive Party in 1915 and 1916 that at first hounded President Wilson's "weak-kneed wishy-washiness" in the time of crisis and then lauded him for finally deciding to employ American troops in an effort to "save the world for democracy."

If American Progressives and German national liberals believed that war was a practical means to cultural achievement, the thought of civil insurrection was distasteful, for it connoted a peril to that guardian of morality and justice, the nation state. In particular, the small independent businessmen, professionals, and clergymen of local society who made up the cadres of the Progressive movement saw their society of honesty, hard work, neighborliness, and private property beseiged on two sides by radical and alien forces. Their concern was that if either the robber barons or their hated enemies, the socialists, were to become completely omnipotent and seize control of the legislatures and the courts, then the safeguards of social harmony would perish. And as Ward told them, ". . .[I]t is clear that progress presupposes order. Order is therefore the necessary basis of progress, its essential condition."[42]

---

41. Documentation for this hypothesis is found in William E. Leuchtenburg, "Progressivism and Imperialism: The Progressive Movement and American Foreign Policy, 1896-1916," *The Mississippi Valley Historical Review* XXXIX (Dec., 1952): 483-504. See also Hofstadter, "Progressivism and War," *The Age of Reform.*

42. Ward, *Pure Sociology,* p. 223. Cf. Ibid., p. 222.

If Ward clearly stated the nature of the problem facing America, some, like Albion Small, also apparently found a degree of comfort from the thought of revolutionary disaster in his synergic cosmology. In *Pure Sociology,* the reader discovered that at least a temporary prescription to social health would be the existence of forces countering the demand for revolution. In America, for example, the monopoly capitalist and the proletariat are fighting each other. Thus each will obstruct the force of the other and prevent him from unilaterally controlling society's affairs. And if things turn out for the better, the conflict might even move the nation on to a higher creative synthesis of their good qualities. As Ward reassured his audience:

> We talk of progress but the fact is that there can be no progress without resistance. . . . Unopposed progress is simply motion of translation and accomplishes nothing. . . . To be effectual and constructive it must meet with resistance and encounter opposition. The conservative party, party of reaction or of order, represents this wholesome opposition which looks so much like antagonism, strife and struggle, transforms force into power and builds political and social structures.[43]

Like the German national liberals, however, Ward and his followers were not content to rely upon the mere genetic intelligence of workers and industrialists to discover their mutual dependencies and establish a basis for *modus vivendi* through the trial and error method of conflict. Instead, Ward advocated that the state hire sociologists to consciously propose and implement techniques for social advancement on the basis of their expertise.

It will be remembered that Ward distinguishes between genetic and telic intelligence. While the first is a capacity involved in the "unconscious" reciprocal con-

43. Ward, "The Sociology of Political Parties," p. 440.

trol of social forces, the latter becomes manifest only in the *conscious* control of such energy. Telic thinking finds its original expression in the application of physical laws to harness natural elements for man's own benefit. But Ward proposed that telesis now be extended to a radically new field beyond the realm of wind and fire, to human behavior itself. He believed that the recent discovery of social "laws" made it possible for the first time to consciously engineer social progress. In a manner analogous to the doctor's use of science to cure his patient, he felt that for *its* health, society should submit its problems to the detached diagnoses and surgical techniques of sociological experts.

On the basis of what he considered to be his sound scientific knowledge of human history, Ward became a determined spokesman for legislation that would grant to each American the opportunity to obtain an adequate education. This was his reasoning: Since with the secularization of society, religious institutions naturally lose their importance as a means of social control, the state will come to assume this responsibility in modern life. Obviously the state can use force, if need be, to gain the compliance of otherwise dissident individuals. But a less costly and in the long run more effective means of insuring conformity would be to instill in the minds of society's members internal psychological controls. In other words, instead of wasting effort by attempting to coerce its subjects against their wills to comply to society's directives, the state should teach its citizens in public schools that what is socially useful and therefore obligatory, is also individually desirable. Only now will each person feel a moral compulsion to behave, and voluntarily carry out what society wished him to do in the first place. But for education to replace external coercion as the ground of social control in America, its school system must no longer cater exclusively to the small minority of rich in the community. To guarantee that every citizen will be taught his social duties, education should be made a democratic right, indeed be made compulsory up until a certain age.

Ward had such great faith in public education as a means of social reform that he even proposed that it be employed to alleviate the possibility of class conflict and to liberate the masses from economic exploitation. This has direct relevance to our study, because it demonstrates the precise point at which Ward left the teachings of Gumplowicz and struck out on an independent path.

In explaining the existence of social classes in America, Ward followed Gumplowicz to the letter. It is not, he would say, because the rich are genetically intellectually and morally superior to the proletariat that there are vast differences in wealth and culture in all societies—a position, by the way, held by serious social Darwinists of his time. Rather, class differences originate from the simple fact of violent conquest of one race by another. The conquering race in conspicuously consuming its wealth, uses its vast leisure time to develop the martial arts that are called upon to defend its dominant position from usurpers. More significantly, they alone have the opportunity to further their intellects, to cultivate refined artistic tastes, and to train themselves in the conventions of civilized political rule, all of which serve to legitimize their superior position in society. This renders it increasingly unlikely that military force will ever have to be resorted to at all to maintain order.

The race struggle has been universal, and everywhere it has produced the same effects. The first important institution to grow out of it is that of caste, and social classes even of the most modern times and in the most advanced nations are all consequences, modified forms, and true survivals of the original system of caste. Their ethnic character is never wholly lost sight of, and notwithstanding the great and universal panmixia of races, enough ethnic traits remain to preserve a crude distinction between the higher and lower social classes in every country of Europe, and even in America.[44]

To alter this totally unjust situation, radical means are called for. And the choice of appropriate tools is made even more difficult because of the fact that appeals to the altruistic sentiments of the ruling class will invariably fall on deaf ears.

All attempts to soften the human heart must fail. Without assuming to dictate what human nature ought to be, the only rational course is to recognize what is, and to act accordingly. Instead of trying to dissuage men from taking away the property of others, society must render it impossible for them to do so.[45]

These realistically harsh words should not be mistaken as a call for the proletariat to take up arms and throw off the yoke of its oppressor. As indicated above, Ward was abhored by the thought of revolution, in spite of the fact that his books were banned in Russia.[46] On the contrary, "the proper way to induce men to desist from unjust action," he claims, "is to

---

44. Lester F. Ward, "Social Classes in the Light of Modern Sociological Theory," *AJS* XIII (March, 1908): 622.
45. Ward, *Dynamic Sociology,* I, 518.
46. Ward has been linked by some historians of social thought to Karl Marx because of the fact that the Tsarist Committee of Ministers condemned his *Dynamic Sociology* on March 26, 1891. However, the content of a letter sent to him from George Kennan demonstrates the fatuousness of this inference. Not only was Ward's first sociological treatise ordered to be burned, but also the work of Herbert Spencer who was himself explicitly apolitical, and also that of the nonrevolutionary Thomas Hobbes. In none of these cases did the official reason for the condemnation have anything to do with the "radicalism" of the authors. Thus, for example, the explanation for the censure of Ward's book was that it "is saturated with the rankest materialism." Albion W. Small, "The Letters of Albion W. Small to Lester F. Ward," ed. by Bernhard J. Stern, *Social Forces* XII (Dec., 1933): 166.

make it of their own interest to do so and teach them in an unmistakable manner that it is so. This is the work of intelligence and education."[47]

One of Ward's biographers, Samuel Chugerman, has summarized nicely Ward's melioristic approach to the class problem in the following way:

> Ward often spoke of the people taking what was rightfully theirs. Yet the acceptance of force in advance of its inevitable necessity, was to him the very negation of rational action. Where Marx chose to fight for human emancipation with the weapons of class warfare and economic cataclysm, Ward advised the masses to educate themselves, wake up to their own interests and by collective effort, make force unnecessary. By fighting with the weapons of education, there is a strong possibility of transforming utopian visions into a practical working reality.[48]

Ward's Rejection of Gumplowicz's Pessimism

In his development of the idea that sociological expertise should be used to consciously plan for increasing social happiness, and his belief in public education as a technique of human progress, Ward found himself attacking the moral position of "pessimism" of which Gumplowicz was a well-known proponent. It is true that in their writings, both men seem to have shared a crude and more or less implicit Schopenhauerian psychology, hypothesizing that man acts on the basis of his (usually material) interests, in conjunction with what he believes are the most practical means for their realization. And there is a similarity in the prediction that inasmuch as there is almost always a scarcity of food and facilities relative to an individual's desires for

47. Ward, *Dynamic Sociology,* I, 518.
48. Chugerman, *Lester F. Ward: The American Aristotle,* p. 355.

complete biological gratification, then men are constantly thrown together in a struggle for power. But unlike his pupil Ward, Gumplowicz stopped at this point. Believing these propositions to have the status of natural laws, he thought it both naive and pretentious for man to attempt to alter his fate from that which was already predetermined. In his characteristically blunt way of expressing himself on this subject, he once said that "man can make and unmake many things, but he can not make himself other than what he is."[49] Because he thought this to be the case, he found little comfort in the hopeful forecasts of universal social advancement made by such analysts as Ward, whom he derisively labeled "optimists." And he counted himself among the small elite of philosophers courageous enough to continue life even while appreciating the terrible dilemmas of human existence. In one of his attempts to persuade Ward to throw away his illusions, Gumplowicz wrote:

> To you Mr. Ward, I do not believe in the moral advance of human beings. I do not therefore believe in a significant improvement of the social circumstances. The human spirit is very inventive. The one group finds means to improve the social condition. The other group discovers new ways to maintain its position. For instance, take slavery: it appears to be done away with, but is it really? In Poland serfdom was done away with, but under the *Robot* farmers are still in indebtedness. While weak ones find new ways to overcome dominance, the strong ones find new ways to maintain it.[50]

In the fourth chapter, it was pointed out how some aspiring young American scholars doing graduate study in Germany during the nineteenth century,

49. Ludwig Gumplowicz, "An Austrian Appreciation of Lester F. Ward," *AJS* X (March, 1905): 645.
50. Gumplowicz, "The Letters of Ludwig Gumplowicz to Lester F. Ward," August 7, 1902, p. 9.

while impressed by its intellectual fare, were shocked by the pessimistic storm and stress of German cultural life; and how E. A. Ross longed for this very reason to go "back to America the land of optimism, of progress, of freedom of will and wealth!" Apparently his nephew was not the only American in contact with German scholarship who felt the call of its frontier optimism, because Ward built into his own sociology the possibility for man to overcome his beastly political and military behavior through the use of his mind. Knowledge of the natural laws governing social interaction, he argued, need not necessarily lead to Gumplowiczian despondence, but can be turned around to control the very conditions giving rise to social evil in the first place.[51] With a sociological cognizance of reality, plus an awareness of the presumably shared end of all men for "happiness," the reformist can institute those legal imperatives that will be most effective in the promotion of true progress.

If one feature stands out as constant in Ward's otherwise continuously changing view of history and society, it is his almost classic liberal assent to human rationality as the means of eradicating human difficulty. In one of his earliest essays written at the age of twenty-eight, entitled "Reason," he spoke of his faith in humanity in the following terms: "It is the common error of mankind to underrate the importance of his reason. . . . Indeed the progress of the world has probably always been in almost exact proportion to the estimate which has been placed upon the reasoning power."[52] Several decades later in 1904, while he was an American delegate to the Geological Congress in Vienna, Ward had the long-awaited opportunity to personally visit for the first time with his old friend Gum-

---

51. Cf. Ward, *Pure Sociology,* p. 144.
52. Lester F. Ward, "Reason," unpublished essay quoted by Chugerman, *Lester F. Ward: The American Aristotle,* p. 291.

plowicz. According to the Austrian, the two men spent
one half day in Graz debating over Ward's program of
meliorism through telic intelligence. Gumplowicz later
confessed that in the face of arguments from "an intellectual giant of a type that I had never before met in
reality, . . . I had to acknowledge myself defeated."[53]

By now, of course, it can be appreciated that Ward
did not, like the old-time liberals, Rousseau, Kant, and
Jefferson, introduce the category of reason out of context of the overall process of human evolution. For him,
the ability to think is not something that stands aloof
from social life, adjudicating its affairs from a distance,
but is itself an unintended product of historical development. Through the wholly blind means of natural
selection, man discovered that he could choose the most
practical means to gain his selfish ends by reflecting on
the consequences of acting in different ways. It is this
"genetic intelligence," as he called it, that has enabled
man to realize that the use of unlimited violence
against his enemies is prohibitively costly for the realization of his *own* selfish interests. It is this utilitarian
consideration, and not sentimental moralizing, that has
compelled men throughout history to restrict the
savagery of the tactics employed in attempting to overpower one another. And this is the reason why
"scarcely any of the shocking acts that blacken almost
every page of the history of every country, would be
even possible in any country."[54] Besides the growth of
houses of parliament within which otherwise disruptive
conflicts can be peaceably played out, "today there is a
code of 'civilized warfare' and any nation or race that
violates it is considered uncivilized. Not only this, but
in fighting uncivilized races, civilized nations must
conform to this code."[55]

53. Gumplowicz, "An Austrian Appreciation of Lester F. Ward," pp. 646-47.
54. Ward, *Pure Sociology,* p. 450.
55. Ibid., p. 451.

But the story of reason's role in human evolution does not stop here. According to Ward, the semi-subconscious genetic mind has imperceptably become fully cognizant of its own place in history. Thus it has become possible for man to consciously control social forces, to calculatedly create social progress, rather than to rely upon the slow and silent effects of synergy. Sociologists are now aware of the laws of evolution and can apply this knowledge to purposively improve man's place in the world.

Because of the important role that reason plays in Ward's cosmology, Samuel Chugerman has likened him to the Greek philosopher, calling him "The American Aristotle." But perhaps it would be no less correct, and certainly just as suggestive if, taking into consideration his indebtedness to German erudition, he were compared to another proponent of mind in history and dubbed "The American Hegel." Such a classification would acknowledge not only Ward's faith in man's ability to think, but it would recognize that this capacity is the fruit of a cosmic dialectical process.

Hegel theorized that the Idea of Right unintentionally evolves from its first manifestation in the conflicting actions of selfish individuals, to the World Spirit of Reason, of which the nation state is a necessary component. Through its power, the state guarantees that the purposes of individual citizens are made consistent with the goals of the community, so that the egoistic actions of the subjects fulfill the needs of the whole. Ward argues in a remarkably similar form that individual action, motivated exclusively by selfish purpose plus genetic intelligence unconsciously gives rise through social conflict to the conditions for its own demise in the purposive control of human behavior by means of the public education of the state's citizenry.

7

Albion Small's
Sociology of Conflict

In the previous chapter Lester Ward's theory of social conflict was described, pointing out in just what ways it can be understood to have resulted from the influence of Ludwig Gumplowicz. It is appropriate now to consider Albion Small's sociology, for more than any other person, he was responsible for the positive reception that Ward's cosmology received from American literati.

But it might be asked whether Small's work really deserves to be analyzed on the same plane as that of his three contemporaries, Ward, Park, and Bentley. Generally speaking, Small is lauded by modern intellectual historians primarily for his knack in organizing the first, and what was for several decades, the most important graduate department in sociology at Chicago. But when his substantive donations to sociological theory are considered, he is spoken of most highly as a historian of his field. Most analysts do not look upon him as an independent researcher in his own right at all, but rather as a vehicle for the dissemination of German sociological literature to American audiences.

There are few grounds for denying that Small was a great historian of sociology. And there is little question but that in his nonhistorical research into e.g. class conflict, he approached the object of study from the viewpoint of those under whom he had previously studied. But this is no less true for Park, Ward, and Bentley. Their thinking too reflected the contacts they had made with the great minds of nineteenth-century Europe and America. All things considered, it may well be that Small was simply more aware of the social context that influenced his thinking, and consequently was more inclined to acknowledge the debt he owed to those around him than were the other three Americans.

Moreover, no more than his fellows did Small simply parrot in his own words the theories of his teachers. In his work is found a synthesis of the ideas of such diverse scholars as Gustav Schmoller, Gustav Ratzenhofer, and Karl Marx, which is no less creative than the sociologies of Ward, Park, and Bentley. Just like Ward, for example, he selected something he liked in the systems of each of his mentors, molded it into a social theory compatible with his own world view, and with no qualms rejected what he believed was the chaff.

This chapter will be devoted to describing in detail the manner in which Small fit realpolitik into his overall philosophy of life. Emphasis will be placed, naturally, on his exploitation of the pronouncements of the German sociologists of conflict; in particular, those of Gustav Ratzenhofer. For if Gumplowicz helped Ward to formulate his sociology of conflict, and Simmel that of Park, it was Field Marshall Gustav Ratzenhofer who

led Small to the paradoxical discovery that social conflict is not necessarily inconsistent with human progress.

Early Views of Social Conflict

Small developed an interest in the subject of conflict
long before he even became aware of Ratzenhofer's existence. And as early as 1894 in a book written at
Chicago with one of his first graduate students, George
Vincent, he presented a rudimentary theory of social
strife.[1] These early statements on conflict should be reviewed briefly because they provide an excellent standard for measuring the degree to which their author
later altered his outlook to conform with that of Ratzenhofer.

If during the latter part of the nineteenth century
Small and Ratzenhofer attempted to construct
sociologies of conflict independently of each other, they
apparently drew from some of the same intellectual
sources. Utilitarian social psychology, introduced first
by Ratzenhofer's fellow countryman Albert Schäffle,
and then elaborated upon by Karl Menger, comprises
the basis for both Small's and Ratzenhofer's explanations for social phenomena. The utilitarian
psychologists, and Small and Ratzenhofer after them,
argued that while much of social life is a matter of unconscious routine, at least in the political and economic
world, action is motivated by conscious purposes in conjunction with practical knowledge.[2] Thus the only way
that the economic and political organizations of a
community can be properly understood are as func-

1. Albion W. Small and George Vincent, *An Introduction to the Study of
Society* (New York: American Book Co., 1894).
2. For a well-documented analysis of social psychology from a utilitarian
point of view, see Small, *Origins of Sociology*, pp. 295-314.

tional tools for the attainment of its spiritual, moral, and material interests.

While Menger and Schäffle moved from this position to detailed analyses of the different ways of insuring biological survival through economic cooperation, using the heuristic device of the organism to illustrate their claims, Small and Ratzenhofer attempted in the former's words "to penetrate mere outward manifestations and seek to learn about the nature of the influences which lie back of them."[3] In other words, they seemed to have concluded independently of each other that if it is the task of science to discover causes of events, then it is no longer sufficient simply to describe the forms that social order takes. The task of the researcher who is true to his calling is to trace such structures back to the psychological desires and intellect giving rise to them.

> It is the psychical potencies of society, knowledge, taste, and criteria of conduct which persist and constitute the real life of the organism. Material structures, technical devices, groupings of individuals, conduct, private and public are simply the expression in tangible things, or in visible actions, of these mysterious forces.[4]

Small argues that all corporate activity, from religion and economics to family life, can be interpreted as the result of shared motives among individuals. Common psychic energy "transmutes" itself, he says, into "a genuine common will," that finds manifestation in the goings-on ordinarily associated with the term "society." There can arise circumstances, however, when the interests of some of society's members will become inconsistent with those of others. Now instead of cooperation and social order, one will find conflict as the dominant form of interaction. As Small describes it:

3. Small and Vincent, *Introduction to the Study of Society*, p. 305.
4. Ibid.

Inasmuch as a large society is made up of countless aggregates and organs, each with a body of knowledge and standards of judgement, peculiar to itself and in some respect different from that of any other group, it is manifestly impossible so to unify and render authoritative all these psychical impulses as to produce in all matters a common volition—a general will with which all individual wills actually coincide.[5]

Thus, while any society may be identified by a consensus of wills among its members, within its boundaries the population will almost always be "divided into many antagonistic groups," each "struggling for supremacy" to get its own purposes "put into execution."[6] The outcome of this struggle for power, or as Small terms it, "the right to be obeyed," "does not involve merely the definition of different group wills, and the victory of the stronger in its original form," for the conflict may be quite complex, involving many groups "as forces exerted in correspondingly diverse directions."[7] Furthermore, the force of hostile groups acting in different directions, has the effect of neutralizing in part the potential power a group has when in isolation from other groups. Thus the result observed when antagonistic groups encounter one another, is a direct function both of their "trajectories" and their respective powers. Those familiar with classical mechanics will appreciate at once the analogy of social conflict as pictured by Small, to the theory of vec-

---

5. Small and Vincent, *Introduction to the Study of Society,* p. 350. In a more formal sense: "At any given moment the psychical force of society, together with the efficiency of the psycho-physical mechanism is a fixed quantity." Ibid., p. 332. And "if special psychical force is at a given time, concentrated on one social activity, the additional energy must either be taken from the potential resources of society, or withdrawn from other activities." Ibid., p. 333. Thus, scarce resources of energy and authority, plus conflicting wills creates conflict.

6. Ibid., p. 350.

7. Ibid., p. 353.

tors in physics. And, in fact, in his early propensity to use models from the biological and physical sciences to bolster his claims concerning social life, he explicitly tells the reader that this intuitive parallel is no mistake. Borrowing from the language of physics, he argues that "the psychical forces encounter each other at different angles, as it were, and certain resultant determinations and actions follow by virtue of the impact."[8]

A situation of conflict, says Small, always constitutes a danger to the social consensus that gives a society its integrity. Since this is true, it is necessary for there to be some means for regulating power struggles into directions that will both guarantee order and will enable the social organism as a whole to make decisions among conflicting wills and execute them.

> Peoples and parties may entertain a great variety of different opinions, may be governed by equally divergent standards of instinctive judgement, and may have a corresponding number of conflicting desires, without involving society in difficulty or danger; but the moment they attempt to embody their varying wills in overt acts, regardless of each other, they threaten social order and welfare. It is obviously necessary, therefore, that some means should be available for coordinating the peculiar volitions of individuals and social organs into a single determination, which can result in definite and orderly execution.[9]

8. Ibid. Thus, the forces may "reinforce each other, "neutralize each other," or "result in a determination whose force and direction are in general proportioned to the original forces, and the degree of opposition in which they meet." Ibid.

9. Ibid., p. 351. Small and Vincent go on to say that "within every organ, whether it be a church, a factory; or a family, different ideas and feelings may coexist; indeed, such diversity, if it does not result in antagonisms is desirable; but the welfare of the group requires that there shall be some means of securing orderly and unified executive activities." Ibid. The authors do not explicitly define what "antagonism" means, but the following example seems to intimate that it would be synonymous with the destruction of social structure: "Church quarrels furnish illustrations of antagonis-

The structures that fulfill this necessary condition for the survival of society comprise what he calls the "regulative system" of the social organism.[10] The modern state with its legislative and executive character is the best example of an organ functioning in the regulative system. "The state in its legislative aspect," Small concludes, "provides an apparatus for determining the collective will, and in its executive character, a mechanism for transforming that general volition into appropriate action."[11]

Thus ends Small's first essay on the subject of conflict. It is brief, but in some ways surprisingly modern. With his vector analysis, one is reminded of Kurt Lewin, the father of group dynamics. The functional explanation of the state, on the other hand, seems to anticipate the theories of Talcott Parsons. At any rate, it does indicate that as was the case for Ward before he came upon Gumplowicz's work, Small had seriously thought about the question of social strife prior to any contact with Ratzenhofer. But no more than Ward, was Small completely satisfied with his early approach to the issue of conflict and its relationship to social order and the state. Thus, when he became aware that Ratzenhofer had made significant contributions to these subjects, he began reading his books avidly, and soon assimilated these doctrines into his own sociology. Commenting on this sometime later, Small replied

tic volitions. The congregation is split up into two or more factions, each of which insists upon having a given minister or a certain form of church music. Feelings of antagonism are aroused, and often times the trouble results in the dissolution of the church, because it is impossible to form a common will or a decision in which all are willing to acquiesce." Ibid.

10. The authors say that "the regulative system of every group may be tested by its ability to render this important service. In proportion as a social organ can reach a definite conclusion, in which the members acquiesce, and can put it promptly into execution, will the group, other things being equal, do its appointed work efficiently." Ibid., p. 352.

11. Ibid.

that "I have no record to show when I discovered Ratzenhofer. The four volumes [constituting *Wesen und Zweck der Politik* and *Die Sociologische Erkenntnis*] . . . came into my hands at the same time, and they impressed me as so much of a find that I began to absorb them into my own thinking and writing."[12]

The Intellectual Relationship of Ratzenhofer to Small

Small's principle work, *General Sociology*,[13] was published a decade after the Vincent text. The content of this treatise allows one to observe the decisive manner in which its author changed his sociology to take Ratzenhofer's ideas into consideration in a relatively short period of time.

Small's and Vincent's appeal for an analysis of the psychological causes presumably underlying and giving rise to social structures to the contrary notwithstanding, *An Introduction to the Study of Society* is devoted almost exclusively to describing how, like in a biological entity, the organs of society all function to maintain its existence.[14] But in *General Sociology,* what Small derogatorily calls the "static" theorizing of persons like Schäffle and Lilienfeld, is relegated to a pre-

12. Small, "Fifty Years," p. 818.
13. Albion W. Small, *General Sociology* (Chicago: University of Chicago Press, 1905).
14. Thus there is a book on "The Natural History of Society," which illustrates in "narrative" form that society, like all "organisms," has "tendencies toward integration, specialization, and interdependence of parts." This is followed by a book on "Social Anatomy" where the concepts of social "organ" and "social nervous system" are introduced. Finally, there is a book on "Social Physiology and Pathology" where the characteristics of "social disease" are elaborated upon.

viously mythical age in sociology's past.[15] Now, what holds precedence in his thought is no longer organicism's structural mechanisms, but a category borrowed directly from Ratzenhofer's *Die Sociologische Erkenntnis*—"social process." "The subject matter of sociology," proclaims Small in one of the first sentences of his book, "is the process of human association."[16]

Small's endeavor to interpret virtually everything as a phase in an overall process of "becoming" is seen with particular clarity in the theory of social conflict and the state he advances in *General Sociology*. In their *Introduction to the Study of Society*, Vincent and Small attempted to model conflict after physical mechanics. In *General Sociology*, however, not only does the biological vocabulary disappear, but also there is a notable absence of parallels drawn between social antagonism and billiard balls automatically bouncing off one another. Under the inspiration of Ratzenhofer, power struggles became to Small, just another form of psychical interaction between purposive groups. Conflict now is pictured as a facet in a continuous, never-ending process occuring between cognizant and intelligent human beings.

Related to this, it can be seen that in Small's later work there is a definite alteration in the way in which he conceives the state, from that revealed in his original text with Vincent. In the earlier book, the state is more or less implicitly thought of as a "mechanism" or at least a static entity, while in *General Sociology*, it is spoken of as a continual process of evolution. After his reading of Ratzenhofer, the state began to appear to Small as if it too were an aspect of a larger "process of associating" in which conscious, purposive men interact with one another to form still larger and more inclusive organizations.

15. Ibid., pp. 76-78; 109-14.
16. Ibid., p. 3.

But Ratzenhofer's place in the American's thinking is much more thoroughgoing and complex than this. Small describes how "my plans for a book on general sociology were not only worked out, but I supposed the material was nearly ready for publication"[17] prior to his coming upon Ratzenhofer. But because

> his [Ratzenhofer's] analytical process following the clue of "interests" was nearly identical with the one I had been following for several years, and his conclusions seemed to me in general to reinforce my own tentative results then a consequence was that in one or two years my lecture notes, intended for incorporation in my book, had become so interlaced with Ratzenhofer's work that it was no longer possible for me to distinguish between the parts which I had arrived at independently, those which had been slightly expanded by drawing upon Ratzenhofer, and those which were entirely his own.[18]

As a result, Small discarded his original plan to use his *General Sociology* for a systematic presentation of his own views exclusively, and chose instead to organize it as a historical study where he would simply become a commentator on Ratzenhofer's notions.

Since at least in Small's eyes there was little to prevent his theories of social life from becoming so easily blended with those of Ratzenhofer, it might be thought that Ratzenhofer's close friend, Gumplowicz, could also claim to have intimate intellectual ties with the American. This inference is based on the fact that so great are the parallels in the two Austrian's sociologies, that historians usually deem it sufficient in analyzing them to describe the system of only one or the other. Oddly enough, however, Small had a great deal of disdain for Gumplowicz's approach to social life. And in a scathing book review of his *Sociologie und Politik* he remarked that

17. Small, "Fifty Years," p. 818.
18. Ibid., p. 819.

a properly descriptive title would be "Professor Gumplowicz's opinions about politics, not hazarded upon their own merits, but tacked as riders upon an assumed science of Sociology. . . ."

Neither sociology nor politics is yet a "science" in such a sense that it can furnish a definite foundation for the other. By yoking the names together in this fashion, Gumplowicz has encouraged incredulity about the possible scientific treatment of either. It is true, as the editor claims that this book and we may add *Der Rassenkampf* as well is "suggestive," so is Jules Verne. It is more to the point that Professor Gumplowicz is unfortunate in his excursions outside the field of Austrian Jurisprudence and legal history. On that territory he is a master. In sociology—and possibly in politics—he is an amusing amateur.[19]

Small's critique of Gumplowicz, together with the knowledge of their mutual admiration of Ratzenhofer, seems to suggest that both scholars were rather selective in their consideration of what they believed was of value in his work. It may have been that both men selected out for positive evaluation only those aspects of his system that were consistent with their own moral and political predispositions. A comparison of the treatments of Ratzenhofer's *Wesen und Zweck der Politik* by both Gumplowicz and Small demonstrates this to be the case.[20]

Gumplowicz on Ratzenhofer

Gumplowicz was always very appreciative of

19. Albion W. Small, *"Sociologie und Politik* by Ludwig Gumplowicz," review of *Sociologie und Politik* by Ludwig Gumplowicz, *AJS* IV (July, 1898): 105-6. See also Small, *General Sociology,* pp. 420-23. Apparently Gumplowicz knew about Small's critical attitude, because in one of his letters to Ward, he thanked him for offering "to help me against the German professors who want to silence me to death, under whose influence Small fell." Gumplowicz, "The Letters of Ludwig Gumplowicz to Lester F. Ward," June 1907, p. 24.

20. Gustav Ratzenhofer, *Wesen und Zweck der Politik,* 3 vols., (Leipzig: F. A. Brockhaus, 1893).

Ratzenhofer's realistic and unsentimental portrayal of the dynamics of conflict. And in his book review of the above mentioned text, he singles out the first two volumes as opposed to the third one for special acclaim. The first volume is devoted to the hypothesis of state formation through violent racial conflict. This is followed by a detailed description of the struggle for power between parties within the state. In Volume II, Ratzenhofer applies realpolitik to the questions of war, imperialism, and international balances of power. Gumplowicz says that in these first two books

> Gustav Ratzenhofer is the first to attempt such a treatment and to carry it out in a really ingenious manner. We believe we do not err in asserting that Ratzenhofer's name will from now on be associated with those of the greatest authors of the past, Machiavelli, Comte and Spencer; but with this difference, however, that what were unsuccessful attempts on their part, have been changed by him into success.[21]

The third volume of *Wesen und Zweck* inquires into the ends of each level of the political process, and Gumplowicz assesses it thusly:

> Throughout the first two volumes a realism prevails that certainly will not escape being considered pessimistic by many.... With the first page of the third volume, however, the author enters on a somewhat optimistic course of thought, a fact that will conciliate many opponents of the first two volumes. The author thinks that he can prove that "the influence of the self interest of all taken collectively, upon individual self interest" is growing with the development of mankind, and that the aim of politics is to "harmonize progressive socialization and individualization, the one a social, the other an individual necessity."

21. Ludwig Gumplowicz," *Wesen und Zweck der Politik* by Gustav Ratzenhofer," review of *Wesen und Zweck der Politik* by Gustav Ratzenhofer, *Annals of the American Academy of Political and Social Science* V (July, 1894): 129.

To the extent that politics fulfills this purpose they are civilizing. Following an opposite course will produce "barbarous" politics. "The aim of politics, is the commonweal of mankind."[22]

Gumplowicz adds, however, that Ratzenhofer's analysis of the ethical purpose of politics should not be appraised on the same basis as the first two books, for he did not intend this to be a scientific account.

The author is, of course, careful to say that he is speaking only conditionally of the purpose of politics, because "considered as a phenomenon, politics is of itself, without purpose." This assurance is fortunate, for without it we should be compelled to charge him with having a teleological view of the world. The author seems to appreciate this well, and consequently does not neglect at the outset to surround his statements regarding the purpose of politics with certain restrictions, in order that he might prevent himself . . . against the charge of unwarranted optimism. For the charge of being thus optimistic would be at the door of everyone who claimed that the aim of all politics, domestic and foreign, and policy as well of all societies, is to secure the maximum welfare of all mankind. The author does not make this claim.[23]

Gumplowicz concludes his book review with some reasons as to why, if the third book is not to be subjected to the same criteria of evaluation as the first two, Ratzenhofer even wasted time writing it at all. "Nevertheless," says the Austrian pessimist, "he naturally desires not to leave his large temple of thought without harmonious completion; he wishes, so to speak, to crown his structure with a beautiful dome. . . . Not to do so would, perhaps, be more scientific, though less human."[24] But to be less scientific, is of course to the positivist Gumplowicz equivalent to the

22. Ibid., p. 133.
23. Ibid.
24. Ibid.

tag of interesting perhaps, but not to be taken seriously.

Small on Ratzenhofer

Books I and II of *Wesen und Zweck*

Interestingly enough, Small has a view almost completely contrary to that of Gumplowicz concerning what he thinks is significant in Ratzenhofer's trilogy. As indicated above, in Part I of Volume I, Ratzenhofer describes the evolution of the state through the now familiar process of racial struggles for domination. Without assenting to the details of his mentor's argument, Small agrees that political relations are founded by men who in rationally pursuing their own selfish conflicting interests, agree for practical reasons to abandon their mutual hostility because of its costliness to themselves. In a manner that sounds like Gumplowicz and Ward, Small claims that

> ... between savages of the lowest order there can be no compromise until the one tribe had eaten the other. An advance in the social process is marked by so much of restraint on the part of both victors and vanquished as permits mastery and slavery as the triumph of one interest over the other, with minimum concession to the weaker interest.[25]

Soon, he adds, the contending parties find it reasonable to suppress their antagonism still further. The rulers give their subjects legal rights, and the vanquished agree to compromise by promising to voluntarily abide by their duty.

Still later, the dominant race, say Romans, retains claims

25. Small, *General Sociology*, p. 238.

of tribute from defeated and absorbed states without sub-jecting the conquered citizens to personal slavery. Later still, as in medieval and modern aristocracies, privileges are secured by law upon the shoulders of other classes. In either case the process is that of accomodating interest to interest through total or partial expression, on the one hand, and repression, on the other.[26]

While these few brief remarks do seem to indicate Small's indebtedness to Ratzenhofer, he is, in fact, quite critical of the latter's hypothesis concerning state formation. According to Ratzenhofer, absolute hostil-ity is the psychological force that drives the social proc-ess in this its early "barbaric" stages. And once states have developed through conquest, this same hatred motivates them to continually extend the territory over which they rule. "The struggle of political persons," he says, "is subject to the law of absolute hostility. *Diese Absolute Feindseligkeit* is the essential characteristic of all politics."[27] As might be expected, Gumplowicz ad-mired Ratzenhofer's insistence on using the only con-cept that he believed could fruitfully account for the ferocity of men locked in combat. He realized, of course, that when an observer makes no attempt to palliate political events, he will wound many a sensitive na-ture. But, he retorted,

> we can no more reproach Ratzenhofer because the 'politi-cal persons' carry on a life and death struggle, that they thereby pursue selfish ends and employ every means that will secure to them these aims, than we can Adam Smith because of his economic motive, . . . [or] Darwin because of the 'struggle of existence.'[28]

Small, however, thought differently. The employment

26. Ibid., pp. 238-39.
27. Quoted in Gumplowicz, *"Wesen und Zweck der Politik* by Gustav Rat-zenhofer," p. 130.
28. Ibid.

of such terms is both misleading and unscientific, he tells his reader. It is true, he admits, that "the conspicuous element in the history of the race, so far as it has been recorded, is universal conflict of interest...."[29] "Yet we must not even provisionally assume as Ratzenhofer does that 'absolute hostility' is literally absolute, as a general relation between men."[30]

> In the cases of blood-feud, or wars of extermination, the notion of 'absolute hostility' has its evident application. For practical purposes the formula means that human relations range upward from a state in which men will fight each other to the death.... So understood it is not an essential human principle, but merely a mode of social relationship under peculiar circumstances.[31]

In addition, he submits, debate over the actual psychological predispositions of warriors in primitive phases of political development are really irrelevant because there is little available empirical evidence to use as a basis for judgement of the issue either way. Since this is true, sociology should avoid attempts to theorize about such questions as the origin of statehood, and focus their attention instead upon conflict as it occurs within already existing political entities.

> In the main his [Ratzenhofer's] generalizations may be held to the test of fact. He seems, however, to have been led by the desire to round out his system into discoursing about phases of the prehistoric process in a way not

29. Small, *General Sociology,* p. 203. He adds more emphatically: "It may be that philosophers will some day be able to reconstruct views of the social process, throughout historic time, in terms which will present implicit consensus of interests as the ultimate motor of the process, while they will construe the obvious conflict of interests as merely secondary incidents in the development process. It would be mere dogmatism to pretend that the facts in sight at present justify such a rendering." Ibid., pp. 203-4.
30. Ibid., p. 204.
31. Ibid.

sanctioned by the present state of evidence. . . . The records deal chiefly with peoples already organized in states.
If we restrict our attention to the social processes within
states, there is not only at our disposal an enormous mass
of partially sifted evidence, but this material permits
comparative study of the process within many states.[32]

Small's proposal to limit the scope of sociological inquiry to modern politics, however, did not result solely
from neutral methodological considerations, as is indicated by the following facts. In the first place, the main
part of Volume II of *Wesen und Zweck,* which traces
absolute hostility as it finds manifestation in war and
colonialism (an analysis not only upon which Gumplowicz lavishes his praise, but also a subject on which
there is substantial documentation), is given only a
one-paragraph treatment by the American.[33] But Part
II of Volume I, in which Ratzenhofer describes domestic
conflict of interest, is rewarded by a forty-page detailed
review and commentary in *General Sociology.* Whereas
Small was considerably skeptical of the truth of
Ratzenhofer's (and by implication, Gumplowicz's)
hypothesis concerning the conditions out of which state
relations evolve, there was little doubt in his mind that
Ratzenhofer's sociology of politics internal to the state
was on a par with the most noteworthy of intellectual

32. Ibid., pp. 225-26. Small claims that in generalizing from present day
facts to cases temporally prior to the existence of states, "Ratzenhofer has
furnished a much more innocent case of the same vice" of Smith, Rousseau,
and Bastian, resulting in a "purely speculative picture of the past." Ibid.,
pp. 224-25. In another place, the author says that "there is much reason to
presume that, if we had literal accounts of all the racial metamorphoses
which have taken place, from the primitive tribe to civic government the
methods would often prove to depart widely from the type thus constructed
[by Ratzenhofer]." Ibid., p. 222. On the basis of this argument, Small concludes that "since the state is the social process in the largest unit which it
is profitable to consider, we shall accordingly speak for the present as
though states were the whole of the human process." Ibid., p. 227.
33. Ibid., p. 318.

contributions. Contrast, for example, Small's following appraisal of Ratzenhofer's theory of domestic struggles for power with his somewhat restrained evaluation of the Austrian's notion of the origin of the state:

> It is the most comprehensive sketch of plans and specifications for the objective analysis of the whole social process, considered as an interplay of interests, that has thus far been offered. It does not complete the task of interpreting the social process but it goes farther than any previous attempt toward fairly beginning the work of interpretation. For the present it is best worthy of all the schemes in sight to serve as a pioneer survey upon which to base more critical study of concrete situations. Each title of the foregoing schedule may be regarded as a demand for a specific investigation. Ratzenhofer has done his part toward the necessary inquiry. He has formulated propositions under each title which may stand as tentative conclusions until superseded.[34]

It thus appears as if Small has shifted his research emphasis, not so much because of his methodological conscience, but rather to ignore what might be considered the less civilized aspects of politics; namely, the place of violent coercion in state formation, and the barbarism of war. For within fully formed states, says Small, the "conjunction of interests grows more evident, " and thus absolute hostility, if indeed it ever did exist, disappears, and the brutality of conflict is tempered. Within the state, "the social process continues to be largely in the form of struggle," he admits, "but it is a less and less inexorable struggle."[35] "National life is conflict,"[36] he goes on, but because "the state always brings to bear upon the individuals composing it a certain power of constraint,"[37] then it is "conflict converg-

34. Ibid., p. 286.
35. Ibid., p. 205.
36. Ibid., p. 245.
37. Ibid., p. 242.

ing toward minimum conflict and maximum cooperation and sociability."[38]

Book III of *Wesen und Zweck*

The third volume in Ratzenhofer's trilogy contains
an elaboration of his views concerning the ethical
meaning of power struggles. For Ratzenhofer to claim
that there are redeeming characteristics in a situation
where absolute hostility prevails, seems on the surface
to be a contradiction. And in fact, he emphatically rejects the liberal view of political activity that it can
logically be subsumed under abstract principles of individual morality. Ethical standards, he argues, are nothing more than the product of social conflict, and not
vice versa.

> It is the essence of political doctrines that they are least
> understood by those in whom the political impulses most
> energetically work. It can be accounted for by failure to
> comprehend the essence of politics, when people preach
> morality to the politically functioning individual. . . . We
> can not bring politics and ethics into immediate harmony:
> On the contrary, ethical motives are a prod-
> uct of political development, and the sovereignty of moral-
> ity is not a product of free volitions, but rather of political
> organization which produces the social will for ethical
> motives.[39]

38. Ibid., p. 245.
39. Ratzenhofer, *Wesen und Zweck der Politik*, II, quoted in Small, *General
Sociology*, p. 320. Even Ratzenhofer admits that, "in my description of political phenomena, I have often recoiled from the logic and fact, and I am consequently quite sure that in many of my readers these same facts, and the
conclusions unavoidable from them, will have aroused disagreeable emotions. The science of politics, however, is primarily a psycho-pathology of
human beings, and with reference to such a science the truth is always
rather of a depressing than of an exhilerating nature. For the very reason
that the essence of politics is so repulsive, . . . political science has up to date
displayed a reluctance to use the probe relentlessly in research within political conditions. A consequence of this shyness about political truth, and

One might easily move from this position and the assumption of a diversity of conflicting interests, as many of Ratzenhofer's contemporaries did, to an anarchic relativity of morals, the denial of the possibility of any authentic morality at all, to either the worship of political means for their own sake in the Treitschkean manner, or a resigned withdrawal, a la Gumplowicz, from the world. But Ratzenhofer debunks both of these paths in his third volume, claiming that there *is* a moral sense in the riddle of human conflict. For almost paradoxically, it is through social conflict that larger and larger numbers of individuals and their egoistic tendencies are subordinated under a single normative and legal order.

> The development of the political struggle shows us the growing power of society over the individual. The study of politics thus displays to us the fact that the whole is triumphing over the special. Since, however, every morality rests upon social obligations, that political understanding which opens up to us the growing cooperation of social compulsion must of itself produce moral insight and ethical principles.[40]

Seeking only to gratify their own shortsighted interests in a situation of scarcity, men engage in social strife, says Ratzenhofer. Here they attempt to overcome the resistance of their foes by using any means that they believe are practical. In time, they discover that

hesitation to carry on severe investigation of politics, has been that we have satisfied ourselves with a sort of pseudo-science, which attempted to rouse the belief that politics has an ethical content, and that political theory can be built upon ethical considerations." Ratzenhofer, *Wesen und Zweck,* II, quoted in Small, *General Sociology,* p. 319. The last few pages of volume II of Ratzenhofer's trilogy are given over to a summary of the position he presents in much more detail in volume III. It is the summary of this position that Small has translated, and from which the previous quotation is taken.
40. Ratzenhofer, *Wesen und Zweck,* II, quoted in Small, *General Sociology,* p. 321.

failure to grant concessions to the demands of their opponents is prohibitively costly for the realization of their own interests. So they implicitly consent to restrain their mutual hostility where practical reason dictates this to be a necessity. Thus are formed relationshps that link previously hated combatants into single groups. Because such associations are at least in part consistent with the selfish interests of the parties out of which they are built, then said parties share a desire to defend their community of interests against outsiders with contrary purposes. Thus are begun power struggles on a new level, until the adversaries are once again absorbed into a single and still more inclusive body.

> As the state becomes more permanent in form and spirit, the process approaches universal restraint of each interest within limits decreed by the aggregate of interests.... The state accordingly becomes a moral institution. It is an ethical effect or deposit of the social process.... There has previously been play of individual and group interests, either unregulated, or from the current point of view less appropriately regulated. The interests are now brought together under a common or improved order, in which each restrains itself somewhat, in obedience to the general interests of the community.[41]

The state is the first corporation to evolve from such a process of conflict. And once founded, it is moved to ever higher levels of consensus as its subjects continually rediscover their mutual dependencies through social strife. In essence then, political history is a story of the successful struggle of public groups against the selfishness of individuals, and yet it goes on by means of this unsocial even anti-social spirit. Conflict is a truly dialectical process which unintentionally leads to conditions for its own demise.

41. Small, *General Sociology*, p. 239. Cf. Ibid., pp. 331-33.

It has already been seen how Gumplowicz treats Ratzenhofer's teleological ethics as an unimportant topping on the cake of an otherwise outstandingly realistic account of politics. Small, on the other hand, considered the Field Marshall's discussion of the moral consequences of power struggles to be the most essential component of his whole sociology.[42] Why might this have been the case?

Small's intellectual life was largely a frustrated attempt to find what he sometimes termed a "master key" with which to analyze social life.[43] To be adequate, such a key, he felt, would not only have to permit a realistic examination of social interaction, but more importantly, it must contain at least implicitly a program of humanistic ethics and social reform. His desire to make the sociological method a tool for social reform originally revealed itself in a rather crude form, when in the *Syllabus* published at Colby College, he admonished his fellow social scientists to "set ourselves heartily to the work of bringing the Kingdom of God on Earth."[44] Thirty years later, he still argued, now in a

42. In Small's words, "in our analysis of the social process thus far we have perforce placed undue emphasis upon the mere form of the process. Whether we are observing one part of the process or another, the really significant matter is not the form of the movement that is going on, but the substance of the occurrences. . . " Ibid., p. 344. "The question, what does all the action in the state mean? can not be solved by simply describing that action. As we have urged above, nothing can be described until we know what it is for. . . . On the basis, then, of such analyses and descriptions of actions within the state as are thus far available, our present task is to gather up all that we can discover about the tendencies implied in state action; not what the actors want, but what their actions inevitably tend to bring to pass. In this way only can we reach, on the one hand, speculative conceptions of what social action should be." Ibid., pp. 330-31.

43. For example, see Small, *Origins of Sociology,* pp. 341-43.

44. Small, *Syllabus,* quoted in Maurice H. Krout, "The Development of Small's Sociological Theory," *Journal of Applied Sociology* XI (Jan., 1927): 218. In a second *Syllabus,* published sometime later, Small argued that "sociology frankly proposes the salvation of society." Quoted in Krout, "The

much more sophisticated way, that sociology could not only make categorical judgements of value, as opposed to merely instrumental statements, but that after the *Verein für Sozialpolitik,* it should lobby to get its views instituted in law. "Social science," he always believed, "has no way to complete itself except as the accomplished habit of human beings. The last phase of sociology is the transmuting of valuations into life."[45]

Taking this melioristic mind-set into consideration, there is little mystery as to why Small was so ready to assimilate the content of the third volume of *Wesen und Zweck der Politik* into his own sociology. In Ratzenhofer's "positive monism," he apparently found a doctrine perfectly compatible with his own Christian concern for social harmony and brotherhood. Perhaps too, he was comforted by the Austrian's forecast that in spite of individual selfishness, indeed even with its unconscious aid, the pacifying influence of socialization will inevitably absorb all peoples into a single

Development of Small's Sociological Theory," p. 219. It is true that Small controlled his "idealics" in later publications, with e.g. the admission that "Christian purpose and aspiration can not furnish technical skill or information. Piety without knowledge of facts would work disaster in politics and economics just as in navigation or in pharmacy." Small and Vincent, *An Introduction to the Study of Society,* p. 19. But his religious beliefs persisted until his death. In 1926 he sent a memo to his closest friends in which he attempted to interpret his intellectual work in the following terms: "My religion is my attempt to make Jesus Christ the pattern and founder of my life. . . . It is my attempt to cooperate with all men of like mind everywhere in trying to make this the religion of every individual and of every group of men of good will throughout the world." Quoted in Goodspeed, "Albion Small," p. 263. Such statements by Small were a constant source of contention between the editor of the *Iconoclast,* Lester Ward, and himself. For example, see Small's letters of Sept. 18, 1890 and Oct. 3, 1890 to Ward in Small, "The Letters of Albion W. Small to Lester F. Ward," pp. 163-66.

45. Albion W. Small, *The Meaning of Social Science* (Chicago: University of Chicago Press, 1910), p. 26. For the author's discussion of the necessity for sociologists to make value judgements, see Ibid., pp. 214-43. For his description of the "constructive" phase of the sociological process, see Ibid., pp. 244-71.

worldwide community. But more importantly than this, only after Small became aware of the meaning of history, of its telos, was he in a position to inquire into the question of what men of good will *should* do toward hastening its realization. After Ratzenhofer's work, sociology could finally set itself to its true vocation of discovering what legal regulations will be most practical in promoting social progress.

Some Concluding Notes on Small and *Wesen und Zweck*

In conclusion then, it can be seen that although both Small and Gumplowicz congratulated Ratzenhofer on his theoretical accomplishments, they really were not admiring the same thing at all. Both critics selected out for special consideration only those aspects of the Austrian's sociology that were already congruous with their particular moral values. Gumplowicz seems to have discovered in his friend's hypothesis of absolute hostility, a notion agreeable to his own pessimistic *Weltanschauung*. But Small avoided writing about situations where this concept would conceivably be of some utility; specifically, in explaining the dynamics of war and the origin of states. Moreover, while Small's optimism apparently gave him reason to see the truth in the meaning that Ratzenhofer imputed to history, Gumplowicz believed this digression into ethics to detract from the uncompromising realism of his theory of social conflict.

The reader will remember that Lester Ward, who otherwise was intellectually inspired by Gumplowicz, explicitly attacked the pessimistic implications of his sociology. This demonstrates that in spite of their differences in regard to formal religious matters, Small and Ward both shared a fundamentally hopeful outlook toward the world.

It is always difficult to explain the presence of psychological attitudes, but there are similarities in the life experiences of the two men that were certainly not incompatible with the development of an optimistic philosophy of history. Both lived their formative years during a period in American history that commentators now refer to as "The Era of Confidence." This was a time when, among other things, the prevailing collective myth held that any man with gumption enough and the proper opportunities could better himself in the world. Surely Ward and Small were aware of the large discrepencies between this—the American Dream—and the actual situation. In fact, their cognizance of this discrepancy was one of the main reasons motivating them to search in Europe for a more fruitful interpretation of American social stratification than was available to them in American scholarship. But there was little in their own backgrounds to suggest that universal self-improvement. as a goal, could not be realized. From a situation of uncultured destitution, Ward ascended through individual effort, as Chugerman describes it, "like an Alger Hero," to occupy an honored position in American intellectual circles. And Small too, while not enjoying such an astronomical advance as his cohort, could also point to instances where upward social mobility was a distinct possibility for the hard-working person. As a young man, his father, at one time a parson in an isolated rural church, came to hold the pulpit in one of the largest Baptist parishes in Maine. This was accompanied by such an increase in pay that the son could be afforded the finest education available during that time. Small, in turn, capitalized on this opportunity to achieve, through diligence, preeminence in his chosen field.

Thus, both Small and Ward were living confirmations of an argument that maintained the distinct possibility of individual improvement and collective progress. This probably increased their receptivity to, and eventually enabled them to internalize the precepts of, an optimistic cultural ethic. This provided them with the generally rose-colored glasses that later biased their observations of social phenomena. And it made it difficult for them to sympathize with the despairing conclusions to which their German mentors were driven as a result of their own analyses.

Small and the Conflict of Classes

The state, says Small after Ratzenhofer, is a process of becoming. It finds its first manifestation as sort of a dictated peace that represents, almost exclusively, the interests of a single powerful race, to the detriment of its vanquished foe. But this is not its final development. In the first place, it continues to extend its domination over more subjects primarily through military conquest. And secondly, within its borders, domestic strife alters its legal structure until it comes to express the purposes, not just of one party, but of a vast plurality of interest groups. Finally, in principle, the state, originally founded by the brute force of one race, can become the protector of the commonweal of society as a whole.

Any historical case, he goes on, can be located as a phase in this overall process, and thus it can be ranked as either more or less "civilized," on the one hand, or "barbaric," on the other. But no state presently occupies either of the two extreme types. Instead, what the researcher finds in his field surveys of any situation is a "union of disunions, a conciliation of conflicts, a harmony of discords. [Any historical] state is an arrangement of combinations by which mutually repellent forces are brought into some measure of concurrent action."[46]

46. Small, *General Sociology,* pp. 252-53.

America, Small claims, is just one of many tenuous, ever-changing balances of opposing groups. Besides the obvious consensus of interests among its people, it still suffers from extreme divisions. The most drastic power struggle it is now experiencing is that between propertyless workers and factory owners, or "class conflict."

It is a grieved and indignant denial that such a thing as class conflict exists in the world. We need not stop to parley with this insanity. No one gets through a primer of social science without learning that class conflict is to the social process what friction is to mechanics. It is one of the elemental reactions between human beings. . . . The fact of class struggle is as axiomatic today as the fact of gravitation.[47]

According to Small, as in any conflict, victory in the economic struggle will be on the side of those who have superior force. Although, he admits, it is often difficult to measure the respective powers of opponents prior to the conclusion of their fight, several predictors of the outcome can be used by sociologists. In the first place, the amount of wealth controlled by a combatant is a good indication of his ability to demonstrate the dependence that his foe has upon him. But more important than this, is one's capacity to organize his supporters into concerted political action.[48]

Using these criteria to assess the relative strengths

47. Albion W. Small, "Socialism in the Light of Social Science," *AJS* XVII (May, 1912): 812.
48. Small is expressly indebted to Ratzenhofer for this analysis of social power. According to Small, "in general, the political power of the industrial classes depend upon their facility in combining their forces for political action. . . . The struggle capacity of the classes to which they severally belong will vary, first, with the quantity of the wealth, either actual or potential; second, with the degree of physical contact between members." Small, *General Sociology*, p. 267.

of the participants in American class conflict, Small concludes that the capitalists, with their substantial wealth and intimate social intercourse, will prevail over their opponents in most circumstances. But factory workers, who are thrown together under the same roof for a large portion of their waking hours, are increasingly coming to discover their shared grievances. Thus, they may be able in the long run to bring their great numerical resources to bear against the riches of their employers. Farmers, he forecasts, are going to find themselves in a worsening position vis-à-vis both the robber barons and the proletariat. This is because their monopoly of surplus economic production, and even their once overwhelming size as a stratum, are wasting away. Add to this their geographical and psychological isolation and consequent inability to organize together, and one can easily see that this interest group is the least powerful of the three.[49]

Despite the sense of detachment in this analysis, Small felt no compulsion to adopt a neutral, value-free stance in regard to the issue of industrial conflict. Even the lecture room, he thought, should provide a podium for the issuance of normative imperatives concerning

---

49. Says Small: "Capital and the advantages of property give, to the classes possessing them both legitimate means of calling governmental agencies to their assistance, and also more or less questionable power to enlist physical force necessary to carry out their aims (e.g. the Pinkertons, armed cowboys, fights of street and steam railway builders, etc). On the other hand, the industrial classes that lack property have only a minimum of concerted unity. They must for a long time act in an unintegrated fashion. They work at cross purposes. They obstruct each other, and pose no strong resistance to the united classes. . . . The wage-earners in factories and mines, though individually possessing less property in general . . . have the compensating advantage of physical contact. They are in close contact with each other. They share a common lot. . . . They can develop, not only group consciousness, but campaign programs. They are thus more frequently in powerful battle-array as strong factors in social contact." Ibid., pp. 267-68.

contemporary social problems.[50] This tendency is seen with particular clarity in the lecture notes of what was perhaps his most well-attended seminar, entitled "The Conflict of Classes."[51]

The basic cause of class conflict, he told his students, is the desire by those who work with their hands to end the monopolization of social wealth by those who do not work at all. In other words, he would say, their purpose is to overthrow the "double standard of justice" in America, where the landlord or capitalist is rewarded whether he labors or not, but the proletarian is paid a wage only if he actively participates in production. But for this very reason, the political efforts of the lower class to liberate itself from exploitation is ethically just, for "there is no ultimate moral sanction for a claim to economic goods which is not based on the presumption of service in the economic process."[52] The immorality of absentee landlordism and inherited wealth, rests precisely upon the fact that the beneficiaries in both cases are getting something from a society to which they are contributing nothing in return. "The great capitalistic fallacy, is that *property* (irrespective of its social function, rightfully) constitutes a title to income. The next great moral revelation will be that *function* alone confers a moral title to income."[53]

It will be recognized almost immediately that there is a distinct similarity here between Small's more or

50. It is possible that Small's disposition to preach was reinforced during his graduate studies at Berlin, where e.g. Schmoller, Treitschke, and Mommsen explicitly argued in support of teachers asserting their values in the classroom. For example, see Weber's discussion of this in Max Weber, *The Methodology of the Social Sciences*, ed. and trans. by Edward A. Shils and Henry A. Finch (New York: Free Press of Glencoe, 1949), pp. 1-47.

51. Albion W. Small, "The Conflict of Classes," University of Chicago Library, Small Papers, Box 11, Folder 4.

52. Ibid., p. 27.

53. Ibid., p. 21.

less implicit advocacy of class conflict, and Marxist socialism. And indeed, in one of his many articles on this subject, he defended the argument that "socialism has been the most wholesome ferment in modern society."[54] He was one of the few Americans of his time who had not only studied Marx, but who also believed that there was some truth in what he said. Thus, he one-time eulogized the father of modern Communism in the following words:

No man has done more than he [i.e. Marx] to strengthen the democratic suspicion that the presuppositions of our present system are superficial and provisional.... I confidently predict that in the ultimate judgement of history Marx will have a place in social science analogous with that of Galileo in physical science.... He is still a voice in the wilderness. But I for one have no more doubt that he was essentially right, and that conventionality was essentially wrong, than I have that Galileo will hold his place to the end of time as one of the world's great discoverers.[55]

But even with his indebtedness to Marxism, Small went to great lengths in several places to distinguish his own proposals from those of the socialists. Thus fol-

54. Small, "Socialism in the Light of Social Science," p. 808. In another place, Small said that "there is hardly a more elementary social generalization than the struggle of contending interests is a perpetual factor in human progress. No competent sociologist any longer attempts to make a point against socialism on this nondebatable proposition." Albion W. Small, "*Sin and Society* by Edward A. Ross," review of *Sin and Society* by Edward A. Ross, *AJS* XIII (Jan., 1908): 568). Small made this comment in response to the "weakest passage of the book," which was the following letter from President Roosevelt in the Preface: "You [Ross] reject that most mischievous of socialistic theses, viz.: that progress is to be secured by the strife of classes. You insist as all healthy-minded patriots should insist, that public opinion, if only sufficiently enlightened, is equal to the necessary regenerative tasks and can yet dominate the future." Ibid., p. 567. Small skeptically replied to this statement that " 'public opinion' whether enlightened or not, is merely a euphemism for one method of mobilizing interests always engaged in the industrial struggle." Ibid., p. 568.
55. Small, "Socialism in the Light of Social Science," p. 810.

lowing his favorable commentary on Karl Marx, he sought to balance his assessment with the confession "that Marx's ideal of economic society has never appealed to me as plausible, probable, desirable, or possible."[56] And he repeatedly attempted to defend his ideas from *ad hominem* criticism of his students by emphatically declaring, e.g., that "I am not a socialist. I think the socialist theory is so defective that I can compare it with nothing more fatuous, unless it would be one of the many varieties of socialistic programs."[57]

Small's main argument against Marx was a position he attributed to him that only work with one's hands comprises a moral claim to a share of societies' goods. He invoked the authority of Adam Smith's *Wealth of Nations* to substantiate a contrary claim that there are three "divinely ordained" ways of contributing to economic production: through labor, through the loaning of land, and through the investment of capital.[58] Consequently, he concluded, there should be in any society, three distinct manners of remuneration for economic service; through wages, rents, and capital gains, respectively. Thus, for Small, "the laborer is worthy of his hire, whether he sits in a Wall Street office or toils in the stoke hole of a ship."[59] Furthermore, he continued, no person, even if he wears a blue collar, deserves a portion of society's production unless he adds, in at least an indirect way, to its totality. "The non-laborer is not worthy of hire, whether he grafts in the guise of a political boss, as president of a railroad

56. Ibid., p. 816.
57. Small, "The Conflict of Classes," p. 28.
58. Ibid., p. 24; 33-34. Small's belief that Smith had said virtually the last word on economics is indicated by his detailed study of his doctrines and their application to sociology, in *Adam Smith and Modern Sociology* (Chicago: University of Chicago Press, 1907).
59. Small, "The Conflict of Classes," p. 33.

system, as a master of high finance, or as a sabotaging workman on a plumbing job."[60]

Apparently, prior to the Russian Revolution, Small was skeptical about the possibility of building a viable economy on any but Smithian dictums. But following World War I, he discovered to his horror that a socialistic revolution was imminent, not just in places like Germany, where with its long tradition of collectivism it might be expected, but in America, presumably the land of rugged individualism. According to Small, the reason for this dire turn of events, was that the war had for the first time demonstrated to Americans the effectiveness of thoroughgoing government intervention in the economic affairs of the nation.[61] War profiteering, high emergency wages, and full employment all were tempting their benefactors to use the state increasingly for their own selfish interests. This, plus the invention of new means like radio for the transmission of revolutionary doctrines, led Small to predict "that Americans are on the eve of the most serious economic class struggle we have ever known." But if the proletariat succeeds in its efforts, this "means the suppression by violence of everyone who resists the exclusive rule of those who work with their hands."[62] In Small's mind,

the most dangerous single factor in each European country today is the organized campaign to put capitalists out

60. Ibid.
61. Said Small: "For war purposes we are now in grim practice of programs which were regarded as impossible only two years ago. We have acted upon a theory of the relation of the government to the citizen which reverses presumptions and doctrines that came over in the Mayflower and had dominated our imagination in spite of much contrary practice until 1917. . . . We have temporarily out Germaned the Germans." Albion W. Small, "The Church and Class Conflicts," *AJS* XXIV (March, 1919): 485-86.
62. Ibid., p. 492.

of existence and, to use one of the phrases which have become commonplace among these agitators, 'to socialize
capital'. . . . Moreover, the idea is spreading through
Europe, and coming across the seas, that it is right to
realize this ideal by any kind and degree of violence
necessary to gain this end.[63]

It can thus be seen that while Small was extremely
critical of what he considered to be the unproductive
uses of capital in political bribery, trust formation, and
short weighting, he was by no means an apologist for
such "asocial" working class activities as work slow-
downs, on the job thievery, and fomenting revolution.
Rather, he identified himself in the end as a spokesman for what he believed were the worthwhile tradi-
tions of Americanism. From his ideological position, he
observed that the "general interests" of the people were
threatened, not simply by the radically disposed immigrant laborer, but also from the concentration of
wealth by the high financier. As he described the situation facing middle America to his seminar,

at one extreme, men have contended that only the laborer,
and the manual laborer at that, deserves any income at
all, and that one man's day's work deserves no more pay
than another's. At the opposite extreme, men are more
strenuously insisting, the more the others challenge the
doctrine, that the proprietor of land or capital deserves a
regular income in the shape of rent or interest, simply because he owns the land or capital.[64]

This picture of the social problems of his day allows
one to clearly place Small as a representative of the
"man in the middle," an idealogue, in other words, of
the Progressive movement. When interpreting Lester
Ward's sociology earlier, reference was made to this
same political reaction of small rural businessmen, in-

63. Ibid., p. 491.
64. Small, "The Conflict of Classes," p. 34.

dependent professionals, and clergy to the social changes after the Civil War. There, the fear that the Progressives had of the power of big business and labor, was mentioned. And it was pointed out how they despairingly forecasted the destruction of civilization, as they knew it, were either of these forces to realize their will at the expense of the collective purposes of the nation as a whole. Like Ward, Small was able to express this concern of local society in the technical vocabulary of sociology, when he said:

> Whensoever the machinery of the state begins to be used to protect one interest within the state against another, from that moment mischief is afoot. The Pandora's Box of political evils is wide open. . . . Henceforth, the life of the state is a series of rapes of the law by the interest or interests temporarily able to control civic power.[65]

Since this is true, then the only ethical choice open to men of good will, is to defend this protector of shared interests, the state, from all would-be usurpers. "The social problem," Small disclosed to his audience, "is to defeat all interests which in content or possibly even in form subordinate general interests to special interests."[66] But what sorts of techniques can be effectively employed in overcoming the resistance of such formidable groups as the socialists and the corporate capitalists? In the first place, says Small, the state can not shirk from its duty to use *any* means practical and necessary to maintain its integrity. Thus,

> there can be no effective program in the state without the use of forcible means. Whatever physical force would be necessary to carry out a program in the interest of unsocialized selfishness . . . is also necessary . . . to defeat that program . . . Every struggle against the enemies of socialization requires superior force than the opponent

---

65. Small, *General Sociology*, p. 270.
66. Ibid., p. 279.

possesses or uses. To this extent and in this sense, Napoleon was right that 'providence is on the side of the strongest battalions.'[67]

Of course, enough has been said by now to show that regardless of the extent to which these comments smack of Ratzenhoferian realpolitik, Small can not be accused of being a collectivist in the classical Prussian sense. No good American Progressive, and Small seems almost to have fulfilled the ideal-type, could possibly have advocated the maintenance of social order above all values whatsoever. "It is a mark of obstructive, anti-social self-seeking," he would caution the reader of the above statement, "to persist in employing force to maintain an obsolete order, or fragments of such an order."[68] Yet Small and those for whom he wrote, did not place American society in this forbidden class of "obsolescence." There is, he often said, no "radical vice" in America. The basic institutions upon which this country was founded are perfectly sound. "I do not believe," he submitted in the course of dismissing the

67. Ibid., p. 340. According to Small, "the state, the national group organized as a unity, is a certain conception, idea, purpose, conscious in certain persons, and committed at all hazards to self assertion. The state is a certain vague or definite theorem to be maintained. It is a body of interests to be guarded. It is a claim, to be defended against all comers. . . . It must succeed. It must prevail over every possible opposition." Ibid., p. 244. See also Ibid., pp. 245-49.

68. Ibid., p. 238. It is educational to consider Small's evaluations of German collectivism made some twenty years after the publication of *General Sociology*. Even at this later date Small maintains that "American domestic problems at this moment are the natural outgrowth of principles which we have published as the final terms of human wisdom [namely, individualism]." Small, *Origins of Sociology*, p. 240. But, he adds, "our appraisal of the successes which the Germans have gained by their application of collectivism by no means makes for the conclusion: Therefore a stampede to Germany! The moral is rather: There may be more in the collectivistic idea than we individualistic Americans have imagined. It is worth while for us to get all the instruction we can from German experience in a working system based on an opposite presumption from ours." Ibid.

demands for a thoroughgoing revolution as inappropriate for America's needs, that "the correct statement of our present social problem will be made in terms of institutional structure at all. . . . It is probable that changes to be made in these institutions, in any visible future, will be more the effect than the cause of solving our present social problem."[69] In other words then, it appears that Small would have gone quite far in supporting the government's use of force to maintain social order in the face of internal subversion.

But however much this is the case, Small never believed that if the state was to effectively squelch radicalism, it would be sufficient to rely solely upon governmental violence. On the contrary, through his study of Ratzenhofer, he became convinced that in the last analysis, it would be more utilitarian for the state to partially acquiesce to the demands of those very classes now clamoring for more freedom, by extending to them Constitutional rights. "The progressive extension of political communities in the socialization process always involves, as one of its incidents," he argued, "an approximate equalization of the power at the disposal of individuals. Within each political community there must exist in principle a fundamental equality of right."[70] Only when federal law begins to protect the interests of the poor, the propertyless, and the outsider, will they in turn find it reasonable to defend the nation

69. Small, *General Sociology,* p. 379. "Our American problem is not, in the first instance," he goes on, "that of reconstructing institutions. It is the problem of the spirit which we will show in working the institutions that we have." Ibid., p. 380. Cf. Small, "Socialism in the Light of Social Science," p. 817.

70. Small, *General Sociology,* p. 341. In Small's view, "as zeal for common welfare is an enobled zeal for individual welfare, so equalization of political influence is a refinement of the strife for political power. Since socialization involves progressive dissolution of lesser political communities, there is also involved extended equalization of political power in general." Ibid. See also Ibid., pp. 342-43.

state against its enemies, instead of working together to undermine it.

Small recognized that the granting of legal rights to newly enfranchised interest groups would naturally augment their political influence. For instance, he knew that giving the working class the opportunity to unionize and to engage in collective bargaining would enable them, for the first time, to balance the strength of the robber barons. But this, he felt, could actually be a constructive consequence, for now at least, the railroad and steel magnates could no longer demand such unjust shares of the national wealth. And vice versa, of course, in a situation where all classes have political rights, the proletariat will find a powerful check on its own selfish wish to establish socialism, in the capitalist and landlord. In other words, Small somewhat pessimistically thought that all groups within the state are driven to maximize their own selfish interests, at the expense of other collectivities. "Each class, in its own manner and degree," as he described it, "is using all the means at its disposal to change the balance of power."[71] The only possible preventative that the People have against this fact, is not legal repression, but rather the Constitutional cultivation of a balance of power among the plurality of conflicting parties, so that no one special interest can unilaterally usurp power.

Although the implementation of Small's policy of equality actually increases the probability of domestic strife, he paradoxically predicted, after Ratzenhofer, that such a situation comprises less a danger to national order than otherwise. This is because only now, do the struggling foes find it increasingly difficult not to equate the realization of their own goals with the at-

71. Ibid., p. 302.

tainment of overall national goals. The equality of rights entails that the interests working at cross directions within the state, find their completion only in the fulfillment of common interests. Thus "struggle in the constitutional state, in spite of heat and passion, bars absolute hostility. . . . The typical working of the social process progressively eliminates the possibility of such episodes, by assuring to each interest its proportionate freedom within the state."[72]

Summary of Small's Views on Class Conflict

When considering American society, Small gives the impression that above all, the thing he most treasured was social order and unity. It is of course correct to say that he not only saw class conflicts as more or less inevitable, but that he also labeled them as progressive. But this was not because, like Ranke or Treitschke, he placed any great value on the actual fighting that occurs in a struggle for power. Rather, he was led to believe, both by his observations of Bismarck's Germany and by such thinkers as Ratzenhofer, Schmoller, and Wagner, that one of the consequences of class strife is an increase in equality. And inasmuch as a more just distribution of political and economic rights is a precondition to greater national harmony, then class conflict is indeed progressive. Nor, it is obvious by now, was Small's apology for equality the result of his socialist revolutionary ideals. He did admire Marx' work, but when it came to the question of workers violently overthrowing the state and establishing a proletarian dictatorship, he balked. Instead, he urged

72. Ibid., p. 297.

cooperation between laborers and capitalists.[73] And
when conciliation was not voluntarily forthcoming, he
advocated that the government use any effective means
to coerce the compliance of the dissidents to the collective interests of the People as a whole.

To say that Small's most preeminent value concerned
"sozialization," and consequently equality, does not
mean that he did not worry about the welfare of the
individual. In fact, he believed that only in a situation
of complete citizenship, could each subject fully realize
his inherent potentialities. The fully progressive nation
state, he said, is one "in which each person shall be
equally free with every other person to develop the
type of personality latent in his natural endowment."[74]
But again, he showed that, when an individual's
achievement is used instead of ascriptive ties to
evaluate his worth, a more rational allocation of
human resources is made possible. And since this is
completely consistent with the state's achievement of
its own interests, then "individuals and groups, from
the least to the greatest have to be suppressed or destroyed if they are incapable of accomodation to this
equalizing program. . . ."[75]

To conclude then that the basic question in Small's
sociology is how to institute and preserve a viable so-

73. After praising Marx, Small clarifies himself, saying that "we had no
sooner formulated the primary sociological generalization of the universality
of conflict than we made out the equally primary generalization of the universality of cooperation. For certain immediate purposes, human beings may
and do forge themselves into groups of friends for better or worse to fight
against other groups regarded as absolute enemies. . . . [But] opposing
groups presently discover that it is the best policy for cooperation to control
conflict. Thus it comes about that our last rendering of the social process
today expresses it in terms of one stage further along in its evolution than
that which most impressed Marx. We assert the universal fact of class conflict as he did. We assert the universal fact of cooperation more strongly
than he did." Small, "Socialism in the Light of Social Science," p. 815.
74. Small, *General Sociology*, p. 349. Cf. Ibid., pp. 350-52.
75. Ibid., p. 341.

cial order, is to show once again the ideological underpinnings of his work. It demonstrates the close
philosophical ties between him, American progressivism in general, and German national liberalism.
The members of the *Verein für Sozialpolitik,* just as
Small and his colleague Ward, believed that all interests must be subordinated to the superior goals of
the state, for it represents the highest stage of civilization. The state, in turn, desires both to spread its peace
over larger territories, and to guarantee order within
its own borders. Thus, to Ward, while war was an ad-
mirable phenomenon because it joins men into ever
greater communities, internal subversion was judged to
be evil, for the opposite reason. And also for Small,
while anarchy is the worst of crimes, because "it is violence that destroys some of the foundations or roots
necessary to progress,"[76] imperialistic expansion of
"progressive" states should be supported.

> In a word, the impulse toward socialization moves to-
> ward extension and increase of communities . . . up to the
> compass of states. There are . . . cases in which opposition
> to enlargement of the state is, like anarchy, a symptom of
> a tendency back from socialization to individualistic isola-
> tion from the inevitable social process. . . . There is need of
> delicate discrimination between righteous refusal to sanc-
> tion aggression, and blind resistance to liberal widening of
> the range of socialization.[77]

There will doubtless be arguments by American
sociologists against drawing such inferences about the
founders of their profession. Much current scholarly
opinion has it that sociology can trace its roots back to
classical liberal social thought.[78] Yet I believe that it is
absolutely necessary in order to successfully carry out

76. Ibid., p. 338.
77. Ibid., p. 336.
78. For example, see Thomas Ford Hoult, "Who Shall Prepare Himself to
the Battle?" *The American Sociologist* III (Feb., 1968): 3-7.

objective research, for sociologists to clearly understand that the theoretical perspective into which they have been socialized, has significant parallels with the non-liberal, nay anti-liberal world view of German political scholarship. Some will admit that it is true to say of Ward and even of Small that their philosophies of history are indeed consistent with realpolitik. But after all, these men had no great effect on later developments in the discipline that they helped establish. Even granting this to be the case, these two were not the only early sociologists to be influenced by German higher learning. Among others, Robert Park and Arthur Bentley, both of whose basic assumptions about social life *have* been taught to new generations of graduate students in sociology and political science, were also theoretically inspired by German *Sozialwissenschaft*. The following two chapters will be devoted to analyzing in detail the manner in which realpolitik penetrated their own thinking.

8

Robert E. Park's Sociology of Conflict

Progressivism, Muckraking, and Sociology

One of the convictions shared by American reformists who lived and wrote during the early part of the twentieth century concerned the basic importance of general education for the attainment of social progress. This can be understood in part as a result of their socialization into a populist ethic that proclaimed the common man as the true agency of social change. According to this doctrine, only if the facts concerning a particular evil are revealed to them, will men be motivated to engage in discussion, collective opinion formation, and finally in political activity that will ultimately solve the social problem.

This notion found various forms of expression in the work of American Progressives. For example, with Ward, it apparently provided the basis for his program of telic meliorism through compulsory education. Small too, had an important place in his philosophy of history for politically conscious educators. In fact, he felt that one of the moral responsibilities of sociologists was to teach their students the difference between social justice and asocial sin. He hoped, in this way, that his profession might cultivate a tolerance in the minds of opposing parties for the views of their enemies, and thus lower the potentiality of uncontrolled hostility in domestic conflicts.[1]

These proposals to make the process of formal education more amenable to the realization of national goals were not limited to Ward and Small. For instance, both Edward Ross and John Dewey[2] made their reputations by advocating similar measures. But now that such ideas have been fully instituted into the American school system, it can be observed that the effects of a progressive pedagogy were always bound to be limited to a relatively narrow circle of professional social scientists and school-age pupils. However, this was not to be case for another way in which the same democratic faith in public opinion manifested itself during the Progressive Era. This was later to become known as the phenomenon of muckraking. For some thirty years, beginning around 1890, exposés of poverty, crime, and corruption, appeared in both newspapers and in periodicals like *McClures, The Nation,* and *The American*. These revelations were written in a

1. Albion Small told his students that the object of his lectures on "The Conflict of Classes," was not to justify any class theory, but rather to "promote progress in human welfare." Small, "The Conflict of Classes," pp. 39-40. This would be done, he said, by altering their opinions concerning domestic affairs. In his view, public opinion was going to play an increasingly significant part in the forces leading to social change. He recognized that "millions of men had [already] gone to their death for the . . . opinions that had been put in shape by philosophers." He added, "my prediction is that the changes which must take place in society in the near future, will be less often . . . wrought . . . by fighting of any sort, and more and more often largely by modified opinion." Ibid., p. 43.
2. For example, see Edward A. Ross, *Social Control* (New York: Macmillan Co., 1901). John Dewey, *Democracy and Education* (New York: Macmillan Co., 1916).

sensational language that appealed to mass literary tastes, and thus much more effectively than traditional teaching methods, were able to mobilize reform activities throughout the country.

Robert Park sometimes listed his name among those like Lincoln Steffens, Hutchins Hapgood, and Upton Sinclair, by calling himself "one of the first and humbler muckrakers."[3] As was typical for educated members of local society, he shared Small's and Ward's belief in the significance of opinion formation for law making. "We are interested in public opinion, I suppose," he once said in a paper on this very subject, "because public opinion is, in the long run, the sovereign power in the state. There is not now, and probably never has been, a government that did not rest on public opinion."[4] It appears that this was not a position that came to Park late in his life. For the story is told of how, while an undergraduate at the University of Michigan, he was introduced by John Dewey to one Franklin Ford. Together, the two young men developed the notion of scientifically polling public opinion, and presenting the findings in a publication to be entitled "Thought News" to legislators.[5]

Like his fellow Progressives, Park believed that cultural workers could play a relevant part in social reform movements, by influencing the exchange of ideas on contemporary issues. It was his hope, as he describes it in his autobiographical note, that with the somewhat detatched reporting on social problems, "the historical process would be appreciably stepped up, and progress would go forward steadily without the interruption and disorder of depression or violence, and at a

3. Quoted in Howard W. Odum, *American Sociology: The Story of Sociology in the United States Through 1950* (Toronto: Longmans, 1951), p. 132.
4. Robert E. Park and Ernest W. Burgess, *Introduction to the Science of Sociology* (Chicago: University of Chicago Press, 1921), p. 820.
5. See Hughes, "Park, Robert E.," p. 416.

rapid pace."[6] In accordance with his desire to advance
the course of history, Park labored for twelve years following his graduation from college, as a feature reporter for newspapers in New York, Chicago, Detroit,
and Denver. Here, he was given the task of disclosing
to his readers the facts about such symptoms of local
"social disorganization" as prostitution, suicide, and
juvenile delinquency.

While searching for arousing Sunday supplement
stories, it occured to Park that in places like Denver,
social evolution as a whole was being played out on
quite a miniscule, and thus easily observable, level.
Consequently, he thought, the city itself might constitute a cheap and accessible sociological laboratory
within which to study social change. Later, when at
the University of Chicago, he sought systematically to
capitalize on this idea by sending his students in
droves to conduct research on the various deviant sub-
cultures that presumably were the unintended products
of social transformation.

In retrospect, Park's intellectual life seems to have
consisted of a cyclical movement from academia, back
to the street, followed by a return to the cloistered
halls. Such a career pattern was not novel for this
time. One observes in the biographies of many of the
early Progressive ideologues, the tendency to begin by
writing for mass circulation media (and subsequently,
to adopt a colorful vocabulary), only to revert later to
the less sensational theorizing about contemporary
events in professional journals.[7] This may have re-

6. Park, "Autobiographical Note," p. vi.
7. For example, Ward not only wrote for the *AJS*, but also contributed to
Forum such explicitly crusading pieces as "Broadening the Way to Success,"
"The Use and Abuse of Wealth," and "Plutocracy and Paternalism." His
nephew Ross is now remembered for his strictly sociological work, but in his
time he gave public lectures on labor, socialism, and tax and monetary reform. Furthermore, he tried his hand at muckraking in *Sin and Society* and

sulted from a real indecision in the minds of these men regarding the most effective way to reach a responsive public with their writings. At any rate, whatever his motives, after spending over a decade of his life as a journalist, Park returned to graduate school at Harvard, and then followed the footsteps of his contemporaries to Germany. With a *Dr. Phil.* from Heidelberg, Park could almost have dictated the terms of his employment at any prestigious American university. But, by this time, he was once again "sick and tired of the academic world, and wanted to go back to the world of men."[8]

Park's first new job was as a secretary to the Congo Reform Association, where he was introduced to the man for whom he later worked for many years as a personal secretary, Booker T. Washington. This Negro reformer was one of the first to turn Park's attention from the city to the subject of race relations. And he once admitted that "I probably learned more about human nature in the South under Booker Washington, than I had learned elsewhere in all my previous studies."[9] One of the results of their lengthy collaboration was *The Man Farthest Down*,[10] a description of the efforts by subservient European nationalities to liberate themselves from feudal bondage.

For present purposes, however, Park's engagement with the Congo Reform Association is even more im-

Latter-Day Sinners and Saints. Lastly, Small attempted to popularize the notions more formally presented in "the Conflict of Classes" in a book entitled *Between Eras: From Capitalism to Democracy.* Most of his politically motivated papers appeared in the *AJS*, under such titles as "Vision of Social Efficiency," "The Significance of Sociology for Ethics," and "The Evolution of A Social Standard."

8. Park, "Autobiographical Note," p. v.

9. Charles S. Johnson, "Robert E. Park: In Memoriam," *Sociology and Social Research* XXVIII (May-June, 1944): 355.

10. Booker T. Washington, *The Man Farthest Down* (New York: A. L. Burt & Co., 1907).

portant. This is because during this period, he wrote several articles for *Everybody's Magazine* that exposed, in the finest muckraking tradition, the brutalities of Belgian colonial policy. In these manuscripts, he exhibits a well-instructed capacity to see behind such "fronts" as the African International Association, The Belgian Congo Press Bureau, and the Society for Studies in the Upper Congo, to the essential violence of capitalistic imperialism. According to Park, all of these agencies were established by King Leopold primarily to collect tribute from the native with the help of mercenary soldiers, and secondly, to legitimize this enterprise in the eyes of Europeans by doing it in the name of civilization. The following excerpt from "The Terrible Story of the Congo," is indicative of the moralistic fervor with which Park approached the subject of what he considered to be racial exploitation.

> Men, women, and little children are either dragged away as "hostages" to be held until their fellow villagers have contrived to make up the deficiency or are shot down like dogs, and their right hands cut off and turned over to the state as evidence of duty done....
> ... Meanwhile, making the most of his opportunity, the Vampire [King Leopold] sits sucking the life blood of the victim that has slowly ceased to struggle. By the time the powers have bestirred themselves to action, he fully gorged, will fling the carcass of their [Europe's] feet and say: "Take it—what is left is yours."[11]

11. Robert E. Park, "The Terrible Story of the Congo," *Everybody's Magazine* XV (Dec., 1906): 771-72. Park pointed out to his readers that the Belgian Congo was not established on the basis of military occupation, but rather through the export of capital. This new type of imperialism, he claimed, "means that the men who are supreme in the world of finance are endowed, by the very necessities of the great interests that they represent, with an arbitrary power, like the authority imposed by military necessity, which supersedes the ordinary political rights of human beings. It means that the 'divine right' has been transferred from the king to the financier.... The socialists are right when they point to King Leopold as the crowned incarnation of the aspirations and tendencies of a business peo-

After nine years of uncovering the evil in contemporary race contacts, Park began to question whether his true calling really lay in the direction of advocacy journalism. For the more he traveled, the more he became convinced that the race relations that he was observing in the Belgian Congo, in Eastern Europe, in the American South, and out in the Pacific, were not simply isolated events occurring at random with no relationship to one another, but that they represented incidents in a single overarching historical process. What was needed, he felt, was a statement of this process, a theory of some sort that would subsume all these diverse incidents under a few general categories.[12]

Fortunately for Park, the discovery of his theoretical interests coincided with an offer from W. I. Thomas to lecture on the Negro in America at the University of Chicago. Park's acceptance of this invitation foretold of the radical alteration that his style of writing on race relations was to undergo in the following years from that represented e.g. in his contributions to *Everybody's Magazine*. What strikes the reader of Park's work after 1920 is the apparent absence of a quality that is readily observable in his early muckraking; that is, the tendency to sermonize. Not only in his writing, but also

---

ple and a business age." Robert E. Park, "A King in Business," *Everybody's Magazine* XV (Nov., 1906): 633. Park used his knowledge of mass media and their relevance in the formation of public opinion to unmask the true intentions of the Belgian Congo Press Bureau: "Consider the aged monarch's position: very well he knows how fragile is his hold on the Congo Free State, and that as the Powers entrusted it to him, so they can take it away. . . . But between Leopold and this danger is the intangible but mighty protection of his realization of the great force of public opinion and his mastery of swaying it through the press, founded, as that art must always be, on a deep knowledge of human nature. . . . He knows what stories allay suspicion, what carry the strongest conviction; knows what to suppress, what to emphasize." Robert E. Park, "Blood-Money of the Congo," *Everybody's Magazine* XVI (Jan., 1907): 61.

12. Park, "Autobiographical Note," pp. vii-viii.

in the classroom, he began to debunk attempts to derive ethical imperatives from sociological analyses. According to a fellow faculty member, he "told . . .[his students] flatly that the world was full of crusaders. Their role was to be that of the calm, detatched scientist who investigates race relations with the same objectivity and detatchment with which the zoologist dissects the potato bug."[13]

With limited data, it will never be known for sure what caused this reversal in Park's perspective. However, two facts that seem to have had some relevance in this regard, should be mentioned. In the first place, an atmosphere conducive to the consumption of politically shocking literature disappeared after World War I. When faced by a foreign enemy, the grounds for persistent domestic quarreling may have appeared to many to be unjustified. And this movement toward consensus was no doubt reinforced by postwar prosperity. Ironically, the same big enterprises that had previously run the small merchant and farmer out of business, began creating after the war, service jobs for adequately trained sons of local society. This, plus the accumulation of work opportunities in government bureaucracy, meant that liberal crusaders such as Park were increasingly faced with a well-fed and indifferent group of readers. Indeed it is not too far-fetched to suggest that Park's skepticism toward the possibility of his remaining in journalism was reinforced by the job insecurity that faced one-time muckrakers as the market for political criticism in postwar America began diminishing.[14] Secondly, there is the point that Lewis

13. Ernest W. Burgess, "Social Planning and Race Relations," *Race Relations: Problems and Theory, Essays in Honor of Robert E. Park,* ed. by J. Masuoka and Preston Valien (Chapel Hill: University of North Carolina Press, 1961), p. 17.

14. According to C. Wright Mills, only *The Nation* and the *New Republic* of all the crusading liberal magazines, remained after the war. See Mills,

Coser has made, concerning the fact that the change in Park's mode of presentation corresponded to a transition from a relatively unsophisticated magazine audience, to the more demanding expectations of his students and colleagues at Chicago. If the members of the Department of Sociology were to maintain their prestige in the eyes of the University community, claims Coser, it was absolutely necessary for them to become more scientific and theoretical, and less melioristic and journalistic.[15] Furthermore, Park himself tells us that when he was beseiged by his pupils to study different social phenomena, he began to critically question the loose way in which such concepts as "race," "public," and "gang," etc. had heretofore been used in commentaries. "I did not see how we could have anything like scientific research," he said of his feelings in this context, "unless we had a system of classification and a frame of reference into which we could sort out and describe in general terms the things we were attempting to investigate."[16]

Park's *Introduction to the Science of Sociology* contains his "first rough sketch" of the frame of reference that he spent the remainder of his intellectual career specifying and elaborating.[17] The "Green Bible," as it was later called by sociology graduate students, consists primarily of excerpts taken from a large variety of original sources. In what was then a relatively unique format, each set of readings was integrated into Park's overall conceptual framework through an introduction. The content of these preliminary statements clearly demonstrates the sway that scholars like Charles Darwin, and especially John Dewey, Hugo

Sociology and Pragmatism, pp. 331-32. Cf. C. Wright Mills, *White Collar* (New York: Oxford University Press, 1956), pp. 327-32.

15. Coser, *Masters of Sociological Thought,* pp. 377-83.

16. Quoted in Odum, *American Sociology,* pp. 132-33.

17. Ernest Burgess was the junior author in this venture.

Münsterberg, and C. H. Cooley held over their author's thinking. However, in his discussion of social conflict, it is the influence of Georg Simmel and the sociologists of conflict, particularly Franz Oppenheimer, that is evident.

It is not exactly clear as to when or how Park came upon the writings of the sociologists of conflict. One of his students who knew him best, Everett C. Hughes, believes that "most certainly" Park read some of their literature while doing graduate study under Simmel and Windelband in Germany.[18] This would not be completely unexpected considering the fact that Simmel's notion of conflict fits easily within the perspective of realpolitik as it was then being developed by two of his associates, Max Weber and Oppenheimer.[19] On the other hand, although Park was over fifty years old when he came to the University of Chicago, it is not difficult to think that Albion Small, more knowledgeable than any other person of his time concerning German sociological developments, might have made him aware of at least Ratzenhofer's theory of race relations, and maybe Gumplowicz's as well.[20]

18. I received a lengthy personal letter from Everett C. Hughes in which he revealed that as a student under Park he read Gumplowicz, Oppenheimer, Gerland, and others. He told me that in the days before sociology became an established profession, it was customary for persons like Park to read widely in a good number of fields and in several different languages. It was, Hughes has little doubt, in the course of this general quest for knowledge that Park discovered not only Gumplowicz and Simmel, etc., but also the French and German geographers, Darwin, and even Max Weber's *Sociology of Religion.*
19. Georg Simmel, *Conflict and the Web of Group Affiliations,* trans. by Kurt Wolff and Reinhard Bendix (New York: Free Press, 1955). One can fine an excellent analysis of Simmel's views in Lewis Coser, *The Functions of Social Conflict* (New York: Free Press, 1955). For a short biographic essay on Simmel that mentions his study under such proponents of realpolitik, as Droysen, Sybel, and Treitschke, see Georg Simmel, *The Sociology of Georg Simmel,* trans., ed. with an intro. by Kurt Wolff (New York: Free Press, 1950).
20. It could be argued that by fifty years of age, Park would no longer be

Conflict and Competition:
Realpolitik and Social Darwinism

But irrespectve of the truth of these speculations, there is little question but that realpolitik permeates Park's social theorizing. In fact, the effect of this German intellectual tradition on his sociology is great enough so that his teachings can be used to differentiate at depth between two philosophies that are sometimes confused: realpolitik and social Darwinism.

Many historians of sociology have dismissed the theories of Gumplowicz and Ratzenhofer and their followers Ward and Small, as provocative, but really insignificant contributions to sociology, inasmuch as they represent a type of social Darwinism.[21] While admittedly, there can be debate concerning the meaning of "Darwinism," the two previous chapters have argued that Ward and Small relied not upon the authority either of Darwin or the English Darwinists Spencer, Pearson, or Galton to justify their claims as to the causes, nature, and ends of conflict, but rather upon realpolitik and two of its most eminent representatives, Gumplowicz and Ratzenhofer. And as was indicated earlier, German realpolitik was apparently formulated prior to and generally independently from Darwinism.

receptive to new intellectual innovations from such sources as Small. Hughes, I think, would question this. He wrote me that throughout his acquaintance with Park, "he took ideas wherever he could find them and would go on in a very speculative way, proving the other man's ideas and facts, without rancor and always with the aim of learning." In regard to Small's influence in particular on Park, however, Hughes is more skeptical.

21. For example, see: Nicholas S. Timasheff, *Sociological Theory: Its Nature and Growth* (New York: Random House, 1967), pp. 63-68. Pitirim Sorokin, *Contemporary Sociological Theories* (New York: Harper & Bros., 1928), pp. 309-56. Harry Elmer Barnes and Howard Becker, *Social Thought from Lore to Science,* 3 vols. (New York: Dover Pub. Inc., 1961), II, 693-742. An important exception to attempts to categorize Gumplowicz and Ratzenhofer as social Darwinists is found in Don Martindale, *The Nature and Types of Sociological Theory* (Boston: Houghton Mifflin, 1960), pp. 127-210.

Furthermore, a thorough perusal of the political writings of the most influential Prussian historians, their students, and the sociologists of conflict, clearly reveals that they make few significant positive references at all to Darwin's work.[22]

Most interesting of all, however, is the fact that in realpolitik, social conflict is not even spoken of in the same terms as Darwin's struggle for existence. It is quite correct to say that like Darwin, the Germans and their American students Ward, Small, and even Park, believed that a necessary condition for social strife, is a scarcity of such things as material goods relative to human desires. But certainly, it would be nonsense to equate realpolitik and Darwinism on this basis alone. After all, Polybius, Turgot, Hobbes, and Hume, to name only four, all reduced the causes of power struggles to the same situation of scarcity. Moreover, irrespective of its causes, according to the Germans, conflict is not analogous to the wholly mindless "struggle," as Darwin might call it, for sunlight or soil nutrients that takes place among plants. Nor is it similar to the more "passionate," yet completely instinctual "fight" that can occur between the crocodile, for instance, and his prey.

German historiographers and sociologists of the nineteenth century had a characteristic appreciation of the vast differences separating human from biological and physical affairs. One consequence of this awareness, as was mentioned in the second chapter, was

22. Gumplowicz argued in one of his papers that if persons like Schäffle were going to borrow the organismic analogy from biology to illustrate the static features of society, then perhaps they "should also have attempted to employ Darwin's theory of the survival of the fittest to explain social development." Ludwig Gumplowicz, "Darwinismus in der Soziologie," *Soziologie und Politik,* in *Ausgewählte Werke,* IV, ed. by F. Oppenheimer, F. Savorgnan, M. Adler, G. Salomon (Innsbruck: Universitäts—Verlag Wagner, 1928), 249. Beyond this, there are few places where he mentions Darwin's name.

their proposal that social phenomena be submitted to a radically different form of scientific methodology, than to a mechanistic logic more appropriate to natural events. In their writings, scholars such as Ranke, Treitschke, and Roscher, all proclaimed that unlike lower levels of animal life, man is imbued with purposes and spirit. Thus, while the movements of planetary bodies, for example, can be explained by reference to laws concerning repulsion and attraction, human behavior can only be understood (*Verstehen*), by tracing it back to its psychic source—the will.

It is not necessary at present to describe all of the nuances of this development in German intellectual life. Suffice it to say that it was apparently this "romantic" view concerning the peculiar nature of human action, as compared to biological movement, that inspired the proponents of realpolitik to place social conflict, not on an organismic basis, but rather squarely on a psychological foundation.[23] According to all of the scholars whose work has been reviewed in this book, conflict is a type of psychological interaction that can reside only between conscious, goal-directed persons. These purposive and thus in principle morally responsible, although not necessarily fully rational "persons" can be either individual humans (as Ratzenhofer supposed), groups such as races or classes (as Gumplowicz maintained), or states (as Treitschke argues).

Of course, this is not to say that Gumplowicz's conception of human purpose was identical, e.g., to that of the great psychological historicist, Wilhelm Dilthey. In fact, the Austrian pessimist explicitly denied, in a way that would probably have made the German historians shudder, the possibility of freedom of the will. But this

23. See Hofstadter, *Social Darwinism in American Thought,* p. 57 for a concurring analysis.

was not because he attempted to explain social behavior by subsuming it under biological principles. As
Gumplowicz said:

> Social science can never "obtain a basis as real as that of
> natural science" until the fantastic view that "society" is
> an "organism" has been thrown overboard and all biologi-
> cal analogies cleared away.
>   Lilienfeld's query whether social organisms do not obey
> the same laws as all other beings must be emphatically
> answered in the negative. The distinction between social
> organisms and organic beings is somewhat more than a
> simple . . .[matter of degree]. They are distinct species of
> phenomena and different laws control them. Laws of or-
> ganic development and laws of social development are *toto
> genere* unlike and ought not be confounded.[24]

In Gumplowicz's mind, man's psyche must of necessity
be invoked if social interaction such as conflict is to be
properly explained. His argument against the doctrine
of free will was only directed to the mistaken notion
that the content of man's personality has a source
other than in social interaction. The psychological
make-up of the adult, Gumplowicz would claim, is
neither the result of his biological instincts, nor the
consequence of free choice.

> The whole belief in the freedom of human action is rooted
> in the idea that man's conduct is the fruit of his thoughts
> and that his thoughts are exclusively his own. This is an
> error. He is not self-made mentally any more than he is
> physically. His mind and thoughts are the products of his
> social medium, of the social element whence he arose, in
> which he lives.[25]

Ratzenhofer, Oppenheimer, Small, and Ward all
agree with Gumplowicz that the distinguishing feature
of social activity is the psychical interaction of the par-

24. Gumplowicz, *Outlines*, p. 35.
25. Ibid., p. 243. See also pp. 240-51.

ticipants; the conscious awareness of the actors involved that the attainment of their own purposes entails either the cooperation, conflict, or compromise with their fellows.[26] This same view also informs the theorizing of both Georg Simmel and Max Weber. For instance, Simmel believed that sociology should limit itself to the study of the "forms of sociation"; that is, the basic processes of psychological interaction going on among goal-directed human beings.[27] One form of sociation, he argued, is social conflict. In other words, what makes conflict a subject worthy of sociological investigation, said Simmel, was not that it is a biological phenomenon, but precisely because it is not. Weber spoke in generally the same manner as Simmel. He proposed that the proper subject matter of sociology consists only of human action, or what he called "behavior to which individuals give some subjective meaning." Where an actor's behavior is based on the conscious anticipation of the possible responses to it by

26. As Small would say it: "So long as biological interests control, the process does not reach the plane of the social; when choices, as distinct from physiological cause and effect begin to modify individual action, the human plane is reached." Small, *General Sociology,* p. 207. Ward in his "Social and Biological Struggles," begins by emphatically denying that either himself or Gumplowicz and Ratzenhofer can properly be called social Darwinists. "I wish to protest in the strongest possible terms against the application of the term Darwinian to the race struggle. I know of no ... sociologist among those who see the real effect of the struggle of races who has accepted this designation for that law." Ibid., p. 293. The basic reason for his denial lies in the fact that unlike a "synergic" relationship between human beings, the "struggle for existence" is really no struggle at all. "A struggle implies some sort of reciprocity between the parties to it. But between a sheep and a wolf [for example] there is no mutuality. All the 'struggling' the sheep can do is to escape from the jaws of the wolf. Even the most robust ram in such a case would have no instinct except that of flight." Ibid., p. 295. On the other hand in social conflicts, the opponents "collaborate" to create a unity between themselves, rather than trying to escape from the situation.

27. Simmel, *The Sociology of Georg Simmel,* pp. 9-10.

others, Weber dubbed this a "social relationship."[28] And in his system, "a social relationship . . .[was] referred to as 'conflict' insofar as action within it is oriented intentionally to carrying out the actor's own will against the resistance of the other party or parties."[29] Weber went on to distinguish on these grounds between conflict and "selection"; "the struggle, often latent, which takes place between human individuals for types of social status, for advantages and for survival, but without a meaningful, i.e. psychologically conscious mutual orientation in terms of conflict."[30]

Interestingly enough, Park explicitly distinguished between conflict and competition on exactly the same basis as Weber does. There is little to support the claim that he actually received his definitions of these terms directly from Weber. But, he was schooled, both here and abroad, in the same point of view that led Weber to appreciate the relevance of man's "telic" capacity for understanding his activity. Specifically, as a pupil first of Dewey, and later of James and Münsterberg, who

28. See Max Weber, *The Theory of Social and Economic Organization,* trans. by A. M. Henderson and Talcott Parsons (New York: Free Press, 1965), pp. 88-118.
29. Ibid., p. 132.
30. Ibid., p. 133. Weber continues: "In so far as it is a matter of the relative opportunities of individuals during their own lifetime, it is 'social selection'; in so far as it concerns differential chances for the survival of inherited characteristics, 'biological selection.' " Ibid. While not as clear as Weber's discussion, Simmel seems to use this same criterion, the presence of psychological contact, to distinguish between conflict and competition. In conflict, the parties actually attempt to interfere with their enemies' behavior in order to prevent him from realizing his goals. This is because the enemy is viewed as controlling the prize (such as territory) over which they are fighting. But in competition, a third party such as a buyer, has the scarce reward, say money, which the two opponents, sellers, are striving after. Thus, as sprinters racing on independent lanes for a trophy held by a judge, "each party fights its adversary without turning against him, without touching him, so to speak" (Simmel, *Conflict and the Web of Group-Affiliations*), p. 59.

themselves were all carriers of the German social psychological outlook, he could not easily have approached sociology from an exclusively biological perspective. Furthermore, as a graduate student listening to Simmel, and while at Heidelberg with Weber's philosophical father, Windelband, and lastly, as a person well-read in both the American and German sociologies of conflict, Park almost assuredly had his original lessons repeatedly reinforced into his thinking.

For this reason, it is not surprising that while in his first sociological treatise, Park equated competition with the "struggle for existence," and argued that it is a "universal" occurrence in all plant and animal life,[31] he added that "it is interaction without social contact. For it is only when minds meet, only when the meaning that is in one mind is communicated to another mind so that these minds mutually influence one another, that social contact, properly speaking, may be said to exist."[32] On the other hand, because conflict is the struggle for scarce facilities and rewards, plus the parties' conscious awareness of their intentions to control the interaction in which they are engaged, then it comprises a type of social contact. "Competition takes the form of conflict or rivalry," he says, "only when it becomes conscious, when the competitors identify one another as rivals or as enemies."[33]

Park felt that war was a classic example of an event in which the combatants consciously alter their strategies to account for the possible reactions of their enemies, in order to more easily defeat them. Thus, he believed, contrary to the hypotheses of social Dar-

31. Park and Burgess, *Introduction to the Science of Sociology,* p. 505.
32. Ibid., p. 507. The authors go on to say that "the members of a plant community adapt themselves to one another as all living things adapt themselves to their environment, but there is no conflict between them because they are not conscious." Ibid., p. 506.
33. Ibid., p. 506.

winists, it could not be fruitfully accounted for by invoking only instinctual biological categories which are
more appropriate for explaining goings-on in the realm
of competition. In one of his last published papers on
this subject, he reiterated the position that he had
taken for over twenty years, when he argued that

> the amount of effort that man puts forth in war, as well
> as the passions and sentiments that these efforts arouse
> are not due merely to the fact that man is here competing
> with other men but that he is conscious of those with
> whom he is in competition, not only of their acts, but of
> their purposes and intentions. Under these circumstances
> competition becomes conflict; a competitor an enemy.[34]

Because conflict involves an interplay between the
minds of the opponents, it has a characteristic result
that allows the analyst to distinguish it in still another
way from competition. In particular, says Park following Darwin to the letter, competition is the source both
of the dispersion of plant and animal species (including
man) over a territory, and of their diversity. In these
two cases, the silent struggle for existence favors those
species who are better adapted to the environment,
while it either eliminates the genetically unfit, or
drives them, so to speak, to fill specialized niches in
the ecological community. The final result is a system
of symbiotic relationships that ties all the surviving
species into a single "economy," where each type of life
is at least indirectly dependent upon all the others for
its survival.[35]

Conflict, on the other hand, has as its consequence,
neither an ecological system, nor the elimination of the

---

34. Robert E. Park, "War and Politics," *Society,* in *The Collected Papers of
Robert Ezra Park,* III, p. 61.
35. See Park and Burgess, *Introduction to the Science of Sociology,* pp.
63-64. See pp. 514-20; 525-44 for attempts to explain the ecological processes
of segregation, migration, and selection. These are among the processes that
constitute the subject matter of what the authors call "human ecology."

weaker by the "more fit." Instead, according to Park, it results in the survival of the weaker race or group, but at the expense of its conscious exploitation by the victor. In other words, power struggles, as opposed to the Darwinian struggle for existence, lead to the psychical control of one group of persons by another. It completes itself in a corporate order or "society," which maintains its integrity, not because it relies upon the biological instincts of its members, but because the powerless consciously obey the expectations of those who rule over them. The "function" of conflict, says Park, "is not to destroy but to ultimately assimilate the vanquished. This involves the imposition upon them of the status of a subject people and, incidently, the assignment to them of a function in the territorial economy within which the victors are dominant."[36]

In Park's view, the organizational outcomes of conflict are not limited to the forcible unification of enemies into a single body dominated by the more powerful adversary. Another unintended product of social strife is the formation of in-group unity in the face of opposition. Park approvingly paraphrases William Graham Sumner in elaborating upon this feature:

> The relation of comradeship and peace in the we-group and that of hostility and war towards other-groups are correlative to each other. The exigencies of war with outsiders weaken the we-group for war. These exigencies also make government and law in the in-group in order to prevent quarrels and enforce discipline. . . . The closer are the neighbors, and the stronger they are, the intenser is the internal organization and discipline of each.[37]

36. Park, "War and Politics," p. 62.
37. Ibid., p. 64. To be more precise: "Conflict is an organizing principle in society. Just as the individual, under the influences of contact and conflict with other individuals, acquires a status and develops a personality, so groups of individuals, in conflict with other groups, achieve unity, organization, group consciousness, and assume the forms characteristic of conflict groups—that is to say they become parties, sects, nationalities, etc." Park and Burgess, *Introduction to the Science of Sociology*, p. 639.

Regardless of whether one is speaking of conquest or of social order within struggling groups, insofar as conflict leads to the psychical control of some persons by others, its final end is the limitation of individual freedom, as it finds expression in competition. Thus, not only is conflict fundamentally different from Darwin's silent struggle for existence, it has the paradoxical consequence of actually restricting it. Small, Ward, Gumplowicz, and Ratzenhofer all appreciated this fact, and this is exactly why they tended both to support war and nonrevolutionary quarrels. They saw in unregulated competition, or what they sometimes called "anarchy," not an advance in civilization, but a reversion to barbarism, to man's animal roots. And they believed that in large measure, only out of power struggles could the political controls necessary to quell man's biological instincts grow. Although Park was certainly not an explicit advocate of war, he too apparently shared this same hopeful outlook, at one time saying that "the effect of conflict has been to extend progressively the area of control and limit the struggle for existence within these areas. The effect of war has been on the whole to extend the area over which there is peace."[38]

It can be seen then, that Park's writing on conflict clearly falls into the school of realpolitik, and that this perspective and social Darwinism are basically incongruent. As the previous chapters have indicated, the proponents of realpolitik also assume a stance that is drastically opposed to liberal political thinking. However, the sociologists who analyzed the subject of conflict from this simultaneously non-biological and anti-liberal point of view, did not ignore the two other ap-

---

38. Park and Burgess, *Introduction to the Science of Sociology,* p. 512. Cf. similar statements in Robert E. Park, "Our Racial Frontier on the Pacific," *Race and Culture,* p. 150 and "Human Migration and the Marginal Man," *Race and Culture,* p. 347.

proaches altogether. Gumplowicz, Ward, and Park had an intimate acquaintance with Darwin and Spencer; and all of the sociologists knew their Kant, Rousseau, and Locke. Furthermore, among those like Ratzenhofer, Ward, and Small who developed complete philosophies of history, the three theoretical outlooks seem to be spoken of in such a way as to "represent" three separate stages of political development—the stage of animal-like competition which leads to the stage of power struggles, which culminates in a liberal society of peace and reason.

In the course of the biological struggle for existence, only those of man's apelike ancestors who by chance were gifted with a rudimentary capacity to think, were ultimately able to reproduce themselves in great enough numbers to insure the survival of their species. But if the mind of Homo sapiens' progenitors guaranteed their biological survival, it also preordained man himself to be a political animal; to be, that is, a beast wholly unique in respect to the fact that he alone would consciously attempt to control the behavior of his fellows for his own benefit. Thus, out of the struggle for existence, evolved its peculiarly human analogue, the struggle for power. Civil strife and war are indeed brutal, but over and above the selfish and shortsighted intentions of enemies grow the state, a more rational political administration, and finally functional equality. In other words, just as the struggle for existence has blindly produced politics, the unplanned consequence of social conflict will be the realization of liberal values.

The Process of Race Relations

There seems to be implicit in Park's theory of race relationships these same assumptions regarding the di-

rection of historical development. Thus like Small and
Ward, Park too apparently saw human experience moving from the biological struggle, through politics, to the
fulfillment of liberal humanism. This proposition may
displease a great number of sociologists, for the simple
reason that contrary to Small and Ward, Park, as a
sociologist, did not believe it to be part of his responsibility to interpret in moral terms, the run of contemporary events. Moreover, he was not a system builder
in the manner of his predecessors. His outlook concerning race contacts was never presented completely in
any one place. What one finds instead are smatherings
of a theory, in a wide variety of papers, some of which
went unpublished, and others of which appeared only
as introductions to his students' books.

Is it justified then to attempt to reconstruct for Park
a single over-arching social philosophy from a plurality
of relatively disconnected, nonmoralistic sources? How,
after all, is one ever to confirm that his reconstruction
is correct? Philosophers of science have, after long debate, concluded that any work written in ordinary language can in principle be formalized in an infinite
number of ways, and that perhaps there is no final
answer to such queries as these. It may be, they add,
that the most that can be required of any analyst is
that he document his claims, and that he not take
statements issued by his subject out of "obvious" context. Beyond this, he can only be requested to make the
basic assumptions guiding his formalization explicit.

In regard to Park's sociology, I assume that there is
a constant theme underlying and informing all of his
work on race relations. Thus, I accept at face value
Park's admission in his "Autobiographical Note" that
he believed he was studying in America, not an isolated and unique phenomenon, but rather, "the historical process by which civilization, not merely here but
elsewhere, has evolved, drawing into the circle of its

influence an ever widening circle of races and peoples."
Secondly, I believe that this historical perspective re-
lects the influence of those people whom he explicitly
acknowledged in his writings, such as Simmel, William
I. Thomas, Oppenheimer, and Small. Thus, to the extent that at least three of these scholars, and possibly
Thomas as well, described conflict and change using
the language of realpolitik, it is to be expected that
Park would follow suit.

Park begins his story of the race process, like the
sociologists of conflict, by hypothesizing the existence
of a plurality of hordes locked in a state of unconscious
competition for life's necessities. In this situation, the
fear of neighboring hordes provides one of the main
bases for what unity there is within each "in-group."[39]
Out of this struggle for existence evolves an ecological
organization of hordes, a "society" in the zoological
sense of the word, both with each other and with the
surrounding flora and fauna. Here, each species of life
is adapted to the others, all instinctively contributing
in a distinct way to the biological maintenance of the
whole community. The territorial population is, according to Park, during this time "held together in an unstable equilibrium of competitive cooperation," in a
"type of association that is fundamentally economic in
the sense in which plant and animal ecologists use that
term."[40]

Apparently through natural selection, some of these
ethnic groups become cognizant of this silent struggle
and its concommitant dependency relations and seek to
use it to their own advantage by consciously exploiting
the labor of rival hordes. What follows is no longer a

39. Robert E. Park, "The Nature of Race Relations," *Race and Culture,* p.
87. Cf. Robert E. Park, "Cultural Conflict and the Marginal Man," *Race and
Culture.* p. 372.
40. Park, "The Nature of Race Relations," pp. 88-89.

biological, but a political fight, where the goal of the opponents is not the elimination of the vanquished, but his enslavement. Citing Oppenheimer as an authority on the subject, Park argues that in historical fact it has been nomadic peoples with an instinct for discipline bred by generations of hard life on the unrelenting Asian plains that have been the victors in such struggles, conquering neighboring peasant populations and setting themselves up as the original political rulers.

> City states came into existence, not always perhaps, but often, when some nomadic chieftain with his tribal followers invaded and conquered a settled and sedentary population. In that case he made the market place the seat of a totalitarian government. Every city as it became a center of political power acquired its local diety, just as among more primitive peoples every clan had its totem.[41]

Thus beginning with forcible enslavement, the essential nature of racial contacts begins shifting radically. What was at an earlier time a purely unconscious relationship of symbiosis, is suddenly changed into a conscious social relationship of class and power.[42]

Park realized that no corporate order, if it is to be stable, can rest solely upon military might. For this reason, he claims, superior races have historically sought to legitimize their rule by cultivating a belief in the natural inferiority of their defeated subjects, and by inventing an appropriate normatively enforced "code of etiquette" to regulate the interaction between races. It is the success with which this strategy is implemented, he maintains, that explains the persistence of segregated social facilities in the American South, many decades after the legal emancipation of the Negro slave. While the plantation caste system was originally established as an uneasy truce between two

41. Ibid., p. 91.
42. Ibid.

deadly enemies, it soon acquired such a degree of moral solidarity that it was able to withstand nothing less than the "shock of a Civil War" in which its objective basis was destroyed militarily.[43]

So much for the society where the subordinate race is completely assimilated into a single unified culture with its conquerors. But what of the fate of the society where such a thoroughgoing assimilation has not taken place? These societies, says Park, contain the seeds for their own destruction through racial conflict. This is because a partial fusion of two alien groups invariably creates a stratum of people who become in time leaders of revolutionary movements. This occurs in the following manner.

House servants, native mercenary soldiers, plantation "strawbosses," and village tax collectors are occupational roles that all colonial rulers and slave states have seen fit at one time or another to create. Although these roles are intended to shore up the sagging power of the slave masters, those who work at them often evolve into "marginal men," men who both live in their masters' culture while partaking of that of the native. By occupying a marginal status, never completely accepted by their superiors, yet at the same time partially distrusted by their own people, "living in two worlds, in both of which they are strangers," such persons develop the disconcerting capacity to assume a detached and objective stance toward both cultures

---

43. Robert E. Park, "The Etiquette of Race Relations," *Race and Culture*, p. 184. A necessary condition for the assimilation of separate races into a single culture is intimate contact between them. Inasmuch as the relations between a slave and his master may be particularly close, then "slavery has been historically the usual method by which people have been incorporated into alien groups. . . . On the other hand the assimilation of the Negro field hand, where the contact of the slave with his master's family was less intimate, was naturally less complete." Park and Burgess, *Introduction to the Science of Sociology*, pp. 761-62.

simultaneously.[44] They become liberated, so to speak, both from their own tribal loyalties and from the ruling myths of their conquerors. And as such, it is they who are the first to become aware of the nonrational or even irrational basis of their people's lowly status in society. It is they, in other words, who form the ranks of movements of national liberation and racial emancipation.[45] First they become the leaders of nationalist renaissance, transforming the folk idiom into a literate language, cultivating archaic native art and poetry, and self-consciously insisting on wearing traditional costume and eating native food. And later, more seriously, they take up political weapons and attempt to seize equal rights from their one time masters.[46]

When the subordinate race acts in accordance with the conceptions of its inferiority held by its masters, there are often friendly relationships between the two. Park believed that the kinship terms "uncle," "son," "man," and "father," as used by southern American whites and Negroes when describing each other, were typical of the warm attitudes that races could hold for each other in a stable situation of racial contacts. The American Negro, the African native and Chinese coolie are invariably "all right in their place," for in their rightful place they are conveniences and not competitors. Indeed, to this extent, says Park, slavery, when voluntarily accepted as morally just by the slave is a "natural solution" to the problem of racial

44. Park, "Human Migration and the Marginal Man," p. 356. Cf. Ibid., pp. 350-55 and Park, "Cultural Conflict and the Marginal Man," pp. 373-76.

45. Park, "Human Migration and the Marginal Man," p. 355. Park indicates that both Simmel and Oppenheimer are the primary sources for his notion of marginality. Cf. Ibid., p. 354 and Park, "The Nature of Race Relations," pp. 97-98.

46. Robert E. Park, "Manuscript Notes on Invasion, Conquest, Migration, Racial Mixture, etc.," University of Chicago Library, Park Papers, Box II, Folder 4. Cf. Park, "The Nature of Race Relations," pp. 98-100.

prejudice.[47] However, at the first moment that the man of lower caste fails to maintain his proper distance as defined by convention; when he becomes "too pushy" by consciously struggling to improve his prestige, power, and wealth in society, then he will be identified as an enemy of social order by those whose positions he threatens.

This attempt to explain racial hostility by tracing it back to the conflict of interests that presumably underlies it, is indicative of the sway that realpolitik held over Park's thinking. For all of those writing from this perspective, psychological antagonism was said to be caused directly by the foreboding experienced by men who believe that their material and ideal interests are threatened by others. "Absolute hostility," as Ratzenhofer hypothesized in one of the first sociological formulations of this notion, "is the guardian *(Wächterin)* over the continuation of common interest."[48] W. I. Thomas, one of Park's most important teachers, was simply applying this same notion to a new setting when, in his famous article on the "Psychology of Race Prejudice," he theorized that the human disposition to describe other races than his own in derogatory terms is a practical necessity if he is to maintain a state of readiness to defend his interests from intruders.[49] And Park's graduate lecturer at Berlin, Georg Simmel, argued in a similar vein when he said that the basis for animosity lies not in a subconscious nonrational need for enmity, but rather in the identification of one's opponent as a rival in a struggle for scarce values. In such a situation, "it is expedient to hate the adversary with whom one fights."[50]

47. Park, "The Nature of Race Relations," p. 98.
48. Ratzenhofer, *Die Sociologische Erkenntnis,* p. 245.
49. See W. I. Thomas, "The Psychology of Race Prejudice," *AJS* IX (March, 1904): 593-611.
50. Simmel, *Conflict and the Web of Group-Affiliations,* p. 34.

There is an interesting consequence that follows from this notion, if it is taken to its logical conclusion. If it is indeed true that "we hate people because we fear them; because our interests, as we understand them at any rate, run counter to theirs,"[51] then there is little hope for programs of general education to achieve racial harmony. Park apparently came to exactly this somewhat pessimistic realization when, after many years of studying race relations, he spoke the following words:

> It has been assumed that the prejudice which blinds people of one race to the virtues of another, and leads them to exaggerate that other's faults, is in the nature of a misunderstanding which further knowledge will dispel. This is so far from true that it would be more exact to say that our racial misunderstandings are merely the expression of our deep-seated, vital, and instinctive impulses. These antipathies represent the collision of invisible forces, the clash of interests, dimly felt but not yet clearly perceived.[52]

In drawing such a conclusion, Park was undoubtedly contradicting both Ward and Small who, in spite of their contact with the same German realpolitik, successfully resisted all temptations to disregard their liberal faith in knowledge as a means of social reform. It is difficult to say on the basis of limited information, whether Park's apparent skepticism here is really a rejection of his earlier beliefs as a muckraker that the education of public opinion would "move history forward," or whether it just reflects the neutral stance he believed he should adopt as a professional sociologist. One should certainly not overlook the fact that during

51. Robert E. Park, "Race Prejudice and Japanese-American Relations," *Race and Culture*, p. 227. Cf. Robert E. Park, "The Basis of Race Prejudice," *Race and Culture*, p. 233; Park, "The Nature of Race Relations," p. 98; and "The Etiquette of Race Relations," p. 186.
52. Park, "Race Prejudice and Japanese-American Relations," p. 227.

the high point of Park's tenure at the University of Chicago, the first violent Negro riots occurred not only a few blocks from his place of work, but also in New York and Philadelphia. This, plus the growing influence of the Ku Klux Klan at this same period, with its cross burnings, lynchings, and virulent denunciations of Negroes, might certainly have dispelled any hope he once had in the possibility of different races discovering the basis for cooperation through education and mutual understanding.

But, if Park had some doubts concerning the efficacy of mutual understanding for overcoming racial antagonism, he like most other proponents of realpolitik, believed that such conflicts would lead to social advancement. Thus, he thought the struggle of racial and national minorities for increased status would alter the power relationships within a society and make it more possible for its members to freely compete for wealth and prestige on the basis of their abilities. He recognized, of course, that the actual outcome of any racial struggle as measured by the degree to which irrational and "mythical" ethnic characteristics still are used to allocate functions and rewards would differ from civilization to civilization. Yet, he predicted in a manner virtually identical to Oppenheimer, that the ultimate end of racial strife and the race relations process altogether, will be the creation of a free society, where only rational criteria are used in the assessments of a person's worth and in the distribution of rewards. In the previous chapter, it was described how Small too, hopefully thought that conflict within the state would unintentionally give rise to an equality among interests. This will not be merely a "crude" democratization, he forecasted, where each individual, regardless of his blood ties, has the liberty to employ his talents under favorable conditions, but rather a situation of distributive justice, "where every human effort, whether moral or mental or physical, which contributes to the economic result...[receives] its proportional share of that result;... [And where] every man or class that secures a share of economic results without contributing to the production of those results, is bound to show cause why that advantage should be permanent."[53] And Ward's espousal of "sociocracy" as the direction toward which society is moving, shows distinct similarities both to this theory of Small's and to Park's prophecy. The coming sociocratic society, he believed, will be neither an anarchic individualism "which creates artificial inequalities" between races and classes on the basis of brutality, nor a leveling socialistic regime "which creates artificial equalities" by maintaining that all men are identical in ability and service to society. On the contrary, "it [will] recognize natural inequalities and [will] aim at getting rid of artificial inequalities,... by confer[ring] benefits in strict proportion to merit,...[after making certain] that equality of opportunity exist[s]."[54]

The Evolution of a Liberal World Society

Park applied these same principles of race relations to several different settings. Racial occurrences in Hawaii, Europe, and on the American continent, despite their vast peculiarities in detail, all have been exemplifications, he felt, of the same basic process of conflict, accommodation taking the form of conquest, partial assimilation, followed by further conflict, and a more democratic accommodation. In fact, Park was apparently of the belief that a world civilization comprising all races and peoples was evolving along these

53. Small, "The Conflict of Classes," p. 35. See also Ibid., pp. 26-27.
54. Ward, *Outlines of Sociology,* pp. 292-93.

same lines, which would eventually culminate in a relatively unified society organized on the basis of liberal ideals.

The first step in this grandiose development was taken from the fifteenth to the late nineteenth century, says Park, when the white-skinned "sea nomads" of Spain, France, Britain, Portugal, and America used their military prowess to conquer Orientals and Africans and establish themselves as colonial rulers over virtually all of the world's remaining population. Those subject to absentee European masters, as in the Belgian Congo, were forcibly conscripted either to work in their mines and plantations, or to control native unrest as mercenary soldiers or "indirect rulers." The final result of European expansion, then, was a more or less vaguely defined worldwide political organization that partially integrated all people into a single division of labor.

> The result of the colonial wars in Asia and Africa, and of the political maneuvers in Europe, has been to create over and above the economic organization of the world not a super-state, to be sure, but a political organization loose and ill-defined but worldwide. This political organization came into existence first of all as a result of exploration, conquest, and settlement. . . . Where Europe has not extended its control by conquest and migration, or by conquest without immigration, it has established political control through the medium of international understandings and treaties.[55]

Park goes on to describe how Christian missionaries followed in the path of military conquerors, not only to coldly legitimize European colonialism, but more often to elevate the natives; to assimilate them into the more "civilized" culture of the white man. The unintentional

55. Park, "Our Racial Frontier on the Pacific," pp. 143-44. Cf. Park, "Cultural Conflict and the Marginal Man," p. 373.

product of such efforts, however, has been the development of politically conscious native freemen. These are the lower level bureaucratic officials, native businessmen, and professionals, who because of their participation in both the culture of their white rulers and that of their blood brothers, are able to view the system of stratification through more objective eyes. They have become envious of the European settler and chafe at what they consider to be the arbitrary restrictions on their own social advancement.[56] This potentially rebellious situation has been aggravated by the fact that the effective exploitation of the natural and human resources of the underdeveloped areas of Africa and Asia, has naturally entailed a significant capital investment by European businessmen. Although the export of capital from Europe originally placed the yellow and black races in financial indebtedness to their rulers, it has by the 1930s finally enabled them to enter more and more viably into economic competition with their one time creditors. Using cheap native labor, Oriental businessmen are beginning to undersell their Occidental counterparts on the world market, because the latter must deal with labor unions whose demands are constantly increasing the overhead of production.[57]

This new found ability to alter the nature of the economic ties linking them with their white rulers, plus their shared belief in the injustice of present forms of exploitation, has manifested itself among African and Asian peoples in the "discovery" of their racial and national identity. This signals the beginning of a new era in worldwide race relations which will be characterized, Park thinks, in the struggle of the previously

56. For the role of missionaries in the development of a world society, see Robert E. Park, "Missions and the Modern World," *Race and Culture*, pp. 338-41.
57. Robert E. Park, "Race Relations and Certain Frontiers," *Race and Culture*, p. 119. Cf. Park, "The Nature of Race Relations," p. 109.

conquered peoples of Asia and Africa for their liberation. Park died in the midst of Gandhi's nonviolent
movement for Indian national independence, before the
successful conclusion of anti-colonial wars in Algeria,
Indochina, and China, and prior to the granting of
political sovereignty to scores of African nations by
Europe. Thus to a certain extent his theory of world
race contacts can be considered prophetic of the events
that were to occur on the international scene in the
twenty-five years following his death. In his words,

> within the organism thus established [by European
> conquest], it was inevitable that there should arise, irres-
> pective of all other interests, a struggle of the subject peo-
> ples to be free and of the peoples occupying an inferior
> position to improve their status. Among the independent
> peoples, status goes by the name of prestige. For a nation
> or a people to be without prestige, is to be without status.
> Among the subject peoples status is defined in terms of
> independence or self-determination.... At bottom the
> struggle to maintain national prestige and the struggle
> for national self-determination are one and the same.
> They are struggles to increase and maintain international
> recognition and status.[58]

Park forecasted that the ultimate outcome of these
struggles for "national liberation," "will be a single
great society," in which national and ethnic considerations play a less significant role in the distribution of
the world's wealth and prestige than is presently the
case.

It would be futile, he argued, for Europe to attempt
to stop the race relations movement from progressing
to this, its final stage; for it to try and maintain its
traditionally superior position in the face of insurrection by its one-time subjects. This is because such re-
bellion is the inevitable product of forces "so vast and
irresistable that the resulting changes assume the

58. Park, "Our Racial Frontier on the Pacific," p. 144.

character of a cosmic process."[59] In other words, the increasing democratization of world society is a predetermined consequence, so to speak, of earlier race contacts.

> The race relations cycle which takes the form to state it abstractly of contacts, competition, accommodation, and eventual assimilation, is apparently irreversible. Customs regulations, immigration restrictions and racial barriers may slacken the tempo of the movement, may perhaps altogether halt it for a time; but can not change its direction; can not at any rate reverse it.[60]

It was because of this that Park felt compelled to forewarn his fellow white Americans that their segregationist racial policies could never prevent the final assimilation of Negroes and Orientals into a world society as equals to themselves. "In the long run," he once stated, it will be "difficult if not impossible to maintain, in America or elsewhere, racial frontiers. All the deeper currents of modern life run counter to a policy of racial or national isolation."[61] This being the case, Americans must prepare themselves to live in a new intimacy with all the world's peoples. They must "adopt new international and interracial manners," and begin treating other men not merely as servants, but as brothers.

Conclusion

It should be obvious by now that like the German and American sociologists of conflict, Park was not interested in the subject of social conflict because he was a revolutionary anarchist who sought to justify the de-

59. Park, "Our Racial Frontier in the Pacific," p. 149.
60. Ibid.
61. Ibid., p. 141.

struction of social order, but precisely for the opposite reason. Living in an age when the antipathies of various factions seemed to imperil American and world solidarity, his basic concern, first as a muckraker, then as a sociologist, was always to discover the conditions for a viable corporate order. In his first attempt to construct a theory of social life in the *Introduction to the Science of Sociology,* he explicitly proclaimed that "sociology, speaking strictly, is a point of view and a method for investigating the processes by which individuals are inducted into and induced to cooperate in some permanent corporate existence which we call society."[62]

Park of course realized that America, with its tradition of individualism and its disdain for big government, "has always had the problem of maintaining national solidarity." But with the emergence of the Negro as a militant minority group and the hostile reaction of the white community to their advancement, he feared that "the problem of national solidarity has assumed a new and increasing importance."[63] "The problem of national solidarity today," he would argue, "is not one of sectionalism, but one of racialism."[64] With the advent of the Second World War, Park's concern for social order apparently increased as now the survival of the whole "Great World Society," and not just American civilization seemed to him to be endangered. In one of his last articles published in 1944, he told his readers that whenever such large empires as Egypt, Rome, or Assyria disintegrated, their peoples underwent terrible suffering. And so it will be for modern man. But because the dependence relations that link men are even

---

62. Park and Burgess, *Introduction to the Science of Sociology,* p. 42.
63. Robert E. Park, "Racial Ideologies," *Race and Culture,* p. 311.
64. Ibid.

more complex and delicate today, "we stand to lose much more by any failure in cohesion."[65]

Since Park believed that racial strife constituted a potential threat to the integrity of America and world society, then the appeal that especially Oppenheimer's writings might have had for him can be partially understood. For as a national liberal in his own country, Oppenheimer's interest in racial conflict, like that of both Gumplowicz and Ratzenhofer in Austria, grew directly out of his concern with defending German unity in the face of the increasingly fervent demands for national independence then being made by a wide plurality of ethnic minorities. To the extent that this unstable political situation was at least formally analogous to the nature of black and white race relations in America during the 1920s and 30s, then to draw upon Oppenheimer's sociology to help explain and predict what might occur here, would have seemed perfectly reasonable to Park.

But why, if this is true, did Park apparently ignore altogether the quite similar work of Oppenheimer's two forebearers, Gumplowicz and Ratzenhofer? While Park does make reference to their notions in the bibliography of the *Introduction,* and he even includes an excerpt from Gumplowicz's system to elaborate on the sociological method, the two Austrians seem to have played a smaller part in Park's overall theory of social life than might otherwise be warranted, if the above hypothesis were correct. It has already been described how both Ward and Small selected out for positive mention only those aspects of Gumplowicz's and Ratzenhofer's sociologies that already accorded with

---

65. Park, "Missions and the Modern World," p. 337. Park adds that "it is by imagining the effect of an actual dissolution of this Great Society that we can make most clear to ourselves the nature of our fear for its future. . . . [And] our prospects are dark enough" (Ibid.).

their own homegrown optimism. Oppenheimer's paradigm as a whole might have been more acceptable to these two founders of American sociology, than the views of the Austrian sociologists of conflict, had they had knowledge of it prior to the publications of their final statements in *Pure Sociology* and *General Sociology*. This is because Oppenheimer was in his own judgement an "optimist." Although he wrote introductions to Gumplowicz's collected works and was cognizant of his intellectual debt to him, he never lost faith in the possibility of social progress. History, he believed, in spite of the violence entailed in political conflict, in fact because of it, was inevitably moving toward the establishment of a liberal Freeman's Society.[66]

It may be then, that notwithstanding his rather pessimistic belief in the necessity of racial conflict, the young Park at least, the same man who was both indignant muckraker and liberal crusader, was imbued with the same sort of optimism as both Ward and Small, and it was this that led him to overlook the dreary philosophies of Gumplowicz and Ratzenhofer. Perhaps the following terms that Park used to describe his one-time cohort Booker T. Washington, can be applied with equal validity to himself in his younger days. ". . .[W]ith an optimism characteristic of other self-made Americans, Washington was disposed to believe that all men were predestined to rise and that those who found themselves behind were, in all probability, merely those who, like the Negro, had started

66. For Oppenheimer's classification of himself as an optimist, see *The State,* pp. 277-78. For Gumplowicz's rejection of Oppenheimer's *Optimismus,* see *Outlines,* p. 317 and Gumplowicz, "The Letters of Ludwig Gumplowicz to Lester F. Ward," Aug., 1902, p. 9. For Oppenheimer's defense of his position against Gumplowicz, see Franz Oppenheimer, "Soziologischer Pessimismus," *Die Zukunft* XXIV (1898): 472-79.

late and were now, or would soon be, on their way."[67] This is not to say that Park necessarily remained an optimist. As suggested on the previous pages, he began late in his life to publically question his faith that those who were down now were "predestined" by cosmic forces to better themselves. "The delight in the 'manifest finger of destiny' and 'the tide of progress'—even the newer belief in the effortless 'evolution' of social institutions," he sadly admitted in his last published paper, "is gone."[68]

---

67. Robert E. Park, "Politics and the 'Man Farthest Down,'" *Race and Culture,* p. 167.
68. Park, "Missions and the Modern World," p. 338. Cf. Ibid., pp. 336-37.

9

Arthur F. Bentley's Sociology of Conflict

Introduction

Generally speaking, Arthur F. Bentley's work is associated with the field of political science rather than with sociology. It can therefore be asked how the inclusion of his writings in a book dealing with that of three persons who at different times all served as president of the American Sociological Association can be justified.

In large part the debate concerning the "proper" speciality into which not only Bentley, but also such encyclopedic scholars as Weber, Veblen, Marx, Ross, and Ely should be fit, is an artifact of the contemporary particularization of social inquiry. Sociologists, economists, and political scientists can in many cases claim exactly the same men as the fathers of their distinctive perspectives. Consider for example the cases of Ward, Small, and Park. If the criterion of time spent were used to classify them, then perhaps Ward would be called a botanist or geologist, or at least a natural scientist, but certainly not a sociologist. Even after he assumed his first teaching position at Brown University, he refused to confine his lectures to the subject of what is today called "sociology"; one of his courses being entitled "A Survey of All Knowledge." Or take the instance of Small, whose basic concern was never to exclusively explain reality in sociological terms, but to develop an overall moral philosophy and then to apply this in the establishment of a just society. His interests, like those of Ward, ranged far, including economics and politics and as a graduate student at Johns Hopkins he wrote his dissertation on American Constitutional history. Park on the contrary, seems at first to fit the image of the professional sociologist. Yet even he did not use this term to describe his intellectual career until well after the age of fifty. Prior to this time his vocation was closer to that of the well-educated literary vagabond who occasionally writes liberal crusading pieces for various newspapers and magazines.

Bentley shared with his three contemporaries this same propensity to exploit not just the literature of an isolated field, but to cultivate as broad a knowledge as possible. His original area of interest was economics, which he pursued under Ely at Johns Hopkins. Ely directed him to the writings of the Austrian economist Karl Menger, whose utilitarian psychology later provided the inspiration for his doctoral thesis. But it was in neither economics nor political science that he made some of his most important contributions, but to philosophy. Both on the basis of his lengthy correspondence with John Dewey and his own independent research, Bentley might be called one of the foremost pragmatic philosophers.[1] However, in spite of this, he

---

1. According to Sidney Ratner, "Dewey had found two of Bentley's books *Linguistic Analysis of Mathematics* (1932) and *Behavior, Knowledge, Fact*

was never a "mainline" professional in any of these specialities. He might more accurately be considered a gifted dilettante, an outsider to academia in the halls of which he taught for only about one year.[2] He spent much more time working as a reporter for newspapers in Chicago exposing, like Park, the social evils of urban America. When in 1911 the market for muck-raking began drying up and journalists searched for more secure positions as university professors or as public relations men for big business, Bentley retired instead to the town of his youth in Indiana to run an apple orchard.

But over and above all of these factors that distinguish Bentley's life style from those of latter-day practioners of the profession, there is a perfectly sound basis for considering him to be an unabashed sociologist at heart. This is because like Small, Park, and Ward, he too sought to penetrate behind the facades of static structures and institutions that most men take for granted, to the "raw stuff" that constitutes the "real life force" of society. And more importantly, no more than for his three contemporaries did he find this elemental energy, the basis for social interaction, in man's unconscious biological drives.[3] In-

(1935) so helpful while working on his *Logic: The Theory of Inquiry* that he singled out the writings of A. F. Bentley as among the few works to which he felt a special debt." Ratner, "Arthur F. Bentley, 1870-1957," p. 573. Bentley and Dewey collaborated in the writing of *Knowing and Known,* a treatise on epistemology.

2. Besides five weeks at the University of Chicago from 1895-1896, Bentley served as a visiting professor at Columbia University where he conducted a graduate seminar on linguistics in 1941-1942.

3. Floyd W. Matson, *The Broken Image* (New York: George Braziller, 1964) calls Bentley a social Darwinist on the basis of his references to Gumplowicz and Ratzenhofer in *The Process of Government.* As was shown in the previous chapter, however, such a classification of either of the Austrians is unjustified. Furthermore, the following statement clearly indicates that the application of this designation to Bentley's work is equally incorrect: "The

stead, although he admitted embarrassment for his proposal many years later calling it "a mentalistic brew concocted out of old conventional wordings, with odors rising close to nauseation,"[4] he argued as early as 1895 that the "basic unit of investigation" in social science should be intelligent, goal-directed activity.[5]

It is not difficult to understand why the content of Bentley's first methodological paper was almost identical to especially Small's thoughts on the same subject. Both drew on essentially the same intellectual sources to develop their ideas concerning the nature of social inquiry.[6] For Bentley in particular the German historical school as represented by Wilhelm Dilthey, Small, and Simmel, and Menger's utilitarianism seem to have provided the inspiration for his early theorizing. Thus, he began his 1895 treatment by rejecting in a very Simmelian manner the notion that sociologists should focus their attention either on liberalism's abstract in-

---

biologically described man is, of course, part of our given fact; but he does not as such, that is without further interpretation, enter into social studies. Where the whole interpretation can be made directly in terms of vital factors, we are still within the field of biology and do not get to anything that we call sociology, or a phase of sociology, at all." Arthur F. Bentley, *The Process of Government* (Chicago: University of Chicago Press, 1908). The edition from which I took my information is that introduced by Peter G. Orleans (The John Harvard Library, Cambridge, Mass: Harvard University Press, 1967), p. 460. Although Bentley claims that the process of government is "a form of truly natural selection," for "there is a representative process involved in the pressures in animal and vegetable life"; he clarifies this by adding "but these things must all be stated as aspects of group activity before they become significant for the interpretation of government or for that matter for any other interpretation of social process." Bentley, *The Process of Government,* p. 461.

4. Bentley, "Epilogue," p. 212.

5. Arthur F. Bentley, "The Units of Investigation in the Social Sciences," *Annals of the American Academy of Political and Social Science* V (May, 1895): 915-41. This is a publication of Bentley's Ph.D. dissertation.

6. See Paul Frederick Kress, "The Idea of Process in American Political and Social Science," unpublished Ph.D. thesis (University of California, Berkeley, 1964).

dividuals or on the equally metaphysical "will of society" or "social soul."[7] To be scientific, he said, sociologists should deal exclusively with that which is directly observable. And "the material that is empirically given us in society to investigate is first of all simply motion, regular and irregular, temporary and permanent changes of situation in both men and things.... Society itself is rather a nexus of actions...."[8] Such motions or actions, he continued, are simply different modes of expression or manners of fulfillment of certain desires. There are three basic forms of want expression; the instinctive, the customary, and the "enlightened egoistic," and Bentley insisted that the fundamental analytical unit for sociology be only the third. This is because it

is only in the class of actions which follow conscious calculations, that the objective formation [i.e. normative and legal systems] is of importance. But it is just such action, basing as it does in reason, that is distinctive of human beings, and by means of which ... the human group is differentiated from the highest aggregation of animals.[9]

It might be added that if this argument reminds one of Small as it should, there is a crucial point at which Bentley began dissenting from Small's position quite early. Where there can be observed at this time a characteristic predeliction on Small's part to make up a list of the wants, desires, or interests that persons act to realize,[10] Bentley always believed this to be a futile exercise. While he agreed that the sociologists of his

7. Simmel, *The Sociology of Georg Simmel,* pp. 1-22.
8. Bentley, "The Units of Investigation in the Social Sciences," p. 917.
9. Ibid., pp. 933-34.
10. See Small and Vincent, *Introduction of the Study of Society,* pp. 173-81, for a list of the psychological elements, "wants" which together with geographical factors can explain all social phenomena. For a similar notion and list, see Small, *General Sociology,* pp. 196-200.

day often attempted to interpret "social motion" by referring to "psychic entities," he claimed that "of necessity only the physical, the outer series" can be observed and thus justifiably be used as a basis for generalization.[11] This was an operationalist position that he was later to present in much more sophisticated terms in *The Process of Government,* a book to which our attention will now be turned.

The Process of Government and Its Sources in Realpolitik

As indicated earlier, Bentley left academic life via a short-lived and disastrous attempt at teaching and worked for nearly fifteen years as a newspaperman in the Chicago area. And it was during this period, using with some reservations the frame of reference originally presented in his Ph.D. dissertation, that he wrote his magnum opus, *The Process of Government.* It seems then that like Park, even though he was a reporter for the Chicago *Times, Herald,* and *Record Herald,* he was meanwhile more interested in systematically interpreting the plethora of political events that were constantly coming to his attention. As Sidney Ratner describes it:

> The rich material that he accumulated concerning the play of specific interest groups in the Chicago City Council and in the Illinois State Legislature on various important issues stimulated him into developing his more generalized study of social pressures for all phases of government in the United States and the rest of the world.[12]

The Process of Government is an important document

---

11. Bentley, "The Units of Investigation in the Social Sciences," p. 918.
12. Ratner, "A. F. Bentley's Inquiries into the Behavioral Sciences and the Theory of Scientific Inquiry," p. 32.

because the interest group theory of politics that is developed therein still constitutes the basic conceptual framework used by modern political science behaviorists. In Floyd Matson's terms: "To review Bentley's contribution is, then, not merely to undertake an exercise in historical exegesis but to come directly to grips with a vigorous and influential movement in contemporary thought."[13] This movement is apparently more indebted to realpolitik than some of its followers readily acknowledge, for Bentley's treatise is filled throughout with positive references to the Germans and Austrians whose sociologies of conflict were reviewed in earlier chapters. Rudolph von Ihering, Marx, Ratzenhofer, Gumplowicz, and Simmel are all congratulated by Bentley as the initial explorers of a territory that he believed was only mapped out more carefully and precisely in his work on politics.

More than any of the Germans, however, it is Simmel's perspective with which Bentley had become directly acquainted while in Berlin, that seems to have informed his theory of government as a process. It would be considered odd if Bentley had not borrowed extensively from Simmel in developing his own outlook, for he believed the Jewish systematist to be the greatest of all sociologists. Some fifteen years following the publication of *The Process of Government* he still felt he could justifiably claim that "in the light of Simmel's work all the current glib and superficial discussions we meet so often as to society and the individual, society and personality, the concepts of society, and so forth belong in the dark ages."[14]

---

13. Matson, *The Broken Image,* p. 117.
14. Arthur F. Bentley, *Relativity in Man and Society* (Bloomington, Indiana: Principia Press, 1926), p. 308, n. 61. ". . . [H]e [Simmel] is vastly more intimate, more subtle, than any other investigator has been, in catching the interinfluencings of social men." Ibid., p. 163.

The Basic Approach

Continuing a line of thought initially developed in his first publication, Bentley begins *The Process of Government* with a scathing critique of attempts by such persons as Ward, Small, and Spencer to explain the process of social interaction by reference to what he disparagingly calls "mind stuff," or unobservable psychological states. For example, Small, according to Bentley, "always comes back to the soul stuff idea. There is a confusion lurking in all his discussions of these desires which can not be cleared away, I think, until he drops the soul stuff entirely. . . ."[15] The reason for Small's disorientation resides in the fact that "although he has been for years arguing it in print he has nowhere and at no time, so far as I am aware, taken the slightest step to isolate these desires or prove their existence apart from the social phenomena they are intended to explain."[16] And to the extent that Small can only confirm that his subject has a particular desire if he behaves in a specific way in certain circumstances, then for Small to impute this desire in an attempt to account for that behavior, logically results in his invoking a mere tautology rather than producing an actual explanation.[17]

But if such words as "interest" or "purpose" can not provide causal explanations for social action, it does not follow that therefore they can no longer be invoked in the course of sociological inquiry. Since these terms really stand for particular behavioral patterns anyway, then they can be usefully applied in a description or better, an "interpretation" of phases of the social process.

The "feelings," "faculties," "ideas," and "ideals" are not

15. Bentley, *The Process of Government,* p. 27.
16. Ibid., p. 35.
17. The author rebukes the use of "ideal," "geist," "zeitgeist," "social mind,"

definite "things" in or behind society, working upon it as causes, but . . . are—or rather, what is meant by them is—society, stated in a very clumsy and inadequate way. . . . I have not denied that this feeling, thinking, ideal following material is the stuff we have before us in interpreting society. What I have denied is that the separation of feelings and ideas, looked on as individual psychical content, from society or from social institutions, or from social activity, is a legitimate procedure in the scientific investigation of society.[18]

The Government and Interest Groups

In Bentley's view then, it is only action, the purposive *behavior* of persons who are cognizant of others and who take their possible responses into consideration in order to insure the maximum gratification of their interests, and nothing else, that can furnish the basis for fruitful sociological theorizing.

[Action] is a "relation" between men. . . . The "relation," i.e. the action, is the given phenomenon, the raw materials, the action of men with or upon each other. We know men only as participants in such activity. These joint activities of which government activities are one form are the cloth . . . out of which men in individual parties are cut.[19]

and "social will" to explain history on the same grounds. This criticism comprises about the first 150 pages of the book.

18. Ibid., p. 166. Thus where Small no longer treats interests merely as psychological states, but instead "rises to an entirely adequate use of 'interest' as forces," then "the 'interests' which are left will prove to be genuine facts, and at the same time forces of society." Ibid., p. 127. For Small's response to Bentley's review, see Albion W. Small, *"The Process of Government* by Arthur F. Bentley," review of *The Process of Government* by Arthur F. Bentley, *AJS* XIII (March, 1908): 698-706.

19. Bentley, *The Process of Government,* p. 176. Explicitly borrowing from Simmel, cf. *Conflict and the Web of Group Affiliations,* pp. 140-54, Bentley speaks of the individual as a point of intersection of "planes" of activities intersecting a Euclidean solid. See Bentley, *The Process of Government,* p. 207. Cf. Bentley, *Relatively in Man and Society,* pp. 107-9.

The sociological investigator, Bentley continues, can differentiate among the parts comprising the continuity of actions and interactions by using criteria which themselves are derived from the research problem he is interested in pursuing.[20] The subsequent classification of aspects or "phases" of the process resulting from the use of such standards will always constitute a particular set of "groups," or what Bentley later referred to as "cross sections" of activity.[21] Thus, at least in principle "the whole social process in all its phases can be stated . . . in groups of active men, indeed must be stated in that way if a useful analysis is to be had."[22]

As the title of his work implies, the group or cross section of the process with which Bentley was primarily concerned is that which is ordinarily called "government." According to the author, this particular group, to begin with, is distinguished from other sorts of activity in the social process by its being "representative" of still other activities. Thus the lobbying, committee hearings, discussions, voting, submissions of amendments to states, ratifications of amendments, Presidential signatures, and all the enforcement behaviors that are usually associated with government "have their fullest meaning and best definitions in

20. This position is identical both to the methodology of Simmel and to his colleague Max Weber. Cf. Simmel, *The Sociology Georg Simmel,* pp. 21-23 and Weber, *The Methodology of the Social Sciences,* pp. 49-112.

21. Bentley's *Relativity in Man and Society* consists in part of an explication of the "attitude of investigation" used in *The Process of Government.* Thus it will be drawn upon to expand upon points not clearly presented in the earlier work. In *Relativity in Man and Society,* Bentley uses the term "man-society" instead of "society" or "social-process." Ibid., p. 90. Man-society for any one investigator is simply activity over a space-time continuum, more or less arbitrarily delimited by the research problem. Ibid., pp. 99-100. Instead of using the term "group," the author introduces "cross-sectional activity." Ibid., p. 91. A cross-section, like an interest, does not refer to some isolated concrete object, but simply to a phase in the continuity of man-society.

22. Bentley, *The Process of Government,* p. 204.

terms of many other activities not specifically described as governmental."[23] The specific activities of which formal governments are representative are designated by Bentley with the term "interest group." "There is," he says, "no group without its interest. An interest. . .is equivalent of a group. . . . The group, activity, and interest are thus one. . . . Sometimes we may be emphasizing the interest phase, sometimes the group phase. . . ."[24]

For the justification of this conception of government not as an idealistic entity standing above and apart from society, but as simply another group that mechanically expresses or "represents" the activities of society's interest groups, Bentley cites the names of Gumplowicz and Ratzenhofer. Although he felt that Karl Marx could be taken as the "starting point for practical purposes" of viewing government as sort of a register of the interaction of organized classes,[25] he gave Gumplowicz credit for presenting the same basic idea in much more acceptable terms:

Turn now to Ludwig Gumplowicz the writer who, so far as my acquaintance with such literature goes, has taken the most important step toward bringing out clearly the na-

23. *Ibid.,* p. 111. For example, "it is possible to take a Supreme Court decision, in which nothing appears on the surface but finespun points of law, and cut through all the dialectic till we get down to the actual groups of men underlying the decisions and producing the decisions through differentiated activity of justices." Ibid., p. 205.

24. Ibid., p. 221. Apparently, the group is activity and the interpretation or valuation of that activity is an interest. "The interest is just this valuation of the activity, not as distinct from it, but, as the valued activity itself." Ibid., p. 213.

25. Ibid., pp. 466-67. In Arthur F. Bentley, "Simmel, Durkheim, and Ratzenhofer," *AJS* XXXII (Sept., 1926), it is said that "if this chapter had to do with the creators of the science of sociology, perhaps the name of Karl Marx should be put at the head of the list. To my regret, I am not sufficiently well acquainted with his work to untangle his theoretical from his practical achievement and gain an opinion. . . ." (p. 251).

ture of the group process. With him we get away from identification with a single class in the community, and we find the group activities given a much wider and firmer foundation. He reflects on the process at longer range, is [sic] as he stands much more remote from the field of acute struggle, but also offers a much more effective agency for any group interests that ultimately avail themselves of his point of view to state themselves in a way to develop their powers in accordance with the requirements of their situation.[26]

Furthermore, Bentley adds, Gustav Ratzenhofer, "apart from compilers of materials and formal systematizers, whose work is of a lesser order," is with Durkheim and Simmel one of "the three great names of modern sociology."[27] He rests this judgment upon the fact that,

> where Gumplowicz, much more concretely still had seen separate hordes or tribes or races grinding together, Ratzenhofer advanced to describing a similar functional process in all large social operations within a society, including political parties, and beyond to various somewhat hypothetical structures of civilization.[28]

Bentley admitted that like Small, "underlying each social operation, whether large or small he [Ratzenhofer] placed what he called an 'interest'."[29] But in his view the Austrian's notion of human interest did not suffer from the same disabilities as that of Small, who conceives psychological motives as unobservable phenomena. Ratzenhofer's

> . . . great merit is that this interest, this system of interest, though psychologically stated comes down in practice to be merely another form of statement for the active procedure of the group and system of groups, a form of statement that emphasizes the living activity side without

26. Bentley, *The Process of Government,* p. 468.
27. Bentley, "Simmel, Durkheim, and Ratzenhofer," p. 250.
28. Ibid.
29. Ibid.

entanglement with individual psychological factors of interpretation. For him, therefore, all the energy aspects of the social facts lie directly within those social facts as such, and are not important to them for the outside.[30]

Domination and Conflict

One of the defining characteristics of realpolitik that both Ratzenhofer's and Gumplowicz's writings admirably illustrate is the capacity to look upon politics with no illusions. In a seemingly cold and systematic way they tried to discipline their thinking on the subject by unflinchingly separating the ends of political behavior from the means peculiar to it. Together, they discovered that regardless of the diversity of long-range motives that men have invoked to justify their engagement in politics, the techniques they use in fact are identical. Specifically, they employ any tactic they believe will be practical to overwhelm those who attempt to resist the realization of their interests. It is not then simply man's psychological goals that must be used to explain the consequences of political interaction, but more importantly the differences in power between the opposing groups. It is not the presumably transcendent ends of the parties that allow the analyst to predict the outcome of social conflict between them, but the degree to which one of them can dominate and force his will on the opponent.

Probably more than for any of the other three sociologists whose work has been studied in the previous chapters, this Machiavellian perspective permeates *The Process of Government*. As Bentley would say in summarizing his theory of politics, "the phenomena of government are from start to finish phenomena of

30. Ibid.

force."[31] Social force manifests itself in two different ways. Not only does the government per se force its subjects to comply to its laws, but groups within the society attempt to seize at least partial control of the government's legal apparatus for their own purposes. In other words, "It is not merely government that dominates underlying activities but underlying activities that dominate government."[32] Since interest groups invariably have inconsistent goals, then their attempts to control the government necessarily result in what Bentley calls "friction." Friction implies some sort of resistance between two or more forces, and is probably equivalent to "conflict" as used by the sociologists of conflict. Consider for example the following characterization of "friction:"

> In each case we have sets of actions diverted from their described trends into wastes and heat. Frictions in each case are called such only by the test of what is outlined for and expected in the action. . . .
>
> Friction in society involves the appearance of representative activities specialized under a new description of phenomena, and appearing under the old descriptions as the retardation of the activities of the latter. These representative activities may use any social technique; any form of violence, blows, imprisonments, killings, spasmodic or in regulated systems; any form of trickery, spasmodic or organized; any form of argument, spasmodic or organized.[33]

Much has been made of Bentley's choice of words to

31. Bentley, *The Process of Government,* p. 258. Bentley elaborated upon what he meant by the term "force" in his *Relativity in Man and Society,* saying: "By dominance in a setting of representative activities, it will be at once evident that nothing more can be meant than the power aspect of representation. The control value of one activity or set of activities, are selected for description, with reference to another activity or set of activities" (p. 179).

32. Bentley, *Relativity in Man and Society,* p. 180.

33. Ibid., p. 187.

describe the goings-on in government. There seems to be an unmistakable proclivity on his part to borrow freely from the vocabulary of physics to elaborate on his claims. But it is unlikely that this can be understood as an aspect of a wholesale move to construct a type of social physics. In fact, there are several places where Bentley explicitly says that classical mechanics as a model can not be fruitfully applied to the realm of social interaction. He once wrote that he wished to avoid "the crude cause and effect statement of the type of the billiard player, the cue and the billiard ball (the player 'aims' and the cue 'pushes' the ball)" because, "however satisfactory it is in its place, such an account is too thin and poor for interpretive use in the study of man-society."[34] On the contrary, the reason why he apparently found terms like "force" and "pressure" more tolerable for his use than such clearly psychological words as "intention," or why he called conflict a situation of "friction," was because of his desire to be an unsentimental political realist. Only these very physical terms, he might have felt, allowed him to overcome the all too human tendency to interpret the vileness of politics in reference to categories that smack of "soul stuff." They would make it possible for him to view the governmental process even more than Ratzenhofer, Gumplowicz, and Weber had done, exclusively from the point of view of the observable strategies that conflicting parties use to overpower one another. "As the mechanist uses it, this key notion [e.g. force] replaces and drives out the alternative idea of purpose in the ordinary sense of conscious effort and intention. It is force and force alone, applied from without, which provides a means of explaining casual relationships and behavioral effects."[35]

34. Ibid., p. 107.
35. Matson, *The Broken Image*, p. 121.

The Origin of Law

Government as a whole is a continual process of contention between interest groups. As Bentley sees it, they "brace each other up, hold each other together, move forward by their interaction, and in general are in a state of continual pressure upon each other."[36] There are an uncountable number of possible outcomes of any power struggle within government. The particular resolution or balance of contrary group pressures at any one time is called the "state" of the system. The state of the government, says Bentley, is best indicated by the legal expectations that are being enforced at that specific time.

> Law matches government every inch of its course. The two are not different things but the same thing. We can not call law a resultant of government. Rather we must say it is government—only stated from a different angle. . . . When we talk about law we think not of the influencing or the pressure as a process, but of the status of the activities, the pressures being assumed to have worked themselves through to a final balance, and law, stated as a completed balance, is therefore highly abstract.[37]

As this quotation suggests, law can not be understood to mean merely a concrete written statute. The operational test of whether or not an expectation is in fact legally binding upon those who are formally subject to it, is the probability of its being implemented by a specially delegated governmental agency. In other words, according to Bentley, law itself is nothing but a phase of the social process, another type of activity. One may be reminded of Weber's behavioristic definition of "law" in this, Bentley's delineation.

36. Bentley, *The Process of Government*, p. 218.
37. Ibid., p. 272.

The law then is specified activity of man—that is, an activity which has taken on definite social forms—embodied in groups which tend to require conformity to it from variant individuals [i.e. deviants]. . . and which have at their disposal, to help them compel these variants to adapt themselves to the common type, certain specialized groups which form part of the governing body of the society, that is, certain organs of government.[38]

In summary then, all law is a type of activity that can ultimately be explained by reducing it to the relative powers of conflicting interest groups. This goes not only for individual legal statutes, but also for complete systems of law. The latter, in Bentley's mind, do not comprise some form of metaphysical entity. Their origin can not be traced back either to a historical telos of the People or to men of "good will" sitting at the table of reason. Rather, "what we can see here from the point of view of law as system is that complexes of groups, working together through the government, combine their pressures. There is nothing absolute about the combination."[39] It follows that not even constitutions, those apparently completely nonpartisan and independent regulators of political activity that one finds in only the most highly developed governments, have an abstract existence apart from the more base aspects of the social process itself.

. . .[C]onstitutions are but a special form of law. They are specially guarded habitual activities of the society, enforcing themselves on all would be variants. The constitution sets up rules through which courts, legislature and executive are played on through interest. . . . Lawmaking and law sustaining pressures are the same.[40]

The reader who remembers the discussion in chapter

38. Ibid., pp. 276-77. Cf. Weber's almost identical definition of "law," *The Theory of Social and Economic Organization*, p. 127.
39. Bentley, *The Process of Government*, p. 287.
40. Ibid., p. 289.

3 will observe an unmistakable similarity here between the view of Bentley and those of Gumplowicz and
Rudolph von Ihering. Both of these men also explicitly
asserted that law is the result of power struggles.
Thus, for example, while Ihering admitted that "the
end of law is peace," he argued that in all cases "the
means to that end is war."[41] This parallel in the perspectives of the Germans and Bentley is not surprising,
for Bentley lauded Gumplowicz precisely for his recognition of this fact, claiming at one time that "he is on
the whole very solid in his insistence that rights are
produced by the conflict of social groups, coming
neither from the individual nor from any 'common
will,' but from a struggle intermediate between these
two statements."[42] Moreover, Bentley had an intimate
knowledge of and a positive evaluation of Ihering's
sociology of law, which is given no less than a thirty-
five page coverage in *The Process of Government*.

Violence and Representation

Bentley believed that even if law has its source in
social combat, its latent purpose, so to speak, is to
lower the potentiality of violence in future strife. As
his graduate lecturer Simmel had taught him, "every
war in which the belligerents do not impose some restrictions in the use of possible means upon one
another, necessarily, if only for psychological reasons,
becomes a war of extermination."[43] It is precisely because there are such legal regulations, that rarely if
ever do either civil power struggles or international
conflicts lead in the end to the victor completely
eliminating his vanquished foe. In both foreign and in

41. Ihering, *The Struggle for Law*, p. 1.
42. Bentley, *The Process of Government*, p. 469.
43. Simmel, *Conflict and the Web of Group Affiliations*, p. 26.

domestic affairs, even deadly enemies have repeatedly throughout history found their tactical thinking limited by the behavior of still other interest groups who are equally "bent on supressing the turmoil." And inevitably,

> when the struggle proceeds too harshly at any point there will become insistent in the society a group more powerful than either of those involved which tends to suppress the extreme and annoying methods of the groups in the primary struggle. It is within the embrace of these great lines of activity that the smaller struggles proceed.[44]

It is this which explains not only the institution of such agencies as the Hague Tribunal, says Bentley, but also the shift first from private vengeance, to intra-clan adjudication of grievances by a monarch, and thence to judicial debate in public courts.[45] In all of these cases, the intensity of involvement of the injured parties has remained the same, but law has made it impossible to express hostility in any but the most carefully restricted, in fact, ritualistic ways.

Within a society, each group strives to realize its interests in the form of legal rights at the expense of other opposing groups. Inasmuch as systems of law simply express the peculiar balance of power between conflicting parties that exists at that time, then they

---

44. Bentley, *The Process of Government,* p. 372. In international affairs, "interests on the old lines are present and will continue to be present, but a new interest grouping forces itself into the field and insists on modifying the process of adjustment. And similarly with regard to industrial disputes between employers and employees." Ibid., p. 385. In the latter case, the interest group seeking to suppress the nuisance of general strikes, violence, etc., will be the consumer, "and whether compulsory industrial arbitration becomes established or not, will depend, not on reasoning—although mediated through reasoning—but primarily on whether the nuisances become violent enough to compel a remedy." Ibid.

45. Ibid., pp. 382-84.

can be arranged on what Bentley calls a "scale of political development."

At one pole of the scale, representing the fact that a single group has unilaterally monopolized power, is the "despotic" government that is indicated by a single legal organ, e.g. a person through whom the complaints of the entire population presumably are expressed.[46] At the other pole, where one observes a multiplicity of equally powerful groups with a diversity of interests, lies the "democratic" government. This, the highest stage of political evolution, is in turn signified by a plurality of government agencies, one representing each interest group in the society.[47]

Depending upon the nature of the interests seeking to find protection in the government, either the democratic or the despotic government will provide a situation for their "smooth" accommodation and thus for effective conflict regulation. However, under certain conditions, it may happen that groups that are defeated in their struggles for formal rights, that are unable, in other words, to get their interests represented by the government, will not have their political strategies fully circumscribed and restricted by legal regulations.

---

46. "Let us set up," the author advises, "say, at one end the hypothesis of a government consisting of an individual who passes personally on every group antagonism at its very inception and allays it by appropriate action." Ibid., p. 305. Consistent with his thesis of representativeness, he realizes that "it is not the despot, but despot plus army, or despot plus landholding class, but despot plus some other class, that dominates, wherein the despot appears merely as a class leader and it is not despot but class dominance that is characteristic of the government." Ibid., p. 314. Furthermore, except in rare cases where a population is under the heel of a conqueror, "the ruling class is to a certain extent the chosen ... ruler of the *ruled* class, not merely its master, but also its representative." Ibid. Emphasis added.

47. Bentley proposes that "at the other end let us set up the hypothesis of a government in which every interest would be able to find a technique for organizing and expressing itself in a system in which every other interest was equally expressed on 'fair' terms, so that in the final course of action all interests would get their due weight." Ibid., p. 306.

For such groups the probability increases that as a last resort, they will find it necessary to employ violence when locked in conflict with their more powerful and thus less violently inclined opponents. Thus in Tsarist Russia, which has a complexity of groups with partial class and territorial interests, and which, according to Bentley, has a government that approaches despotism, "there is at present no available technique for the most depressed groups but violence or a show of force."[48] On the other hand, in England "there is still a swifter and more effective technique for the adjustment of such conflicts that come before it" than there is in America (of the 1900s). And it follows then that a lower level of political violence would be expected in this country than in either Russia or America.

Harking back to his friction analogy, Bentley hypothesizes that if a government finds itself simply unable to accommodate new interest groups then "the result is explosive action, revolution."[49]

As in explosions, so in revolutions, we have accumulations and specifications of activity, temporary statuses, pauses in the more coarsely observed phenomena, and then the disruptive phenomena and the attendant rearrangement of action. . . .

48. Ibid. The situation is similar, although not quite so bad here in the United States, where "a great mass of the population feeling its hurts, but as yet little clear as to the what or the how of revenge and protection, cut off from effective representation in the government, is driven therefore to radicalism." Ibid., p. 346.

49. Bentley, *Relativity in Man and Society*, p. 187. In other words "Where interests must seek adjustment without legislative forms, if they cannot get recognition through the ruling class or monarch, they have no recourse but to take matters in their own hands and proceed to open violence of war. When they have compromised and made adjustments to such extent that their further process can be carried forward in a legislature, they proceed to war on each other, with the killing and maiming omitted. It is a battle of strength, along lines of barter. The process is similar process, but with changes in the technique." Bentley, *The Process of Government*, p. 371.

Slow revolutions are differentiated from violent revolutions in technique, not in underlying forces. The techniques themselves are representative activities. Which kind of revolution comes may be stated in terms of the plasticity of the society, but that again has no statement except in terms of full analysis of cross sectional activities in their varying energies and forms of representativeness.[50]

Since it is true that despotism necessarily evolves into a more democratic type of government, then it follows that the instances of violent domestic strife in any society's history will decrease with the passage of time. As each interest group wins the legal right to present its demands in the public forum, to bargain with its foes in houses of parliament, and when it finally achieves the goal of having its purposes enforced by the law of the land, then it comes increasingly to have a greater stake in maintaining the integrity of the government against revolutionary upstarts. As it begins to identify its own interests with those of the government, it finds less palatable the use of any conflict behaviors that involve violence and serious disruptions of the social order. Thus in a democracy, where the success of almost every interest group is closely tied up with the maintenance of the government as a whole, power struggles continue, but they assume a less angry and uncontrollable character, and become more civilized.

The reader will notice at once the sense in which this forecast is identical especially to Ratzenhofer's view of political history, expanded by Small, that the despotic conquest state founded on the basis of barbarism and slavery naturally develops into a democratic and much more secure cultural state, primarily through the mechanism of social conflict. This seems to indicate that while Bentley by no means was interested in presenting a complete philosophy of history, there *is* such an outlook implicitly informing his work. And this

50. Bentley, *Relativity in Man and Society,* p. 189.

Weltanschauung apparently owed much to persons such as Small and Ratzenhofer, and the tradition of real-politik generally.

Some Concluding Notes on
The Process of Government

Bentley's sociology of conflict then, is distinctly similar at least in form to the comparable notions of Gumplowicz, Ratzenhofer, Simmel, and Ihering. This does not mean that he simply copied everything that these scholars said about social strife and attached his own name to a unique organization of their statements. On the contrary, even more than Ward, Small, and Park, Bentley appears to have been critical in his assessment of what he thought was of value in the Germans' sociologies. In particular, what he most appreciated was their nonapologetic attempt to approach political behavior with a sense of detatchment and neutrality. It was their capacity not only to avoid sentimentalizing and moralizing about politics, law, and government, but also their success in reducing all such phenomena to an observable process of conflict between interest groups for which he congratulated them. This is a stance that I have referred to throughout as realpolitik, and that Bentley later simply was to label "realism." "By a 'realist' in politics we mean one who not only works this way [i.e., 'the power of government must be worked out in terms of the powers that express themselves in it before anything more than a superficial estimate of the extent of that power is arrived at], but does it systematically and with no camouflage or other pretense."[51]

But if he liked their realism, Bentley was less im-

51. Ibid., p. 181.

pressed with their conception of "interest group" as some sort of corporeal body. He thought, for example, that Marx's claim that the proletariat constitutes a sharply identifiable entity, was a "very crude form of group interpretation."[52] And he contended that Gumplowicz's work faltered in the same way.

> The groups which Gumplowicz uses in his interpretations are groups that are concrete in the sense that they are composed of so many different people who can be gathered together in physical separation from other groups. In general they are groups of such character that a man can belong only to one of them. They are not groups as I have used the word in early chapters, but classes of an extreme type. . . . This is one defect in his system as it stands.[53]

To avoid the suggestion that groups were to be understood as individual objects, Bentley sought to do away with the term altogether in his *Relativity in Man and Society*. Here he proposed to call the focus of his research concern not the group, but the cross section. In his view "cross section" was to refer to nothing more than an analytical classification of the social process from the point of view of the sociologist's particular research interest. As he saw it then, there could be no "basic" cross sections or classes; there were as many of them as there were problems that social scientists could conceivably be interested in exploring. "We have different groups of individuals in each plane," he would argue, "each group taken not as so many men as individual wholes with a space line around them, but as a group activity formed of this one aspect of the lives of the men counted in it."[54]

It is difficult to say with any degree of confidence why Bentley attempted to "get away from any pretense

52. Bentley, *The Process of Government*, p. 465.
53. Ibid., p. 470.
54. Bentley, *Relativity in Man and Society*, p. 109.

to uniqueness in any of those structures or systems" that comprised the foundations for Gumplowicz's and Marx's analyses of social life.[55] However, it may well be that nineteenth-century Europe, with its plurality of class-conscious national minorities and its rigidly defined and tightly organized political parties, offered to both the Germans some justification for their notions of "class" and "race" as unambiguous and easily identifiable entities. But to an American scholar attempting to realistically portray political affairs in a society where different classes are not so obviously associated with distinct life styles, and where the blurring of class lines has historically prevented parties from adopting exclusive ideological lines, such a theoretical position might appear to be too simple and thus inadequate. It might be added that like most early American sociologists, Bentley was raised during what was at the time of his youth, an unprecedented era of expanding opportunities and upward mobility. Many historians have imputed great significance to this period for its vindication in the eyes of many (including Bentley, Small, Park, and Ward, who thrived within it) of the optimistic American cultural idea, that at least the New World has escaped from the deadening historical cycle of inflexible class formation and revolutionary conflict.

At any rate, Bentley's selective treatment of the German sociologists of conflict seems to be similar in some respects to that observed earlier, particularly with regard to Ward and Small. Yet, where Small's Christian idealism forced him to reject Gumplowicz's work *in toto*, and while Ward's humanism led him to dispute Gumplowicz's *Pessimismus,* Bentley never compromised his desire to view politics realistically to his liberalism. An indication of this is revealed in a comparison of Bentley's evaluation of what is impor-

---

55. Ibid., p. 182.

tant in Ratzenhofer's sociology, with Small's complimentary treatment of the Austrian's teleological account of politics and his corresponding debunking of the hypothesis of absolute hostility.

> Unfortunately, Ratzenhofer was not content to take the facts as they paraded themselves before the exceptionally well-located window which his positions in life offered him through which to observe them, but instead he felt impelled to swathe them in an exceedingly wearisome and maladroit metaphysics, which he called positive monism, but which one may well describe—with apologies to a jest that was current not so many years since—as neither positive nor monistic.... With his metaphysics he deems himself advancing beyond Gumplowicz, but in reality he is retrograding.[56]

Bentley had even less room in his politics for such "spooks" as liberalism's Reason, than he had for Small's and Ratzenhofer's "the meaning of history." If any sense is to be made of "reason" at all, he would say, it will only be when it is finally associated with a particular interest group (in this case the bourgeoisie) contending for power, and seeking to hide its very this-worldly goals behind a mask of otherworldliness. "When groups are adequately stated, everything is stated. When I say everything I mean everything."[57] As was indicated earlier, this is not to say that psychological phenomena like thinking and reasoning occupy no place in Bentley's overall perspective. Rather, he simply holds that such "processes" can not be analyzed correctly out of context of the observable social process. They are themselves, as his colleague Dewey would agree, nothing more than products of group interaction.

It has been claimed by some of his critics that Bent-

---

56. Bentley, *The Process of Government*, p. 476.
57. Ibid., p. 208.

ley received the inspiration for his endeavor to trace personality attributes back to observable group behavior from Newtonian classical mechanics.[58] But in fact the same position is adopted by another sociologist to whom *The Process of Government* is in part dedicated; namely, Ludwig Gumplowicz. One section of Gumplowicz's *Outlines of Sociology* is devoted to a critique of Adolph Bastian's anthropology because his investigations fail to properly explain cultural events by reference to empirically available social behavior. Instead he "endeavor[s] to attribute all social phenomena to human thought. . . . With him thoughts are always primary and deeds are an emanation from them."[59] However, "in sociology," Gumplowicz maintains, "the point of view must be totally different. The social process must precede. The social fact is primary."[60] For "do we not daily see that it is always the act which excites reflection? Does not the thought follow?"[61]

Following Gumplowicz's lessons, Bentley vehemently

58. For example, see R. E. Dowling, "Pressure Group Theory: Its Methodological Range," *American Political Science Review* LIX (Dec., 1960): 944-54.

59. Gumplowicz, *Outlines,* pp. 38-39.

60. Ibid., p. 39.

61. Ibid., p. 52. Gumplowicz believes that it is "strange that Faust's misgivings did not warn him:
'In the beginning was the thought,
This first line let me weigh completely,
Lest my impatient pen proceed to fleetly,
It is the thought which works, creates, indeed?'
Had he [Bastian] taken to heart the deep meaning of the poet's words: 'in the beginning was the act,' he would have come much closer to the sociological problem." Ibid. pp. 52-53. More specifically: "The great error of individualistic psychology is the supposition that man thinks. . . . A chain of errors, for it is not man himself who thinks but his social community; the source of his thoughts is in the social medium in which he lives, the social atmosphere which he breathes, and he can not think ought else than what the influence of his social environment concentrating upon his brain necessitates." Ibid., pp. 156-57.

denied that appeals to the "general will" or "general welfare" of the people are anything but ideological utterances, which in principle can be reduced to the description of a particular interest group struggling for power. "Each group, . . ." he cautioned his reader, "will bolster up its claim on an elaborate structure of reasoning and assertions. . . . When we go down to the group statement, we get down below *mere* reasoning to the very basis of reason."[62]

Bentley and the Progressives

According to Bentley all ideas of social justice and community good and all notions of political reason are simply effects of the governmental process. They can not be seen as neutral standards that passively adjudicate the social conflicts from which they arise. Several of his reviewers have concluded that therefore Bentley was a "cynical conservative," a scholar who in the realm of politics, could "see no evil, hear no evil, and speak no evil"; a proponent in other words of the Machiavellian doctrine that "might makes [moral] right."[63]

Disregarding the possible fallacious reasoning in this argument, such criticisms overlook the fact that while Bentley did indeed attempt to maintain an objective stance relative to political life, he explicitly recognized that his own thinking on the subject reflected *his* position in the very social process he was studying. While he could try to suspend his value judgements in the

62. Bentley, *The Process of Government*, p. 241.
63. These three assessments are taken respectively from: Myron Q. Hale, "The Cosmology of Arthur F. Bentley," *American Political Science Review* LIX (Dec., 1960): 955-61. Matson, *The Broken Image*, p. 122. Peter H. Odegard, "A Group Basis of Politics: A New Name for an Ancient Myth," *Western Political Quarterly* XI (Sept., 1958): 689-70.

course of the presentation of his research, he realized, more clearly than most sociologists of his day, that he could no more detatch himself from the object of this analysis then he could deny his own existence as a social animal. Specifically, like Ward, Small, and Park, he too was an outspoken ideologist for the Progressive movement; a defender of the bourgeoisie liberal values of private property and equality before the law, and an avid supporter of the virtues of rural small-town life.

From the beginning of his intellectual career when he wrote his senior thesis at Johns Hopkins on "The Condition of the Western Farmer as Illustrated by the Economic History of a Nebraska Township,"[64] Bentley demonstrated his concern for the plight of the farmer in an age of inflated currency and railroad monopolization. Following the First World War, he worked closely with the Non-Partisan League in North Dakota, and in 1924, after he had joined the National Progressive Party, he became chairman of the Indiana state presidential campaign committee of Robert M. LaFollette.

It was on the basis of his political experiences and a detailed personal investigation of Midwest Progressivism that Bentley wrote *Makers, Users, and Masters in America*.[65] The book was begun in 1918 and completed two years later, but due to various apparently nonpolitical circumstances it was not published until some fifty years later. Sidney Ratner has described how its author was motivated to write it because the political conditions of his day appeared to threaten his ideal of a liberal social order. Nineteen eighteen saw both the rejection of the League of Nations by the American

64. Arthur F. Bentley, "The Condition of the Western Farmer as Illustrated by the Economic History of a Nebraska Township," *Johns Hopkins University Studies in Historical and Political Science*, 1893.
65. Arthur F. Bentley, *Makers, Users, and Masters in America*, ed. and intro. by Sidney Ratner (Syracuse, New York: Syracuse University Press, 1969).

people and big business' successful attack on both unionization and Bolshevism, later culminating in the election of the conservative President Warren Harding.

The facts aroused Bentley and other champions of the small business man, the farmer, and the worker, and made them fear for the future of democracy. At the same time, Bentley was concerned about the repression of honest opposition to the war effort by the passage of the Espionage Act in June 1917 and the Sedition Act in 1918.[66]

Rather than dishonestly declaring that he was approaching his study of the American economy from a position of ethical neutrality, Bentley began his description of its workers, consumers, and "masters" with a clear characterization of his own biases. ". . . [F]or a final prejudice, if prejudice it be, he admits a deep-seated and seemingly indestructable desire for civil liberty, for freedom of thought, of speech and belief."[67] While, he continued, he is cognizant of the apparent futility of ever establishing an "organized society without focuses of power and authority . . . he finds himself chronically opposed to increasing absorption of benefits to themselves. . . . That is to say, he is always ready to fight against whatever abuses of power seem worst at any moment."[68] At the time when he wrote his book, Bentley was of the opinion that there were two main collectivities that were becoming increasingly abusive in this sense. There were the captains of industry, the group that attempted to justify its seizure of power by invoking "a philosophy of burglary or piracy,"

---

66. Ratner, "Introduction," *Makers, Users, and Masters in America,* p. xv.
67. Bentley, *Makers, Users, and Masters in America.,* p. 5. "Taken in political, rather than in economic terms," Bentley goes on, "there would probably be no hesitation in characterizing him as typically middle class in interests." Ibid., p. 6.
68. Ibid., p. 4.

and then the socialists, or the group that sought to mobilize popular support by resorting to "a philosophy of . . . anarchy or Bolshevism."[69] This being the case, his main literary task was to unmask the machinations of these devious enemies of the American middle class. Once warned of the threat to their values, Bentley had the muckraker's hope that the common man would then take up arms and run the rascals out of power.

Bentley initiated his exposé with a consideration of the concentration of American wealth by large industrialists, using the frame of reference developed in *The Process of Government*.[70] He describes the capacity that capitalists who are organized into combinations, conglomerates, and trusts have, to control, at least indirectly, the lives of virtually all American workers and consumers. This almost compulsory, essentially territorial monopoly of power by big business (including control over all aspects of production, wages, prices, and even consumer needs) is coming to be so centralized that what has evolved in this country is an "industrial government."

> . . . [T]he industrial organization we now have . . . is a true government itself existing in its capacity of industrial government—a great compelling organization of the relations of men; of the relations not merely of some men with other men, but of all men who live in its territory with each other. An organization from which no man can

69. Ibid., p. 5.

70. The author describes his method of approach in the following terms: "So far as it is possible, they [i.e. 'the facts of wealth and power in the United States] will be stated objectively, not with reference to current theories, not with blind reliance on the symbols which must be used in stating them, but instead in terms of groups, or their interests as related to one another, of their viewpoints as developed out of those interests or as latent in them, and of the probabilities of their political or extra-political action in accordance with those interests." Ibid., p. 3.

break away any more than he can from the political
government.[71]

As is typically the case, the industrial government
contains within it struggles for dominance between
various interest groups. And because of their
"strategic, strong positions in the industrial world" it is
the capitalists who are able to realize their will over
the consumers and workers. Using an ingenious arse-
nal of weapons for appropriating private property, including stock watering, profiteering, high finance,
stock adulturation, short-weighting, and labor rac-
keteering, etc.,[72] the robber barons are no match for
their unorganized and largely ignorant foes. It follows
that inasmuch as the form of a government is simply a
representative expression of the balance of power of the
interest groups within it, then while our "political government is democratic; our industrial government is
autocratic."[73] This means in effect that the concerns of
the makers and users must somehow find protection in
the offices and activities of their appropriative masters.
But apparently this form of representation is not adequate enough to address the grievances of the subject

71. Ibid., p. 32. More specifically, "this industrial government is a government itself, not some lesser form of organization, by the very tests that all
of the people are involved in its workings; that the ramifications of its organization are very wide; that its control is highly centralized; and that the
limitations it puts upon individual action, direct, and indirect, are very
great." Ibid., p. 34. That the industrial government has no formal written
constitution or abstract legal sovereignty is, of course, considered irrelevant
by Bentley, who uses observable activity as the basis for any distinctions he
makes. Even "the modern state did not appear full-fledged in Europe, but
arose out of long sharp struggles. When some future historian describes the
industrial development of the nineteenth and twentieth centuries, he will
have a tale to tell similar in all essentials to that which our present historians now tell of the political development of Europe in the thirteenth to
the sixteenth centuries." Ibid., p. 42.
72. Ibid., pp. 66-69.
73. Ibid., p. 38.

population, for "not organized within the system of industrial government they have been driven to organization without (outside) it, i.e. in the political
government."[74]

> One may almost say that it is against profiteering that
> all labor and industrial and business legislation is
> directed.... Here are the various attempts at the control
> of trusts and combinations. Regulation of banks, usury
> laws, "blue sky" laws, laws against race discrimination
> and against local price discrimination are there....[75]

But to the extent that even the political government
does not offer an effective means for the expression of
the interests of the little people, then "revolutionary
movements also take their roots here. A reform directed against profiteering that becomes hopeless of
success through legislation or politics will readily identify the legislative and political processes with the profiteers, and strike at the government along with the
profiteers."[76]
Although "the first great line of cleavage which
opens itself is that of wage labor, or the proletariat,"[77]
neither socialism nor anarchism are presently (1920) in
a position to win many adherents in America, says
Bentley.[78] This is not only because of the sectarian

74. Ibid., p. 39.
75. Ibid., p. 69.
76. Ibid.
77. Ibid., p. 172.
78. Bentley claims that, "socialism in the United States has insisted on an
orthodoxy and a bigotry that has driven out of its ranks most of its ablest
leaders, and (has) led to such a splitting of its forces as to make it in most
ways insignificant.... In common understanding, socialism is somehow
supposed to be the program of class conscious wage-labor; but despite the
fact that Marxist socialism has dealt much with the proletariat in contrast
with all other elements of the population, it is clear enough that any such
identification of wage-labor generally with socialism, as a political or industrial fact of America today (1920) is far from the truth." Ibid., pp. 173-74.

tendency of left-wing extremism, but more importantly because "the kind of (police and military) force that has always been exerted by masters (of business and industry) when their mastery is threatened" serves temporarily to scare potential revolutionaries into submission.[79] But while the threats of violence and blacklisting have served at least for the moment to dissuade workers from forging themselves into a worthy opponent for the owners of the means of production, Bentley hypothesizes as he did in *The Process of Government* that "such exercise of force, given our present degree of education, and information among the victims, is most clearly pressing, not away from but toward revolution; heightening and deepening conviction, destroying willingness for compromise and mutual understanding, (and) developing fanaticism."[80] Thus,

> these facts stand, not as an argument of the possibility of revolution today, but as evidence that when the shock comes, arising out of the enormously excessive claims in the future upon the possible limit of product, all the conditions exist to turn us from mere crisis of business under its old plan of organization into revolution which shatters that plan of organization itself.[81]

But in his mind, as it was for Albion Small, a proletarian revolution is just as undesirable an outcome of history as is the contemporary status quo, where the capitalist robber barons constitute a closed ruling class. For with a Communist revolution, power relationships will not dissipate as Marx and Lenin predicted. Private property and the middle class of independent entrepreneur-farmers will be even less secure here

---

79. Ibid., p. 178. pp. 207-33 are devoted to a description of the various techniques of legal and extra-legal violence used by big business to protect its power from the thrusts of the Non-Partisan League and the socialists.
80. Ibid., p. 178.
81. Ibid., p. 180.

than they are under an appropriative plutocratic regime. In fact a revolution will simply mean that a different form of property seizure, this time justified in the name of democracy and working class liberation, will replace the old techniques and apologies. And the social problem as it previously existed will persist. In other words, "the trouble with the revolutionary element in the proletariat leadership," Bentley believed, "is not that it is different from the old organization [i.e. big business], but too much that it is fundamentally the same thing. . . . He regards himself as a man out to get something, not as a man with a tool in his hand out to produce something."[82]

Thus instead of climbing on the bandwagon of the socialists, Bentley advocated "A Middle Class Counter-Revolution." It was to be a *counter* revolution because its goal was to institute once again the bourgeoisie value of the productive use of private property.[83] As to the means for effectively implementing this movement, to prevent the calamity of either the plutocrats or proletariat from unilaterally monopolizing power, he was less sure. But consistent with his overall methodological position, he did exhort the middle class in its search for a practical strategem to "turn to the essential realities beneath" the slogans, theories, and party administrations of the opposition; to focus upon the myriad of interest groups that such things represent. ". . . [T]he real parties must be sought behind the formal parties, and especially in non-partisan associations or leagues of citizen voters for the accomplishment of political objects."[84] In other words, if the middle class is not to become merely the trampled ground of opposing forces from the left and

82. Ibid., p. 181.
83. Ibid., pp. 186-90.
84. Ibid., p. 256.

right, "it is for the man in the middle not to permit himself to be misled, nor to permit himself to be made the victim of either side."[85] If there is any hope at all for liberalism it is to be found in temporary nonideological coalitions, pressure groups, or lobbies of clear-sighted citizens with immediate concrete goals. The Municipal Voters League of Chicago, the Anti-Saloon League, and most importantly, the Non-Partisan League of which Bentley himself was a member, are all cited as illustrations of the type of political tool he has in mind.

In summary then, it is totally incorrect to picture Bentley as a wholly disinterested spectator of the human tragedy of political interaction. His ethical neutrality to the contrary notwithstanding, just as for Ward, Small, and Park, he attempted to derive from his politics, solutions to what he considered to be the social problems of his day. As a "man in the middle," he sought, not only in the area of domestic strife, but also in the international realm, to apply the sociological perspective to minimize the "frictions" between opposing interests. Thus, for example, in a manner inconsistent with what might be expected of a cold-hearted cynic who neither sees, hears, nor speaks evil, he proposed in the last section of *Relativity in Man and Society* to

take a position frankly identifying ourselves with certain activities of society, identifying ourselves, if we care to put it that way, with certain interests in society. Let this position be against war, nor war absolutely or war forever, but war in the next generation or the next century between the nations as they now exist. We need not worry, against someone's argument, out of the frying pan into what fire we may fall if we succeed in our project, if we put a check to wars. We answer we will meet those new perils when we come to them, and we have no fear

85. Ibid., p. 182.

that our desires and energies and struggles will disappear all too soon under folded angels' wings if we win out. We point out too the new powers of destruction, the widened range of destruction, the threat to the old men and women and children in the homes as well as to the soldiers in the field, the wastes and after-burdens, the possible weakening of "our" civilization against other civilizations, or against fertile and as yet uncivilized forces of potential mastery. We know that there are profits in wars to certain activities of our own, but we say they are profits of short durations, and we say that in longer durations those profits are losses, and the real profits will come on our side of the argument.[86]

Following this unsparing appraisal of modern war, Bentley addressed himself to "The Resolvability of Frictions." And in so doing, he anticipated a whole new school of thinking on conflict which it will be our task in the next chapter to elucidate in depth. As a start, says Bentley, social conflict "may be overcome by small stages of advance in understanding."[87] But understanding does not mean as it did for Small, Ward, and the young Park, either muckraking, progressive education, or "opinion changing." To Bentley these are simply subtly disguised propaganda techniques, means of political mobilization.[88] What he proposes is a comprehensive sociological analysis of "understanding" of the causes of war itself, which would entail, as it always did for Bentley, a realistic look behind the mere opinions and "theory" of war back to the conflicts of interest underlying them. Not until sociologists are able to reduce war to a process of psychical interaction between opposed interest groups, he argued, will there be any hope of resolving it. But, he promised, once "the hidden things can come to light, [then] the light will

---

86. Bentley, *Relativity in Man and Society,* p. 195.
87. Ibid., p. 198.
88. Ibid., p. 196.

be curative."[89] In other words, despite his advocacy of
"realism," Bentley never lost his optimistic liberal faith
that reason, and especially reason as science, can overcome the irrationality that is war and political violence. It must be added that he went no further than
merely to advance his belief. It remained for the next
generation of American sociologists to put their money,
time, and effort where Bentley had put his faith. And
it is to this generation and its attempt to carry out
Bentley's charge, that we now turn.

---

89. Ibid. Bentley believed that "the conflicts which are now obscure and
concealed, not unlike the analysts' inhibitions in the unconscious he studies,
will come up into full view ready for resolution into something of peace and
harmony of living and effectiveness of action." Ibid., p. 197.

10

Sociology and Conflict

Beginning in 1950 with Jessie Bernard's query "Where is the Modern Sociology of Conflict,"[1] commentators with increasing vocalism have decried the sociological profession for what is thought to be its attempt to avoid dealing with the subject of conflict. These critics argue that contrary to the early German and American sociologists whose theories comprise the subject matter of this book, contemporary American sociologists have since the 1930s come to devote their full attention to the issue of social order, to the neglect of conflict and change.[2] Although there is certainly not

1. Jessie Bernard, "Where is the Modern Sociology of Conflict," *AJS* LVI (July, 1950: 11-16.
2. Several of the most provocative articles on this subject are: Coser, *The Functions of Social Conflict,* pp. 15-38; John Horton, "Order and Conflict Theories of Social Problems as Competing Ideologies," *AJS* LXXI (May, 1966): 701-13; Ralf Dahrendorf, "Out of Utopia: Toward a Reorientation of Sociological Analysis," *Sociological Theory: A Book of Readings,* ed. by Lewis Coser and Bernard Rosenberg (New York: Macmillan Co., 1965); Dahrendorf, *Class and Class Conflict in Industrial Society* (Stanford: Stanfor University Press, 1959), pp. 157-73; Irving Lo·iis Horowitz, "Consensus, Conflict, and Cooperation: A Sociological Inventory," *Social Forces* XLI (Dec., 1962): 177-88.

complete unanimity among them concerning the
reasons for this shift in theoretical perspective, most of
them give the impression that it is at least partially
the result of sociology's intimate consultant-client relationships with the dominant institutions of American
society. For example, in one of the most sophisticated
presentations of this view, Lewis Coser says that "it
appears that the first generation of American
sociologists saw themselves as reformers and addressed
themselves to an audience of reformers. Such self-
images and publics called attention to situations of conflict, and this accounts for the sociologists' concern with
them."[3] However,

> in contrast to the figures so far discussed, the majority of
> sociologists who dominate contemporary sociology, far
> from seeing themselves as reformers and addressing
> themselves to audiences of reformers, either have oriented
> themselves toward purely academic and professional audi-
> ences, or have attempted to find a hearing among de-
> cisionmakers in public or private bureaucracies.[4]

But to the extent that they write for big business, welfare agencies, or the military, then "this new audience
will choose the sociologists' problems and these problems are likely to concern . . . the preservation of existing institutional arrangements," instead of the issue of
how to alter them through political action.[5]

While, on the face of it, there does seem to be substantial truth in this argument, it is obvious that a
final evaluation of its soundness either way will have
to wait for a full-scale empirical investigation. The

3. Coser, *The Functions of Social Conflict,* p. 16.
4. Ibid., p. 20.
5. Ibid., p. 27. Thus it follows that whereas "conflict provided to those
sociologists [he names Cooley, Veblen, and Small] the central category
for the analysis of society and of process," Ibid., p. 16, sociologists today
"center attention predominantly upon problems of adjustment rather than
upon conflict; upon social statics rather than upon dynamics." Ibid., p. 20.

findings presented in the previous chapters have no claim to being the last word on the early American sociology of conflict, yet they do appear to point the way in which this research question, when it is finally asked, can be most fruitfully formulated and answered.

More or less implicit in the above critics' assessments of the profession, is the hypothesis that early American sociologists were concerned primarily with the question of social conflict as opposed to social order. However, the findings reported earlier suggest that just the opposite was in fact the case. Bentley, Park, Ward, and Small, not to mention their German colleagues, were interested in conflict precisely because of their preoccupation with the question of the possibility of social order.

Each born and raised in a small rural community by Protestant parents who were, with the exception of Ward's, also members of the old middle class, their personalities were indelibly etched with the manners, life-style, and ideal and material interests associated with this stratum. Like one of their intellectual fellow travelers, Edward Ross, they could all, with the same justification, have described themselves as he did, as one of the "fiber of the people" who had "homebred notions of what is fit or decent or worthwhile."[6] But if this is so, then, like other members of local society during this time, they too were frightened by the post-Civil War movements that seemed on the verge of destroying their idea of a progressive civilization, led by

6. For Ross' classification of himself in these terms, see Wilson, *In Quest of Community: Social Philosophy in the United States, 1860-1920*, pp. 87-88. For an attempt to explain the content of early American social problems texts by referring to the negative reaction of their small-town Middle Border authors to urbanization and industrialization, see C. Wright Mills, "The Professional Ideology of Social Pathologists," *Power, Politics, and People,* ed. and intro. by Irving Louis Horowitz (New York: Ballantine Books, 1973), pp. 525-52.

independent, hard-working, God-fearing small businessmen, farmers, and professional people. On the one hand, as Ross wrote in his undergraduate oration "The Coming Slavery," there was the modern industrial corporation, owned by "capitalist pirates" who in their quenchless thirst for money, were blatantly disregarding the interests of the common man. Thoughtlessly, they ran their "competitors" out of business, using any means they believed practical to concentrate the nation's wealth in their own hands. And impersonally, they organized thousands of workers under factory roofs, driving them to produce under degrading conditions. In the other direction, Ross cried, stands the equally unappealing urban masses. Recently arrived from Eastern Europe and the Mediterranean region, they are swarthy, uneducated, and inculcated with an alien religion which seems to demand subserviency to a foreign prince, the Pope. Furthermore, their pastimes of gambling and drinking, their "moral laxity," together with the unaesthetic manner in which they wallow in the cities' slums, provides little to admire for the "one-hundred percent old-time Americans."[7]

To make matters worse, both groups, the proletariat and the plutocracy were, in the eyes of America's man-in-the-middle, presently engaged in a war against each

7. In his younger years, Ross was an explicit racist. Concerned over the possibility that the Teutonic peoples with whom he identified were committing "race suicide," and were becoming "mongrelized" through miscegenation with "subnormal and low-grade" Slavs, Chinese, and Italians, he advocated that America shut its borders. In 1912 he wrote that "there ought to be on guard at the Nation's gates a man whose family line is entwined with the national past, and feels a normal American reaction at the spectacle of the country being held back by the constant pouring in of immigrants from progressively lower social grades and from peoples more remote from the orbit of our civilization." Edward A. Ross, "Correspondence to Woodrow Wilson," Nov., 1912, Ross Papers, State Historical Society of Wisconsin, Madison, quoted in Wilson, *In Quest of Community*, p. 112.

other, seeking with the tools immediately available to them, to unilaterally control the government for their own selfish purposes. From one side, big business was attempting to control party nominations, to rig voting, to influence congressional behavior illegally, and to bribe both officials and judges in the administration and interpretation of the law. In the other corner, were the socialists and anarchists, organizing the property-less in an equally concerted way, to engage in strikes, to foment riots, and and destroy private property. Un-aware, perhaps, of the direction where their actual in-terests lay, the lower classes with increasing frequency during the early decades of the twentieth-century, began, like starving animals in close quarters, to turn against each other. Where the immigrant population had a clearly identifiable physical or cultural trait, as did the newly arrived Negro from the rural South, the Oriental in California, or the Italian Catholic, they were attacked as unwelcome intruders by various nativistic and protectionist associations. The violence rendered by immigrant groups to one another often surpassed in intensity, that done by organized social classes to their foes. For the "forgotten American" then, those like Bentley, Park, Small, Ward, Ross, Cooley, and Veblen, the social order they had grown to believe in was indeed seriously threatened. In Ross' customarily colorful way of putting it: "The antipathies of sects threaten to tear society to pieces. The drawing apart into opposing camps of poor and rich, capitalist and worker, functionary and citizen, civilian and sol-dier, as well as the race enmity of white and black, or yellow and white, or Christian and Jew, summons soci-ety to act or perish."[8]

But for many of Ross' contemporaries the question

---

8. Edward A. Ross, *Social Control* (New York: Macmillan Co., 1902), pp. 393-94. See also Ibid., pp. 51-56.

remained of how best to respond to society's plea for help. None of the vocabularies that then held sway over public opinion seemed to provide an adequate program of social reform. Social Darwinism, it was felt, not only failed to properly address the problem of American social order, but in fact apologized for the same material greed that was apparently the main cause of social conflict in the first place. Moreover, Rousseauian-Jeffersonian liberal thought, with its assumption of man as a *naturally* social animal, overlooked the glaring fact that if American civilization was to survive the ravages of industrialization, it would in some cases have to *force* its citizenry to conform to the collective will of the People.

Frustrated in their quest for a convincing interpretation of the dangers to national solidarity in either Darwinism or liberalism, the sons of the old middle class discovered the anti-liberal, romantic, and thus nonbiological literature of German social science. Here at last, in the writings of such persons as Ratzenhofer, Gumplowicz, Oppenheimer, and others, was an appreciation of the significance of the group, and ultimately the nation state, for the moral edification, indeed the moral being altogether of the individual. Furthermore, and implicit in this notion, was an idea that certainly was not lost on men who had received rigorous training as Congregationalists, Presbyterians, and Baptists, that man was qualitatively distinct from lower beasts, in that he alone was gifted with an intellect and a will. Man, in this view does not simply *behave*, or passively respond to environmental stimuli. Rather, he *acts* by giving moral meaning to, and by consciously directing his behavior. From this perspective then, the conflicts that menace America's corporate order, could not be understood as the inevitable consequences of humanity being subconsciously driven to fight by uncontrollable biological instincts. On the contrary, being instead the result of the conscious pursuit of purposes in conjunction with limited knowledge, even the most bloody power struggles could now be seen as susceptable to melioristic intervention. All the social reformer need do to end disruptive conflicts would be to alter by a process of public education, or what was later to be called "socialization," the minds of the combatants. It would be sufficient to solve the problem of American unity, merely to convince potential enemies that their own interests and those of the nation are coincident, and that what appears to be individual gain at the expense of others, is really a collective loss all around.

In conclusion then, it is clear that Park, Bentley, Ward, and Small were no less apprehensive of social conflict than modern sociologists presumably are. They wanted, above all, social peace, an end to the contest of class against class and race against race. They became adherents of realpolitik not generally because they shared Treitschke's or Hegel's romantic belief that in the struggle itself was to be found the source of human virtue, but because only it seemed implicitly to contain strategies for consciously inducing social progress. Thus in part, it was from Gumplowicz's despairing description of politics, that Ward derived the possibility of man becoming cognizant of his situation and using this as a step in his liberation from it. Or consider Small, who discarded Ratzenhofer's hypothesis of absolute hostility only to expand on his "positive monism" to demonstrate to his students the inevitability of evolution to a democratic society. Park, on the other hand, while less advocatory than either Small or Ward, drew upon Simmel and Oppenheimer, if not to provide an outright apology for racial struggles of liberation, to at least point out their (moral?) necessity. And Bentley, in a more uncompromisingly realistic way than any of the others, discovered from his study of Gumplowicz,

Ihering, and Simmel, the only agency that he believed could effectively carry out a middle class "counter-revolution," the nonpartisan citizens' lobby. In each of these cases, the reform program, whether it took the form of educating public opinion as it did with Small and Park, active governmental involvement in the Nation's economic affairs as it did for Ward, or in the common man's participation in conflict itself, according to Bentley, the final goal, the end toward which they all looked, was social unity, solidarity, and order; not just any type of harmony, but one which exemplified their most deeply held values—liberalism's equality and private property, Protestanism's propriety and uprightness, and small-town neighborliness and intimacy.

The repeated failure of historians of sociology, with some exceptions, to recognize their profession's long-standing bias in favor of social order, and its abhorrence of "disorganization," "deviance," "individualism," or "anarchy" as it has variously been called, may have something to do with the word "Progressivism" itself, the banner under which so many early American sociologists wrote.[9] For notwithstanding the forward-looking suggestion of this banner, the American Progressive movement was essentially reactionary in its outlook; a "counter-revolution" as Bentley so aptly put it. It was led by persons who were fighting for the *old* American way, for a life style and status position of the *old* middle class against the dominant drift in America toward big business and big labor. It was a struggle of small property holders against the steady encroachments of big property and anti-property, spurred by in-

9. Among the exceptions are the following authors. Each of them has attempted to explain the basic features of sociological theory by invoking the notion of conservatism: Albert Salomon, *The Tyranny of Progress* (New York: Noonday Press, 1955); Leon Bramson, *The Political Context of Sociology* (Princeton, New Jersey: Princeton University Press, 1961); Robert Nisbet, *The Sociological Tradition* (New York: Basic Books, 1966).

dustrialization, over its traditional domain. To overlook this point renders it impossible to account for the undeniably conservative consequences of Progressivism precisely where it succeeded; from its early and quite vulgar racism and support of Roosevelt's benevolent imperialism, to the public promises of Woodrow Wilson not to lead the country forward, but to turn the clock back to the Golden Age of Thomas Jefferson's farmer-entrepreneurs.

The proponents of Progressivism enlisted the aid of the state in their battle to preserve old-time Americanism, to shut the borders to immigration, establish compulsory education, break up monopolies, and regulate the railroads. But it is naive to assume, as so many historians writing of this era have, that the resulting increase in the power of big government as such was "progressive"; that is, that it in fact helped to further the interests of local society. Indeed, long range perspective now allows us to clearly see that the choice of the state as an ally to protect small business, small-town life, and fundamentalist Protestanism, was a disastrous tactical error on the part of Progressives. Compulsory progressive education meant not the preservation of neighborhood ties and a religiously oriented curriculum, but rather the consolidation of school districts and the loss of local community control over hiring practices and course content. The protection of the "forgotten American" from the predations of labor and business resulted in the even more terrifying specter of government intervention in all aspects of life. Even by 1920, it had begun to appear to some Progressives like Albion Small, that America had already "out-Germaned the Germans." And the irony of it is that big business did not come out of the Progressive Era chastened and meek, but instead, riding the saddle higher than it ever had before. The establishment of a Federal Reserve Bank, uniform commerce regulations across states, food and drug laws, and even strictures against purely speculative merging of companies, did not undermine the control that Standard Oil and U. S. Steel had over the American economy. On the contrary, their holdings became more secure, their competitors more in fetters, and their profits more predictable than they had been twenty-five years earlier.[10]

Tension and Conflict

Nor apparently, is it completely true that relative to early American sociology, influential contemporary practitioners of the profession are less theoretically concerned with social conflict. Since the heyday of the classical sociologists of conflict, a large list of scholars who have devoted considerable effort to this very subject has grown. With no attempt to be exhaustive, it includes, for instance, Kurt Lewin,[11] Elton Mayo,[12] T.

10. Gabriel Kolko, *The Triumph of Conservatism: A Reinterpretation of American History, 1900-1916* (New York: Free Press of Glencoe, 1963).
11. Kurt Lewin, *Resolving Social Conflicts: Selected Papers on Group Dynamics,* ed. by Gertrud Lewin (New York: Harper & Bros. Pub., 1948). This book contains a bibliography of articles on the same subject by some of Lewin's students, e.g. A. Bavelas, Dorwin Cartwright, Gordon Allport, Robert Bales, J. P. R. French Jr., Leon Festinger, etc. These scholars have all been at one time or another attatched to the Research Center for Group Dynamics, a well-endowed institute devoted at least in part to the study of conflict.
12. The classic statement of his views is found in Elton Mayo, *The Social Problems of an Industrial Civilization* (Boston: Graduate School of Business Administration, Harvard University, 1945). Mayo is the progenitor of a line of researchers such as J. O. Low, Lloyd Warner, and Fritz Roethlisberger, who while working out of the Harvard School of Business Administration have expended considerable effort on the study of industrial conflict.

W. Adorno,[13] J. L. Dollard,[14] and Robert Nisbet.[15] In addition, there not only exists *The Journal of Conflict Resolution* for disseminating the latest research in this special area, but also the scores of well-endowed institutes, such as the UNESCO Tension Project,[16] the funds of which underwrite the empirical analysis of conflict. In other words, one is no more justified in claiming that today's sociologists are no longer concerned with social conflict, then he is in arguing that first-generation sociologists avoided the subject of social order.

Yet the fact cannot be ignored that while sociologists have continued to write about social strife with undiminished fervor, they approach it in many cases from an entirely different frame of reference than that employed by the original German and American sociologists of conflict. Specifically, regardless of the otherwise significant theoretical discrepancies separating the above mentioned analysts, they share a fundamentally similar perspective in regard to conflict which, with acknowledgement to Jessie Bernard, might

13. T. W. Adorno, *etal.*, *The Authoritarian Personality*, Studies in Prejudice Series, ed. by Max Horkheimer (New York: Harper & Row Pub. Inc., 1950). See also the other books on racial aggression in this series by persons such as Bruno Bettelheim, Morris Janowitz, Nathan Ackerman, and Marie Jahoda. These scholars make up one research branch of the American Jewish Committee which devotes large amounts of its funds to the analysis of Jewish conflict with other groups.

14. J. L. Dollard et al., *Frustration and Aggression* (New Haven: Yale University Press, 1939).

15. Robert K. Nisbet, *The Quest for Community* (New York: Oxford University Press, 1953). This book is one example of the whole school of mass political theorists to which reference will be made below.

16. Three volumes that have grown out of this project are: Hadley Cantril, ed., *Tensions That Cause Wars* (Urbana, Illinois: University of Illinois Press, 1950); Otto Klineberg, *Tensions Affecting International Understanding* (New York: Social Science Research Council, 1950); Robin M. Williams Jr., *The Reduction of Intergroup Tensions* (New York: Social Science Research Council, 1957).

be called "tension theory," to distinguish it from what has throughout this book been dubbed realpolitik.[17] Tension theory is radically opposed to realpolitik on three grounds, the most basic being the latter's explanation of why there is such a thing as conflict in the first place.

The Causes of Tension and Conflict

The proponents of realpolitik claim that conflict is a form of interaction between rational goal-directed persons that results from their pursuit of mutually exclusive interests in a situation of scarcity of power or wealth. Tension theorists argue instead that social struggles are really the consequence of nonrational and often subconscious psychological "tensions." These in turn stem from a variety of sources from the frustrating and debilitating effects of urbanization and industrialization to restrictive child-rearing practices. But regardless of the wide diversity of causes of tensions, they always drive their sufferer to engage in aggressive behaviors that hopefully, in the end, reestablish some sort of mental equilibrium or consonance. These can include anything from participation in what these analysts call "radical" political activity, to the use of

17. I am indebted for this observation to Jessie Bernard, "The Sociological Study of Conflict," *The Nature of Conflict: Studies on the Sociological Aspects of International Tension* (Mayene, France: Joseph Floch for the United Nations Educational, Scientific, and Cultural Organization, 1958). However, the distinction made by this author has been extended to include many sociologists not explicitly treated by her. The word "tension theorists" is not intended to imply that the sociologists so classified constitute a clearly identifiable theoretical school. On the contrary, the contributors to this overall perspective comprise theoretical approaches as diverse as Freudian psychology and group dynamics. The word "tension theory" then, is intended to

scapegoats, a fervent submissiveness to demogogic leaders, prejudicial intolerance, and hateful stereotyping.

In the tradition of realpolitik, psychological animosity is treated, not as a consequence of "tensions," but of a conflict of interests. Ratzenhofer, for example, maintained that if they had the choice, people would always decide on a life of peace and tranquility before war. But inspite of their best wishes, they will develop an absolute hostility toward strangers because of the scarcity of resources for human survival and the subsequent struggle for existence. Park and Thomas spoke in essentially the same way. For neither of them was racial prejudice considered to be due to a subconsciouis need to hate a convenient scapegoat because of some sort of not fully understood impediment to goal achievement. On the contrary, it arises from a group's fear that an enemy is threatening its material interests. It is the result of a conscious identification of others as a danger to the realization of its purposes. Or take Simmel. In his classic study of conflict, he began by admitting that "it seems impossible to deny an *a priori* fighting instinct, especially if one keeps in mind the incredibly picayunish, even silly, occasions of the most serious conflict."[18] But, he added on reflection, this "instinctual" hostility is not so much biologically based and thus nonrational as it is a psychological reaction to a situation where interests are in conflict. Thus, "it seems probable to me, that on the whole, because of its formal character, the hostility drive merely

suggest that its formulators share only a very general outlook toward social conflict.

18. Simmel, *Conflict and the Web of Group Affiliations*, p. 29. He continues: "The observation of certain anti-pathies, factions, intrigues, and open fights might lead one to consider hostility among those primary human energies which are not provoked by the external reality of their objects but which create their own objects out of themselves." Ibid., p. 31.

adds itself as a reinforcement to controversies which are due to concrete cases."[19]

This theoretical position is unalterably opposed to that of the tension theorist who emphatically rejects what he considers to be an overly rationalistic manner of interpreting racial prejudice. In Elton McNeil's view, expressed in the introduction to a collection of articles by contributors to *The Journal of Conflict Resolution:*

> No attempt to understand the vicissitudes of human aggressive behavior is adequate without concepts similar to that of the existence of an unconscious part of the self. The efforts for centuries to explain the motivation of human actions on a purely conscious and rational basis always produced embarrassing paradoxes or left a host of details unaccounted for.[20]

Rather,

> prejudiced subjects generally tend to feel themselves "forgotten," the victims of usually parental injustice who did not "get" enough of the things they deserved. Thus they tend to resent other people, especially outgroups, of whom they readily conceive as unjustifiably threatening, as intruding on their rights, and as attempting to take privileges away from them.[21]

Marxist-Leninism clearly falls within the outlook of realpolitik, at least in regard to its rationalistic way of explaining the participation of workers in the Communist Party. The revolutionary proletarian, it might be easily said, is one who, conscious of his true class interests, has coolly weighed several alternative plans of action in terms of their utility to realize his goals,

19. Ibid., p. 33. In other words, "It is expedient to hate the adversary with whom one fights, . . . just as it is expedient to love a person whom one is tied to and has to get along with." Ibid., p. 34.

20. Elton B. NcNeil, "The Nature of Aggression," *The Nature of Human Conflict,* ed. by Elton B. McNeil (Englewood Cliffs, New Jersey: Prentice-Hall, Inc., 1965). p. 29.

21. Ibid., p. 28.

and discovered that Communism is the most practical means to achieve what he wants. But according to Robert Nisbet, one of the foremost tension theorists, "to consider the facts of poverty and economic distress as causes of the growth of communism is deceptive."[22] In his view it is the psychological tension of "anomie," the result of a situation of normlessness and loss of community, which in turn follows from social change, that drives people to engage in either left- or right-wing "extremist" politics.

> It is hard to overlook the fact that the state and politics have become suffused by qualities formerly inherent only in the family or the church. . . . Where there is widespread conviction that community has been lost, there will be a conscious quest for community in the form of association that seems to promise the greatest moral refuge, . . . and above all it is the totalitarian Communist party that most successfully exploits the craving for moral certainty and communal membership. . . . Moreover the almost eager acceptance of the fantastic doctrines of the Nazis by millions of otherwise intelligent Germans would be inexplicable were it not for the accompanying profer of moral community to the disenchanted and alienated worker, peasant, and intellectual. . . . Consciously or unconsciously the joiner is in the quest of secure belief and solid membership in an associative order.[23]

22. Nisbet, *The Quest for Community,* p. 35.
23. Ibid., pp. 33-34. Mayo and his student Lloyd Warner, *Yankee City,* one volume abridged edition (New Haven: Yale University Press, 1963), pp. 270-354, give similar explanations for the fact that some workers engage in conflict with management. It is not so much that the workers have authentic economic and/or political grievances, but rather that they seek some meaning for their work experience which drives them to join labor unions. This notion has also found application in several other settings. See for instance Seymour Martin Lipset and Philip G. Altbach, "The Quest for Community on Campus," *The Search for Community in Modern America: Interpretations of American History,* ed. by E. Digby Baltzell (New York: Harper & Row Pub., Inc., 1968), pp. 123-47 for an attempt to explain student activism in these terms. For other examples of this same approach see: Seymour Martin Lipset, "Working Class Authoritarianism," *Political Man*

A vast number of other examples could easily be cited of the dispute between the supporters of realpolitik and tension theory concerning the real causes of conflict. There is Mayo's and his students' attempts to explain labor militancy, not from Small's and Oppenheimer's point of view, but in terms of the tensions attending the depersonalization of factory work, and their proposal that industrial conflict, and even war could be avoided if managers used more humane administrative techniques.[24] Or take Lewin's notion that German militarism was not necessarily caused by the presence on its borders of enemies as Simmel or Park might say, but rather a consequence of the fact that the "field" in which its citizens were educated contained, for many decades, "few degrees of freedom" and "free space of movement."[25] In all of these cases the tension theorists submit that the model of rational man that is implicit in realpolitik is not fruitful enough to account for the most important facts relating to conflict.

(Garden City, New York: Doubleday & Co., Inc., 1960), pp. 87-126; James S. Coleman, *Community Conflict* (Glencoe, Illinois: Free Press, 1957); Eric Fromm, *Escape from Freedom* (New York: Holt, Rinehart & Winston, Inc., 1965); William Kornhauser, *The Politics of Mass Society* (New York: Free Press, 1959); Gino Germani, "Social Change and Intergroup Conflicts," *The New Sociology: Essays in Social Science and Social Theory in Honor of C. Wright Mills,* ed. by Irving Louis Horowitz (New York: Oxford University Press, 1965), pp. 391-408.

24. "The consequences for society of the unbalance between the development of technical and of social skill have been disastrous. If our social skills had advanced step by step with our technical skills, there would not have been another European war." Mayo, *The Social Problems of an Industrial Civilization,* p. 23.

25. For Lewin's attempt to account for the differences in American and German character using such concepts, see *Resolving Social Conflicts,* pp. 3-70.

The Resolution of Tension and the
Strategies of Conflict

Besides the fact that those committed to realpolitik
and tension theory approach the subject of conflict's
causes from substantially different directions, it is also
interesting to note that they disagree about what count
as scientifically relevant research questions. The early
German and American sociologists devoted most of
their attention to describing the strategies used by opponents to overcome the resistance of their foes. And in
so doing, they began with the Machiavellian assumption that regardless of the ends such as peace, *Kultur*,
love, and justice that are purportedly sought by political actors, the techniques they use to achieve these
ends are identical. Gumplowicz, for example told his
readers that

> at present politics is strife after power. Each state, party,
> and faction, even every individual strives after power with
> all the means at command. Material means are sup-
> plemented with as cogent reasons as possible. Such
> reasons and arguments are called the theory of politics.
> But where is the criterion of correctness? From the stand-
> point of success, when the fact has been accomplished, the
> policy which succeeded is recognized as right. . . . So ulti-
> mately, greater might is the better policy, as things stand
> now.[26]

Since this is true, then at least in the short run, the
demands of morality are basically incompatible with
the demands of politics. Bringing the two together, sel-
dom removes barbarism or violence. Instead it simply
scandalizes ethical purposes and animating aims. "Do
we not see," Weber asked his audience in a speech in

26. Gumplowicz, *Outlines*, p. 164.

Munich in 1918, "that the Bolshevik and the Spartacist ideologies bring about exactly the same results as any militaristic dictator just because they use this political means? ' . . . All that take the sword shall perish by the sword'. . . . Hence the Sermon on the Mount."[27]

Tension theorists have generally overlooked the whole area of tactical planning in conflict, and thus have failed to come to grips with many of the dilemmas of human existence that the sociologists of conflict appreciated so well. Instead they have concerned themselves almost exclusively with what they like to call "tension reduction." In other words they have in the language of the contributors to the UNESCO Tension Project focused their full attention on the single question of "how can the social sciences be used in the contemporary world for the prevention or control of tensions which are harmful to peace?"[28]

In various papers Jessie Bernard has argued that sociologists should direct their efforts once again to developing a sociology of conflict in the tradition of realpolitik.[29] Robert Angell, a well-known scholar whose work seems to fit the category of tension theory, has countered this idea with such statements as the following: "But presumably we are not interested in a theory of conflict *per se*. We are interested in it mainly to understand how to avoid the most serious type of conflict—war."[30] The techniques proposed by such per-

27. Weber, *Essays*, p. 119. Cf. Gumplowicz, *Outlines*, p. 229.
28. "Preface," *The Nature of Conflict: Studies on the Sociological Aspects of International Tension*, p. 12.
29. Jessie Bernard, "The Theory of Games of Strategy as a Modern Sociology of Conflict," *AJS* LIV (March, 1954): 411-24.
30. Robert C. Angell, "Discovering Paths to Peace," *The Nature of Conflict: Studies on the Sociological Aspects of International Tension*, p. 205. Dorwin Cartwright, one of Lewin's colleagues and students has argued that one of the main reasons for the establishment of the Center for Group Dynamics was to develop techniques for tension reduction: "Society's skills in reducing inter-group conflicts are pitifully inadequate. . . . Much more specific infor-

sons as Angell to reduce the psychological tensions that are believed to give rise to disruptive conflicts have not been limited by interprofessional parochialism. The following quotation by Gordon Allport is typical of the open-mindedness that tension theorists have demonstrated toward any paradigm that seems to promise some success in reducing the probability of war:

> It is unprofitable to ask whether individual or social factors are basic. The question is rather, how can we effectively interrupt the dysgenic cycle now underway? To attack economic and social barriers to understanding is not incompatible with the social psychiatric approach. Each procedure aids and supplements the other. Both are needed.[31]

With this sort of attitude it is not surprising to observe tension theorists seeking to alter what they take to be aggressive behaviors and psychologies of their subjects by any number of otherwise theoretically unrelated means. Thus, for example, there is the large body of research relating to the direct manipulation of the conflict-prone person's mind through psychoanalytic counseling, the use of cognitive dissonance, and finally through the mass media. Furthermore, there are all the indirect techniques of manipulating the social situation to guide the psychological energies of persons into "constructive" directions. Here, the substantial

mation is needed about forces producing inter-group conflict or harmony and about the ways in which they may be controlled. . . . Until we can know concretely and finally the consequences flowing from efforts to reduce inter-group conflict there is only slight hope that we shall hit upon an effective course of social action. To this end the Center together with a variety of agencies have conducted research projects in close collaboration with action programs." Dorwin Cartwright, *The Center for Group Dynamics* (Ann Arbor: Institute for Social Research, 1950), quoted in Bernard, "The Sociological Study on Conflict," p. 60.

31. Gordon Allport, "The Role of Expectance," *Tensions That Cause Wars*, quoted in "Preface," *The Nature of Conflict: Studies on the Sociological Aspects of International Tension*, pp. 13-14.

number of leadership effectiveness studies, group cohesiveness and participation research, lines of communications experiments, and all the attempts to cultivate Human Relations skills in management come to mind. Although the findings of such studies are by and large still inconclusive, they comprise the subject matter for most social psychology textbooks.[32] And they unambiguously indicate the importance of the goal of conflict resolution to certain members of the sociological profession.

The Outcomes of Tension and of Conflict

The question that naturally arises at this point is why should tension theorists avoid speaking about conflict as the unraveling of carefully laid plans, and concentrate their energies almost exclusively on tension reduction? One answer that immediately suggests itself is that the choice of scientific problems peculiar to realpolitik, and tension theory is merely an outgrowth and reflection of their opposing ideas concerning the causes of conflict. Thus, if as a tension theorist an analyst uses a model of irrational man to explain a person's participation in conflict, it may simply be difficult for him to suddenly discard this assumption and invoke instead a rationalistic notion of decision-making once that person is fully engaged in the fight. Or if, on the contrary, he begins by invoking a thoroughgoing rationalistic interpretation of conflict dynamics, it may be inconsistent for him to resort to a nonrational psychological theory to account for the existence of conflict in the first place.

Upon closer analysis, however, it appears that this

32. For example, see Paul F. Secord and Carl W. Backman, *Social Psychology* (New York: McGraw-Hill, 1964).

query can not be cleared up as effortlessly as this. In the first place, it does not necessarily follow that if a sociologist employs the rational calculus to understand why an actor partakes in power struggles that it is therefore difficult for him to speak about either nonrational political factors or conflict resolution. For example, even though significant aspects of Max Weber's sociology were written from the perspective of realpolitik, especially as it was developed by Oppenheimer, he had an explicit appreciation of how military strategists and propagandists consciously exploit the completely irrational loves, fears, and hatreds of soldiers and citizenry in order to mobilize their active participation in the war effort.[33] And it was the same Arthur Bentley whose work fits as easily as Weber's into realpolitik, who also was one of the first American social scientists to use the term "tension reduction" and to propose a scientific policy for realizing this goal.

On the other hand, it is certainly not logically impossible for tension theorists, even with their stress on the nonrational dimension of political life, to talk about its strategic aspects. There is a distinction common in political sociology that can be usefully applied at this point between the elite of a conflict group who are responsible both for making tactical decisions and assuring that they are obeyed, and the mass membership who gladly carry out the directives of their leaders. In this context it seems that the main reason why tension theorists write so little about strategic thinking is sim-

33. Says Weber, "The history of the last decade, especially the relations between Germany and France, shows the prominent effect of this irrational element [i.e. nationalism] in all political foreign relations. The sentiment of prestige is able to strengthen the ardent belief in the actual existence of one's might, for this belief is important for positive self-assurance in case of conflict. Therefore, all those having vested interests in the political structure tend systematically to cultivate this prestige sentiment." Weber, *Essays,* pp. 160-61.

ply because while they are relatively uninterested in elites, they are almost morbidly fascinated by the ordinary participant in conflict. They are by and large concerned, for example, not with the man who organizes a lynching or coldly plans a strike, but with the individual who has a propensity to join the mob, the fervent rope bearer or picket. It makes little difference whether the work of Mayo, Fromm, DeGrazia, Arendt, Nisbet, or Lipset is cited. In their discussions of intolerance and authoritarianism, they write without exception, not about factory management, military generals, or revolutionary elites, but about the anomic mass man, the little man who is presumably unconsciously swept up in the passion of nationalism and liberation. Furthermore, from Horkheimer to Kornhauser, when elites are rarely addressed, it is generally in terms of the fearful possibility that they will rationally and calculatedly capitalize on the psychological tensions of the isolated, frustrated individual to goad him to engage in disruptive conflicts. In other words, instead of being unable of necessity to account for the rational component of political interaction, invariably, whenever tension theorists shift their attention from the mass man to the elite, they adopt an outlook that is virtually indistinguishable from the old line advocates of realpolitik.

The question posed at the beginning of this section then, might be better rephrased to ask, why is it that when theorizing about conflict contemporary sociologists have concentrated upon the subconscious needs of the mass man instead of the intelligent machinations of their leaders? One response that is commonly proferred is that those in positions of power require both information on the irrational psychological desires of their subjects and simple manipulative techniques to more effectively control them. Upon holding out the promise of lucrative grants for scientific research on such subjects, these authorities have discovered that sociologists are willing to alter their theoretical outlook to accord with their demands. "The tone of this demand is," as one popular protrayal has it, "universally on how to adjust and how to manipulate. The great stress is not on complex understanding, but on simple, but effective techniques. It should not be surprising that those who create the demand for, and pay for, sociology, should exert great influence in determining not only its structure, but also its content."[34]

This is not the place to attempt even a summarization of the vast literature dealing with sociology's relationship to, and collusion with the dominant sectors of American life. However, if only for purposes of clarification, brief mention should perhaps be made of some of the more revealing ties that link the major schools of tension theory with particular institutional-funding sources. It is commonly known, for example, that the Harvard Department of Industrial Research that sponsored Mayo and company's early studies on the morale of workers was established in 1926 concurrently with Small's and Bentley's forecasts of impending proletariat revolution. And there is little doubt but that the idea of financing empirical inquiries into the emotional needs of workers was motivated, if not by management's outright fear of socialism, then at least by their mundane desire to increase productivity. It must also be recognized that in this same vein Lewin's Center for Group Dynamics, originally at M. I. T., was almost solely dependent for many years for its fiscal sustenance upon the good will of big business. Add to this the fact that the Defense Department has been since World War II, a prime source of money for tension-oriented studies in communications, leadership,

34. Al Szymanski, "Toward a Radical Sociology," *Sociology in American Society,* ed. by New University Conference (Chicago: 1971), p. 9.

and mass media effectiveness, then it might be concluded that therefore tension theory itself is mainly a product of the practical concerns of powerful persons.

But even if a completely convincing demonstration of the manner in which the findings of tension research are compatible with the interests of governmental, military, and business elites could be presented, this would not be sufficient to explain the appeal of this theoretical perspective to its developers. The main reason for this is that these same elites have found realpolitik in its mathematical formalization as "game theory,"[35] and the field of "political behavior," which, at least according to its representatives, derives its basic assumptions from Bentley's *The Process of Government*,[36] equally as valuable for their purposes as tension theory. On the one hand, computerized simulations of international confrontations, or to use the jargon of the game theorists, "scenarios," have provided a seemingly scientific basis for American foreign policy decisions, and have thus lent them an aura of legitimacy in the eyes of potential critics.[37] On the other

35. Although much more mathematically sophisticated than traditional realpolitik, game theory shares with this basic perspective both the assumption of the rationality of the opponents involved in a game, and a concern with strategies they can use to maximize their rewards and minimize their costs. It has found a positive reception in such civilian "think tanks" as the Rand Corporation and the Hudson Institute, which are charged with developing a foreign policy that will maximize American global interests in the face of "nuclear blackmail" and guerrilla "subversion." For a critical description of work by what he calls the "new civilian militarists," see Irving Louis Horowitz, *Games, Strategies, and Peace,* Beyond Deterrence Series (American Friends Service Committee, 1963).

36. For example, see David Truman, *The Governmental Process* (New York: Columbia University Press, 1951). The work of Peter Odegard, Donald Blaidsell, Oliver Garceau, and the research on voting patterns and opinion formation by Paul F. Lazarsfeld and William McPhee all seem to fall within the interest group paradigm as it was originally developed by Bentley.

37. For some classic examples of the use of the trappings of game theory to justify possible military strategies, see Herman Kahn, *Thinking About the*

hand, what has been dubbed "the behavioral revolution in politics" has resulted in an imposing body of administratively serviceable information on everything from voting patterns and public opinion to prejudice attitudes. Thus on the surface, there seems to be little in the nature of the funding agency alone to determine a grant recipient's choice of one frame of reference, e.g. tension theory or realpolitik, over another. Business executives, defense planners, and welfare bureaucrats are probably all equally capable of utilizing to their advantage any theoretical point of view that social scientists can invent.[38]

In addition to this, there is very little evidence to support the claim that tension theorists are any less "liberal" or more committed to the "status quo" than were the early American sociologists of conflict. It is true that while Ward, Small, Park, and Bentley can be associated with the Progressive movement, it is difficult to identify Mayo, Fromm, or Lipset with a similar reformist crusade. But it must not be forgotten that no matter how "radical" the proposals of the Progressives were in the nineteen twenties, their advocates understood their political vocation to be the *defense* of small-town, Protestant, bourgeoisie values from revolutionary forces, and not their overthrow. Their preeminent task was to protect and extend the notion

---

Unthinkable (New York: Avon Books, 1968), and his *On Escalation* (Baltimore, Maryland: Penguin Books, 1968).

38. In light of these observations on game theory and political behaviorism, it might be added that the apparent "shift" in sociology of which so many of its critics have spoken, from the realpolitik of its founders to tension theory, may be nothing more than an effect of the professionalization of social inquiry into sociology on the one hand, and political science on the other. In the latter field realpolitik, although in a domesticated form digestible to mdidle class audiences, was flourishing in the work of its most eminent theoreticians, Almond, Key, Dahl, and Truman; at exactly the same time, the 50s and 60s, that sociologists were decrying the absence of studies on conflict, power, and decision making, in their own profession.

they shared of the cooperative Christian democratic community, to create a national group whose solidarity is grounded on principles of the American Creed. But such a goal is not completely alien to e.g. the human relations sociologists, students of Elton Mayo who have advocated the establishment of a community of "spontaneous cooperation" in the otherwise dehumanizing impersonal factory situation as a solution both to individual unhappiness and social conflict. And it is certainly not inconsistent with Lewin and his school's well-studied proposition that democratic participation is not only the most effective situation for the realization of group ends, but the most conducive to high morale among group members. Like the early American sociologists of conflict, those I have listed as tension theorists have repeatedly expressed in their writings their revulsion to totalitarianism of either the right or the left. To a person, they support such ideas as equality of opportunity, private property, and the various bourgeoisie freedoms, exactly as did Ward, Small, Park, and Bentley. Even Jessie Bernard, who is otherwise fairly critical of tension theory, has admitted that,

> perhaps the first impression one gets from a survey of the programme of research based on the social psychological approach to conflict in the United States is the tremendous amount of idealism and goodwill it seems to represent. Here are men apparently urgently serious about hatreds, hostilities, prejudices, violence, and equally serious about applying science to the problem of eliminating them. They are hopeful that science may in time find a way to render peace and love or altruism within reach of men. They are men of faith, liberals in the old tradition.[39]

Some pages earlier, I began this section by asking the question, why is it that modern sociologists in their

---

39. Bernard, "The Sociological Study of Conflict," p. 62.

research on conflict have spent their energies inquiring into tension reduction to the exclusion of conflict tactics. Several alternative hypotheses were offered as possible explanations for this finding, but were all rejected in turn for various reasons. It seems to me that notwithstanding the fact that it may be hard for an analyst with an abiding appreciation of man's irrational nature to speak about strategic reasoning, and even granting that it has been financially rewarding for sociologists to construct inventories of human tensions and psychological control techniques for use by powerful elites, the most convincing interpretation of tension sociologists' deep interest in tension reduction is their phobia of social conflict.

It is true that the early American proponents of realpolitik were originally motivated to adopt the perspective they did because of their concern over the possibility that the social order that they had been brought up to believe in was threatened by domestic power struggles. But they also recognized that conflict was a dialectical process that had created, in spite of its violence, law and the conditions for a semblance of moral action. And they had an optimistic faith that it would eventually produce such strict regulations as to transform power struggles into mere verbal disputes. "Conflict," Simmel told them, "is . . . designed to resolve divergent dualisms, . . . it is a way of achieving some kind of unity."[40] If one party simply has as its goal the annihilation of his enemy, then conflict "does approach the marginal case of assassination in which the admixture of unifying elements is almost zero."[41] But such situations, he reassured them, are rare. More commonly there are found, even among the most deadly of enemies, limitations governing the amount of violence

40. Simmel, *Conflict and the Web of Group Affiliations,* p. 26.
41. Ibid., p. 27.

they can do to one another. "This formal type of relationship is most widely realized in the enslavement —instead of the extermination—of the imprisoned enemy."[42]

Tension theorists do not seem to share with the fathers of their profession this same confidence that out of nature, red in tooth and claw, can civilization grow. In their minds, social strife is either equivalent to, or at least a harbinger of catastrophe. Typical of the pessimistic evaluations tension theorists make of conflict is the following statement by Mayo. It is significant because it appears to be addressed to exactly the same type of conflict that was several decades earlier praised by the American and German sociologists of conflict for its constructive and positive consequences:

> The other symptom of disruption in a modern industrial society relates itself to that organization of groups at a lower level than the primitive. . . . It is unfortunately completely characteristic of industrial societies that we know that various groups when formed are not eager to cooperate wholeheartedly with other groups. On the contrary, their attitude is usually that of wariness or hostility. It is by this road that a society sinks into a condition of *statis*—a confused struggle of pressure groups, power blocs, which . . . heralds the approach of disaster.[43]

With this negativistic attitude toward power struggles, it is not surprising that tension theorists should agree with Elton McNeil that social psychologists turn their attention to developing viable means of reducing the tensions that cause conflicts in the first place. Because man finally has the capacity to exterminate his entire race in the pursuit of selfish and shortsighted goals, then

the urgency of the need for a modern-day solution to the

42. Ibid.
43. Mayo, *The Social Problems of an Industrial Civilization,* pp. 7-8.

puzzle of conflict seems now, as it has in every age to be incredibly great. If the benefits of our historical heritage are nothing but a peculiarly human illusion, then we must search for something more palatable than the bitter and ineffective pills of disastrous human experience.[44]

Realpolitik, Tension, War, and Revolution

No person who theorizes about conflict can have his work understood if it is looked at out of the context of the political situation in which he lives and writes. It is very unlikely that it was just a coincidence that the realpolitik of every German and American scholar whose notions were detailed in earlier chapters was either developed before World War I, or drew upon sources that were composed prior to that watershed of history. The personal experiences of these persons clearly confirmed their belief that even war, the most primitive of all forms of political interaction, in spite of its obvious cruelty, did indeed produce social solidarity. It was through a contest of violent power that the corporate unity of the United States was finally guaranteed. And in Germany too, five years after the Civil War, the question of its existence as a state was decided not through debate, but by the force of arms. But this is not all. With the possible exception of Napoleon's escapades, international conflict had for many decades, worked to preserve the European society of nations by maintaining the balance of power among sovereign peoples. War "was not," says John Herz, contrasting the situation then with what appears to be the case now, "a process of physical or political annihilation but a contest of power in which interests [e.g. prestige and wealth], but not the existence, of the

44. McNeil, "The Nature of Aggression," p. 14.

contestants were at stake."[45] In addition to this, to Hegel, Ranke, Treitschke, Ratzenhofer, and Weber, their invocations of Machiavelli's doctrines notwithstanding, war was collectively thought of as a gentleman's affair, limited not only in reference to its ends, but more importantly, in terms of its means. Essentially they viewed war in the same manner as one might describe the individual combat in the dueling fraternities of which several of them were members. One could receive grave injuries as did Weber and Ratzenhofer, yet the object of the engagement was not to kill the opponent, but merely to "defeat" him in a ritualistically defined way, by using techniques strictly governed by rules. War then, like other sporting events was not seen as a condition of pure anarchy, but in fact as a deftly planned form of mutual collaboration between persons who call one another enemies: The contestants agree on certain definitions of participation and nonparticipation, they agree to limit their strategies to include only certain weapons, they agree when to begin as well as end the contest, and they agree on the division of prizes and trophies after the game has been played. Simmel summarized the peculiar point of view of realpolitik when he said that "one unites in order to fight, and one fights under the mutually recognized control of norms and rules."[46] Even Ward, who had fought in the most bloody of nineteenth century confrontations, the War between the States, and who himself was severely wounded at Chancelorsville, was able to write without fear of contradiction that "today there is a code of 'civilized warfare' and any nation or race that violates it is considered uncivilized. Not only this, but in fighting un-

---

45. John H. Herz, "The Territorial State in International Relations," *War and Its Prevention*, ed. by Amitai Etzioni and Martin Wenglinsky (New York: Harper & Row Pub., 1970), p. 48.

46. Simmel, *Conflict and the Web of Group Affiliations*, p. 35.

civilized races, civilized nations must conform to this code."[47]

The most telling illustration of the political optimism of the early American sociologists of conflict is found in their unanimous consensus that the path of history is progressing from militarism, robbery, despotism, and slavery, to peace, exchange, democracy, and rational governmental administration. From the conquest state to the culture state of equality and harmony, Ratzenhofer told his readers, this is the direction that the motor of social conflict is driving humanity. Or using a different metaphysic, Spencer described how the Darwinian-like struggle for existence is moving man from a condition of war and rudimentary economics, to solidarity and industrialism. For men today, such notions seem almost pathetically naive. We know from experience that it is exactly those highly industrialized, democratic, and bureaucratically organized nations and not "uncivilized peoples" that have not only an increased appetite for war, but also have the instruments for carrying it out in such a way that even pessimists like Gumplowicz could not have anticipated. "Europe," as Raymond Aron has told his sober audience, knows today that industry, far from preventing war, gives it a limitless scope. Consciously or not, contemporary philosophers of history have made this fact central in their thought."[48]

Tension theory is a product of the Century of Total War. It is a perspective that has evolved coterminously as war and civil strife have appeared to men to change from highly regulated fights, to processes of complete devastation. Up to the First World War, even conflicts involving hundreds of thousands of participants took

47. Ward, *Pure Sociology*, p. 450.
48. Raymond Aron, *The Century of Total War* (Boston: The Beacon Press, 1963), p. 56.

place in a setting of technological and organizational limitations and often within at least implicitly understood "rules of the game." But the limitations on war's destructiveness that both an undeveloped physical science and unsophisticated administrative theory afforded men in the nineteenth century, are largely absent today. It has become technically possible for the first time in the twentieth century for states to enlist their entire populations in the war effort and for scientists to construct implements whose capacity for violence is virtually unlimitled.[49] Furthermore, the opponents in modern warfare, unlike the European nations that the early sociologists cited for their examples, commonly represent widely divergent cultures. Consequently, they find it increasingly difficult to agree as to what count as appropriate goals in power struggles, let alone on what are the meanings of "reward" and "cost" in social strife. But without shared criteria for measuring their respective strengths, and devoid of a basis upon which to anticipate one another's responses to purported threats and parries, then even assuming the contestants in contemporary war are rational, the probability of routinizing their conflict into more predictable and thus less violent directions has decreased since the eighteen hundreds.[50] With many of the structural safeguards regulating conflict that the German historians and sociologists took for granted now disappearing, it is not o.ld that men of especially liberal conscience, might find themselves no longer content with merely describing the possible strategies of power

49. For a compilation of several excellent papers on this subject, see Hans Speier, *Social Order and the Risks of War* (New York:, George W. Stewart, Pub. Inc., 1952).
50. For the classic study on the difficulties of communicating threats and promises in a "mixed-motive game," see Thomas C. Schelling, *The Strategy of Conflict* (New York: Oxford University Press, 1963).

struggles, but rather engaged in attempts to control those conditions giving rise to conflicts altogether.

For sophisticated persons observing, and in some cases being victimized in an age of total war and revolution, those like Bettelheim, for example, who experienced first hand Nazi concentration camps, or those like Arendt and Fromm who escaped a similar fate only through good fortune, the claim that it is a form of interaction between conscious and rational persons as realpolitik does, probably stands out at once as contrary to the actual "facts" of the situation. To claim that reasonable men are capable at the same time of relinquishing the responsibility for their own action to a political elite, and then engaging in the detached, unemotional extermination of their enemy, might appear to many to be a self-contradiction. For thinkers of liberal persuasion, with a faith in reason's liberating and civilizing potentiality, to explain the horror of it with reference to the category of reason, would be unthinkable. Rather, they might hold that there must be some not completely conscious, perhaps even irrational needs in modern man that would goad him to construct and then to use the techniques of terror that have now become commonplace in the twentieth century. To them either the vocabulary of neo-Freudian psychology with its appreciation of the ultimately nonrational motivational basis for behavior or the idea of human action as a function of subconscious cognitive imbalances, might seem to offer a more fruitful account of modern political man than the notion of the dispassionate actor coolly weighing different tactics in terms of their utility to achieve concrete ends. It was these scholars then, who first began after World War I (and then with increasing frequency during the Stalin regime, the precipitous growth of totalitarian Communism, and the successful rise of fascist movements) to interpret participation in war and revolution with reference to such theories as mass society, frustration-aggression, and mental dissonance. In other words, it was they who became what are today known as the tension theorists.

Some Concluding Points

To say that tension theory has had its source in liberalism's revulsion to the totalitarian violence of modern conflict, is not to claim that its hypotheses are true or even that it provides workable techniques for resolving these conflicts. In fact it seems that in spite of the perfectly sincere purposes that have motivated the development of tension theory as a program for effective social control, it has glaring weaknesses.

To begin with, while it is certainly true that tension theorists have an understanding of the social context that presumably causes psychological tensions (for instance collective frustrations, mass society, work alienation, and "field restrictiveness") their basic unit of analysis is the individual. They are concerned primarily with helping the individual to cope with, to adjust to, to accomodate himself to the situation in which he lives, so that he will have no need to be hostile to others, so that he will have no desire to persecute minority peoples, or submit himself to a demogogue. Unfortunately, however, this emphasis is misplaced, for it is not the individual as such who engages in political turbulence, but the group; and not just the small "combat group" or informal "work group," but the army and the party; and not even these in an age of totalitarianism, but complete nations and races. It is not necessary to adopt the methodological position that groups have emergent properties that in principle are not reducible to individual behaviors to recognize that in social psychology today, the theoretical gap between group concepts on the one hand and individual concepts on the other is still extremely large. The relationships, if any, that exist between inner peace and inter-group harmony, between psychological and social tension, between individual prowess and national military preparedness, or between individual hostility and racial aggressiveness, all still remain to be discovered. It seems then, if those who are truly interested in lowering the incidence of international and interracial violence are to come up with something more effective than the short-term alteration of individual attitudes through propaganda, psychoanalytic counseling, and the manipulation of primary group structures, they will have to shift their immediate attention from the deviant individual to the corporate group struggling for power.

Yet tension theorists will find it difficult to even focus upon the corporate group because traditionally they have approached conflict as a political candidate might approach his constituency, that is, with the assumption that in conflict all men are of equal explanatory significance. It is obviously the case, however, that in conflicts like war and revolution, particularly in the twentieth century with the new feedback and communications systems that have substantially augmented the possibility for centralized control of large aggregates of persons by small elites, this form of theoretical liberalism is completely without justification. As mentioned above, it is almost axiomatic in political science that there are those who coldly make the binding decisions to engage in combat on the basis of crude cost accounting principles, and then those others, "the masses," who carry out the commands with little if any awareness or concern with the larger strategic issues. And it appears that if social scientists are to play any role at all in putting an end to violent group conflict, they will have of necessity to influence the tactical thinking of the "deciders," rather than exhaust their time and money gathering information on those who simply follow their orders. But in order to persuade the decision-makers not to resort to organized violence, peace researchers will at a minimum have to demonstrate that its use is unprofitable in the achievement of their interests. (I say, "at a minimum," because of course there are some groups with a vested interest in violence itself). If this is true, then it follows that the language of realpolitik would provide the natural vehicle for the presentation of this research. Already the paradigm of realpolitik, with its assumption of the rationality of opponents each with a certain repertoire of "moves," is being appropriated from the military tacticians and being applied to the study of the effectiveness of nonviolent resistance as a form of national defense, the relative costs and rewards of unilateral disarmament, and the profitability of nonviolence as a means for revolution.[51] Paradoxically, then, although the rudiments of realpolitik arose among those who looked upon war as a glorious instrument of human progress, it might provide a frame of reference for the conduct of research into the question of how to do away with war altogether.

51. For example, see Richard Ofshe, "The Effectiveness of Pacifist Strategies," *The Journal of Conflict Resolution* XV (June, 1971): 261-69 for a discussion of this point plus a bibliography of some of the latest research. See also, American Friends Service Committee, *In Place of War* (New York: Grossman Pub., 1967).

Appendix: Letter from Everett C. Hughes to James Aho, July 8, 1970

8 July 1970

Dear Mr. Aho:

I don't think there is any mystery about how Park came to refer to German sociologists or any other, for that matter. He was a man who read widely in three languages: English, German and French—morely widely perhaps in German than in French. I have a good many of his books written by German and other European scholars. You know, I am sure, that he took his Ph.D. at Heidelberg, but that he had also studied at Strassburg which at that time was a German university. You should remember also that when Park was doing his basic reading, sociology was not so organized as it is now and the people who were developing what we now call sociology read widely in a good many fields. In Park's thesis there is a good deal of reference to the geographers in Europe and especially in Germany. In the Park and Burgess *Introduction* there is an immense bibliography at the end of each chapter. You will see that geographers figure prominently in them. There was a tremendous interest in Germany in the relation of the so-called Germanic races to the other races. When Gumplowicz spoke of race relations, he was not talking about black and white or European unpigmented peoples in relation to the more pigmented peoples of the east. He was talking of relations basically within Europe: between Slavs, Germans, etc. And he interpreted politics as the result of conquering of some races by others; the conquering race became the feudal lords, collecting tribute from the others. Park was familiar with this literature and made a good deal of use of it. We who studied with him at Chicago—if we did our homework—read Gumplowicz, Oppenheimer, Gerland, and others. My wife and I translated for Park a good deal of human geography written by the French geographers of the early 1920's. They also saw geography in part as the relations between peoples. Some peoples, said the human geographer, moved more widely and freely than others. They occupied land in an active way by conquest, trade, and the like, whereas other people were passive: they sat down, occupied the land, bred children and animals and kept on no matter what trade went on in the larger world. These were all cases of the relations of peoples. They were the relations of races as races then conceived. More recently the physical anthropologists have tried to clean up our language in this regard and to limit the term race in its usage.

As for the general question of Park, then, the answer, is that he early in his career (most certainly from the time when he went to Germany which was in 1899, I believe,) read widely in German literature. It is not a question of any individual's influence at all. It is a question of his own search for knowledge and for the sources of knowledge and of ideas.

You must have noticed that the Park and Burgess *Introduction to Sociology* has a special chapter on conflict. A good many sociologists were inclined and still are inclined to run away from the topic of conflict. Park, you must know, studied with Simmel in Europe and owned an early copy of Simmel's *Soziologie*. (I now have that copy.) But, remember also that Albion Small had studied economic history in Germany. He came back to this country and took his Ph.D. in Welfare Economics at Hopkins. He started the *American Journal of Sociology* in, I believe, 1895. He published some of Simmel's articles before the publication of Simmel's volume of *Soziologie* appeared in Germany. Simmel was known to sociologists in the United States as early as he was known in Europe. It is not a case of a cultural lag and the reputation of a man gradually crossing the ocean. Simmel was part and parcel of Chicago sociology as soon as in Europe itself. Albion Small evidently knew him and his work or he would not have published translations of his articles back before 1910 as he did.

Note also that Small made wide use of German literature in all of his lectures. His lectures had a certain germanic quality in their very structure. I had a course of his in the fall of 1923 and perhaps again in the winter—January—1924. In these he read letters from himself to other sociologists and from other sociologists of the time to him concerning what sociology should be. I do not remember that any of these letters were from German sociologists, but they may well have been. He read correspondence with Lester Ward, especially, in this country. Small also gave a course on Marx at that time. A point to be made here is this: that while certain people undoubtedly developed theories in Europe which were then brought over here, the actual development of sociology itself was taking place here as early as there and very soon the situation was somewhat reversed. More was going on here than in Europe. You do not specifically mention Max Weber in your letter. Park knew Weber's work; indeed, I have Park's three volumes of Weber's work on the *Sociology of Religion*. But Weber's work had not been put out in any corrected form until the 1920's, after the Park and Burgess volume was published. An additional thing about Park is that he was a very sociable man. He talked to people everywhere. Perhaps it came from his years of experience as a newspaper reporter. At the University of Chicago when I knew him, he would one day be at lunch in the Faculty Club with Emerson, the world expert on the social life of insects. On another day he would be talking to Allee who studied the social life and pecking order of hens. He also was close to Mead, to Ames, and to many others. He took ideas wherever he could find them and would go on in a very speculative way, proving the other man's ideas and facts, without rancor and always with the aim of learning. This quality of the man is more important than the particular source of this or that or the other idea. No doubt Park talked a good deal to Albion Small when he came to Chicago and certainly it is clear that it was he who influenced Small to direct the whole group of social scientists towards study of the city, starting with the city of Chicago. The evidence on that is quite clear. In this case it was Park who influenced Small rather than the reverse, but I would not rule out any possibility of influence of Small upon Park. Small was already interested in the city and in the problems of city life. I do not remember any great concern of his concerning race relations. W. I. Thomas was invited by Park to a conference on race relations in Tuskegee about 1912. It was there that Thomas apparently met Park and from that meeting eventually there came an invitation to Park to come to the University of Chicago, his first regular academic position. He was 50 years old when he came to Chicago. Thomas was quite concerned with the biological relations between the races as was everyone at that time. I do not think that Thomas had any such knowledge of race relations as Park had, and I would not think of any influence in one direction in this case. Thomas and Park were close friends and colleagues. Certainly in some of Park's work Thomas's ideas come through quite clearly. On the other hand I should think that the relationship was decidedly mutual, not a case of one man influencing the other unilaterally.

You should not overlook Park's very great interest in Darwin. He used Darwin a great deal and in it was the notion not so much of conflict as of unending competition and of the other phenomena that go with it, such as symbiosis. He later applied that idea also to race relations.

I'm afraid my information is not quite the sort you want, but it is the best I can give you. I knew Mr. Park very well indeed for the last twenty years of his life, from 1923 to 1944. He was a man who meditated and reflected on his ideas continually. He never let an idea go without having worked it through very well indeed. Yet he was very interested in the news, in what was going on around him. The joining of these two qualities—the reflective, philosophical quality and the alertness to the news and to what was going on—the combination of these two made a very creative man.

Sincerely yours,
Everett C. Hughes

Bibliography

General Works on German Social and Intellectual History and Particular Studies of the German Sociologists of Conflict

Abel, Theodore. *Systematic Sociology in Germany*. New York: Octagon Books, Inc., 1965.

Antoni, Carlo. *From History to Sociology: The Transition in German Historical Thinking*. Translated and edited by Hayden V. White. Detroit: Wayne State University Press, 1959.

Aron, Raymond. *German Sociology*. Translated by Mary and Thomas Bottomore. New York: The Free Press of Glencoe, 1964.

Barnes, Harry Elmer. "The Struggle of Races and Social Groups as a Factor in the Development of Political and Social Institutions: An Exposition and Critique of the Sociological System of Ludwig Gumplowicz." *Journal of Race Development* IX (April, 1919): 394-419.

Barnes, Harry Elmer and Becker, Howard. *Social Thought from Lore to Science*. 3 vols. New York: Dover Publishing, Inc., 1961.

——— and Becker, Howard, *Social Thought from Lore to Science*. 3 vols. New York: Dover Publishing, Inc., 1961.

Becker, Howard and Smelo, Leon. "Conflict Theories of the Origin of the State." *The Sociological Review* XXIII (July, 1931): 65-79.

Berolzheimer, Fritz. *The World's Legal Philosophies*. Translated by Rachel Szold Jastrow. New York: Macmillan Co., 1924.

320

Bendix, Reinhard. *Max Weber: An Intellectual Portrait.* Garden City, New York: Doubleday & Co., Inc., 1962.

Bramson, Leon. *The Political Context of Sociology.* Princeton, New Jersey: Princeton University Press, 1961.

Coker, Francis W. *Recent Political Thought.* New York: Appleton-Century-Croft, 1934.

Honigsheim, Paul. *On Max Weber.* Translated by Joan Rytina. New York: Free Press, 1968; Michigan State University, East Lansing, Michigan: Social Science Research Bureau, 1968.

———. "The Sociological Doctrines of Franz Oppenheimer: An Agrarian Philosophy of History and Social Reform." *Introduction to the History of Sociology.* Edited by Harry Elmer Barnes. Chicago: University of Chicago Press, 1965.

Iggers, Georg. *The German Conception of History.* Middletown, Connecticut: Wesleyan University Press, 1968.

Kohn, Hans. *The Mind of Germany: The Education of a Nation.* New York: Harper & Row, 1960.

———. *Prophets and Peoples: Studies in Nineteenth Century Nationalism.* New York: Macmillan Co., 1947.

Marcuse, Herbert. *Reason and Revolution: Hegel and the Rise of Social Theory.* London: Routledge, Kegan & Paul Ltd., 1968.

Mayer, J. P. *Max Weber and German Politics.* London: Faber and Faber, 1957.

Meinecke, Friedrich. *Machiavellism.* Translated by Douglas Scott. New York: Frederick A. Praeger, 1965.

Nisbet, Robert. *The Sociological Tradition.* New York: Basic Books, 1966.

Oppenheimer, Franz. "Tendencies in Recent German Sociology." *The Sociological Review* XXIV (January, 1932): 1-13; (April-July, 1932): 125-37; (October, 1932): 249-60.

Parsons, Talcott. *The Structure of Social Action.* Glencoe, Illinois: Free Press, 1949.

Philippovich, Eugen von. "The Infusion of Socio-Political Ideas into the Literature of German Politics." *AJS* XVIII (September, 1912): 145-99.

Ross, Edward A. "Turning Towards Nirvana." *Arena* IV (November, 1891): 733-43.

Salomon, Albert. *The Tyranny of Progress.* New York: Noonday Press, 1955.

Schmid, Robert. "Gustav Ratzenhofer: Sociological Positivism and the Theory of Social Interests." *Introduction to the*

History of Sociology. Edited by Harry Elmer Barnes. Chicago: University of Chicago Press, 1965.

Small, Albion W. *Origins of Sociology.* Chicago: University of Chicago Press, 1926.

Von Laue, Theodore H. *Leopold Ranke: The Formative Years.* Princeton, New Jersey: Princeton University Press, 1950.

Willoughby, Westel W. *Prussian Political Philosophy.* New York: D. Appleton & Co., 1918.

Zebrowski, Bernhard. *Ludwig Gumplowicz: Eine Bio-Bibliographie.* Berlin: Prager, 1926.

Writings by the German Sociologists of Conflict and Related Authors Directly Consulted in the Course of Research

Gumplowicz, Ludwig. "An Austrian Appreciation of Lester F. Ward." *AJS* X (March, 1905): 643-53.

———. "Darwinismus in Der Soziologie." *Soziologie und Politik. Ausgewahlte Werke.* Edited by F. Oppenheimer, F. Savorgnan, M. Adler, G. Salomon. Vol. IV. Innsbruck: Universitäts-Verlag Wagner, 1928.

———. "The Letters of Ludwig Gumplowicz to Lester F. Ward." Edited by Bernhard J. Stern. *Sociologus: Zeitschrift für Volkerpsychologie und Soziologie.* Leipzig: C. L. Hirschfeld Verlag, 1933. In German and French.

———. *The Outlines of Sociology.* Translated by Frederick W. Moore. Edited and Introduced by Irving Louis Horowitz. New York: Paine-Whitman, 1963.

———. *"Soziologie: Positive Lehre von den Wechselbeziehungen* by Gustav Ratzenhofer." Review of *Soziologie: Positve Lehre von den Wechselbeziehungen,* by Gustav Ratzenhofer. *AJS* XIV (July, 1908): 101-11.

———. *"Wesen und Zweck der Politik* by Gustav Ratzenhofer." Review of *Wesen und Zweck der Politik* by Gustav Ratzenhofer. *Annals of the American Academy of Political and Social Science* V (July, 1894): 128-36.

Hegel, Georg Wilhelm Friedrich. Hegel's *Philosophy of*

Right. Translated and edited by T. M. Knox. New York: Oxford University Press, 1952.

Ihering, Rudolph von. *The Struggle for Law.* Translated and introduced by John J. Lalor. Chicago: Callaghan & Co., 1915.

Oppenheimer, Franz. "Farm Communities in Eastern Prussia." *Proceedings of the Institute of Public Affairs: Bulletin of the University of Georgia* XXXVI (1936): 121-33.

———. "Japan and Western Europe." *The American Journal of Economics and Sociology* III (1943-44): 539-51; IV (1944-45): 53-56; 239-44.

———. "Principles of Farm Community Organization." *Proceedings of the Institute of Public Affairs: Bulletin of the University of Georgia* XXXVI (1936): 108-20.

———. "Soziologischer Pessimismus." *Die Zukunft* XXIV (1898): 472-79.

———. *The State: Its History and Development Viewed Sociologically.* Translated by John M. Gitterman. New York: Vanguard Press, 1926.

———. "Wages and Trade Unions." *The American Journal of Economics and Sociology* I (1941-42): 45-82.

Ranke, Leopold von. "The Great Powers." *Leopold Ranke: The Formative Years.* Translated by Theodore H. Von Laue. Princeton, New Jersey: Princeton Univesity Press, 1950.

———. "Political Dialogues." *Leopold Ranke: The Formative Years.* Translated by Theodore H. Von Laue. Princeton, New Jersey: Princeton University Press, 1950.

Ratzenhofer, Gustav. Letters of Ratzenhofer to Lester F. Ward. Providence, Rhode Island: Brown University Library. Lester F. Ward Papers. In German.

———. "The Problems of Sociology." Translated by Albion W. Small. *AJS* X (September, 1904): 177-88. Ratzenhofer's address to the 1904 St. Louis Exposition.

———. *Die Sociologische Erkenntnis.* Leipzig: F.A. Brockhaus, 1898.

———. *Soziologie: Positive Lehre von den Menschlichen Wechselbeziehungen.* Leipzig: F. A. Brockhaus, 1907. The introduction to this book was translated by Albion W. Small as "Ratzenhofer's Sociology." *AJS* XII (January, 1908): 433-38.

———. *Wesen und Zweck der Politik.* 3 vols. Leipzig: F.A. Brockhaus, 1893.

Schmoller, Gustav Friedrich von. "Schmoller on Class Conflicts in General." Translated by Albion W. Small. *AJS* XX (1915): 504-31.

Simmel, Georg. *Conflict and the Web of Group Affiliations.* Translated by Kurt Wolff and Reinhard Bendix. New York: Free Press, 1955.

———. Letters of Simmel to Lester F. Ward. Providence, Rhode Island: Brown University Library. Lester F. Ward Papers. In German.

———. *The Sociology of Georg Simmel.* Translated and introduced by Kurt Wolff. New York: Free Press, 1950.

Treitschke, Heinrich von. *Politics.* Translated by Blanche Dugdale and Torben de Bille. Edited and abridged with an introduction by Hans Kohn. New York: Harcourt, Brace & World Inc., 1963.

Weber, Max. *Economy and Society.* 3 vols. Edited, introduced and translated by Guenther Roth and Claus Wittich. New York: Bedminster Press, 1968.

———. *From Max Weber: Essays in Sociology.* Translated, edited and introduced by Hans H. Gerth and C. Wright Mills. New York: Oxford University Press, 1958.

———. *The Methodology of the Social Sciences.* Edited and translated by Edward A. Shils. New York: Free Press of Glencoe, 1949.

———. *Theory of Social and Economic Organization.* Translated by A. M. Henderson and Talcott Parsons. New York: Free Press, 1965.

A Selected List of Works on American Social and Intellectual History

Adams, Henry. *The Education of Henry Adams.* New York: Modern Library, 1931.

Becker, Carl. *The United States: An Experiment in Democracy.* New York: Harper & Bros., 1920.

Berelson, Bernard. *Graduate Education in the United States.* New York: McGraw-Hill Book Co., Inc., 1960.

Burgess, John W. *Reminiscences of an American Scholar.* New York: AMS Press, 1966.

Butler, Nicholas Murray. *Across the Busy Years: Recollec-

tions and Reflections. 2 vols. New York: Charles Scribner's Sons, 1934.

Coser, Lewis. *Masters of Sociological Thought: Ideas in Historical and Social Context.* New York: Harcourt Brace Jovanovich, Inc., 1971.

Curti, Merle. *The Growth of American Thought.* New York: Harper & Bros., 1943.

Dewey, John. *Democracy and Education.* New York: Macmillan & Co., 1916.

Dowling, RE. "Pressure Group Theory: Its Methodological Range," *American Political Science Review* LIX (December, 1960): 944-54.

Ely, Richard T. *Ground Under Our Feet.* New York: Macmillan Co., 1938.

Faris, Robert E. L. *Chicago Sociology, 1920-1932.* San Francisco: Chandler, 1967.

Gabriel, Ralph H. *The Course of American Democratic Thought.* New York: Ronald Press, 1940.

Hale, Myron Q. "The Cosmology of Arthur F. Bentley." *American Political Science Review* LIX (December, 1960): 955-61.

Hall, G. Stanley. *Life and Confessions of a Psychologist.* New York: D. Appleton & Co., 1927.

Hapgood, Hutchins. *A Victorian in the Modern World.* New York: Harcourt, Brace & World, 1939.

Herbst, Jurgen. *The German Historical School in American Scholarship.* Ithaca, New York: Cornell University Press, 1965.

Hofstadter, Richard. *The Age of Reform: From Bryan to F. D. R.* New York: Alfred A. Knopf, 1955.

————. *Social Darwinism in American Thought.* New York: G. Braziller, 1959.

Hofstadter, Richard and Lipset, Seymour M., eds. *Turner and the Sociology of the Frontier.* New York: Basic Books, Inc., 1968.

Kolko, Gabriel. *The Triumph of Conservatism: A Reinterpretation of American History, 1900-1916.* New York: Free Press of Glencoe, 1963.

Kress, Paul Frederick. "The Idea of Process in American Political and Social Science." Unpublished Ph.D. thesis. University of California, Berkeley, 1964.

Leuchtenberg, William E. "Progressivism and Imperialism: The Progressive Movement and American Foreign Policy, 1896-1916." *The Mississippi Valley Historical Review* XXXIX (December, 1952): 483-504.

Martindale, Don. *The Nature and Types of Sociological Theory.* Boston: Houghton Mifflin, 1960.

Matson, Floyd W. *The Broken Image.* New York: George Braziller, 1964.

Merriam, Charles E. *A History of American Political Theories.* New York: Macmillan Co., 1910

Mills, C Wright. "The Professional Ideology of Social Pathologists." *Power, Politics, and People.* Edited by Irving Louis Horowitz. New York: Ballantine Books, 1963.

———. *Power Elite.* New York: Oxford University Press, 1959.

———. *White Collar: The American Middle Classes.* New York: Oxford University Press, 1956.

———. *Sociology and Pragmatism: The Higher Learning in America.* Edited by Irving Louis Horowitz. New York: Oxford University Press, 1966.

Odegard, Peter H. "A Group Basis of Politics: A New Name for an Ancient Myth." *Western Political Quarterly* XI (September, 1958):689-701

Odum, Howard W. *American Sociology: The Story of Sociology in the United States Through 1950.* Toronto: Longmans, 1951.

Potter, David M. *People of Plenty: Economic Abundance and the American Character.* Charles R. Walgreen Lectures. Chicago: University of Chicago Press, 1954.

Robson, Charles B. "The Influence of German Thought on Political Theory in the United States in the Nineteenth Century: An Introductory Study." Unpublished Ph.D. dissertation. University of North Carolina, 1930.

Ross, Edward A. *Seventy Years of It.* New York: D. Appleton-Century Co., 1936.

———. *Social Control.* New York: Macmillan Co., 1901.

Sorokin, Pitirim, *Contemporary Sociological Theories.* New York: Harper and Bros., 1928.

Thomas, W. I. "The Psychology of Race Prejudice." *AJS* IX (March, 1904): 593-611.

Timasheff, Nicholas S. *Sociological Theory: Its Nature and Growth.* New York: Random House, 1967.

Thwing, Charles Franklin. *The American and the German University.* New York: Macmillan Co., 1928.

Turner, Frederick Jackson. *The Frontier in American History.* New York, Chicago and San Francisco: Holt, Rinehart & Winston, Inc., 1967.

Webb, Walter Prescott. *The Great Frontier*. Boston: Hough-
    ton Mifflin Co., 1952.
White, Morton. *Social Thought in America: The Revolt
    Against Formalism*. New York: Viking Press, 1949.
Wilson, R. Jackson. *In Quest of Community: Social
    Philosophy in the United States, 1860-1920*. New York:
    Oxford University Press, 1970.

A Selected List of Biographical Material
on the American Sociologists of Conflict

Barnes, Harry Elmer. "The Place of Albion Woodbury Small
    in Modern Sociology." *AJS* XXXII (July, 1926): 15-44.
————. "Two Representative Contributions of Sociology to
    Political Theory: The Doctrines of William Graham
    Sumner and Lester Frank Ward." *AJS* XXV (Sep-
    tember, 1919): 150-70.
Burgess, Ernest W. "Social Planning and Race Relations."
    *Race Relations: Problems and Theory, Essays in Honor
    of Robert E. Park*. Edited by J. Masouka and Preston
    Valien. Chapel Hill: University of North Carolina
    Press, 1961.
Bentley, Arthur F. "Epilogue." *Life, Language, Law: Essays
    in Honor of Arthur F. Bentley*. Edited by Richard W.
    Taylor. Yellow Springs, Ohio: Antioch Press, 1957.
Burnham, John C. *Lester Frank Ward in American Thought*.
    Washington: Public Affairs Press, 1956.
Chugerman, Samuel. *Lester F. Ward: The American Aristo-
    tle*. Durham, North Carolina: Duke University Press,
    1939.
Commager, Henry Steele, ed. *Lester Ward and the Welfare
    State*. Indianapolis and New York: Bobbs-Merrill Co.,
    1967.
Goodspeed, Thomas W. "Albion Small." *AJS* XXXII (July,
    1926): 1-14.
————. "Albion W. Small." *University Record* XII (n.s.,
    1926): 240-65.
Hughes, Helen MacGill. "Park, Robert E." *International En-
    cyclopedia of the Social Sciences*. 2nd edition. Vol. XI.
Johnson, Charles S. "Robert E. Park: In Memoriam."

Sociology and Social Research XXVIII (May-June, 1944): 354-58.

Krout, Maurice H. "The Development of Small's Sociological Theory." *Journal of Applied Sociology* XI (January, 1927): 216-31.

Park, Robert E. "An Autobiographical Note." *Race and Culture.* Vol. I of *The Collected Papers of Robert Ezra Park.* Edited by Everett C. Hughes et al. Glencoe, Illinois: Free Press, 1950.

Ratner, Sidney. "Arthur F. Bentley, 1879-1957." *Journal of Philosophy* LV (July, 1958): 573-78.

———. "A. F. Bentley's Inquiries into the Behavioral Sciences and Theory of Scientific Inquiry." *Life, Language, Law: Essays in Honor of Arthur F. Bentley.* Edited by Richard W. Taylor. Yellow Springs, Ohio: Antioch Press, 1957.

———. "Introduction." *John Dewey and Arthur F. Bentley: A Philosophical Correspondence.* Edited by Sidney Ratner and Jules Altman. New Brunswick, New Jersey: Rutgers University Press, 1964.

Small, Albion W. "Fifty Years of Sociology in the United States." *AJS* XXI (May, 1916): 721-864.

———. "Lester Frank Ward." *AJS* XIX (July, 1913): 75-78.

Ward, Lester F. *Young Ward's Diary.* Edited by Bernhard J. Stern. New York: G. P. Putnam's Sons, 1935.

A Complete List of Writings by the American Sociologists of Conflict on Conflict and Related Subjects

Bentley, Arthur F. "The Condition of the Western Farmer as Illustrated by the Economic History of a Nebraska Township." *Johns Hopkins University Studies in Historical and Political Science,* 1893.

———. *Makers, Users and Masters in America.* Edited and introduced by Sidney Ratner. Syracuse, New York: Syracuse University Press, 1969.

———. *The Process of Government.* Chicago: University of Chicago Press, 1908.

———. *Relativity in Man and Society.* Bloomington, Indiana: Principia Press, 1926.

————. "Simmel, Durkheim, and Ratzenhofer." *AJS* XXXII (September, 1926): 250-56.

————. "Units of Investigation in the Social Sciences." *Annals of the American Academy of Political and Social Science.* V (May, 1895): 915-41.

Bentley, Arthur F. and Leopold von Wiese. Bentley-von Wiese Correspondence. Lilly Library, Indiana University. Arthur F. Bentley Papers. In Engligh and German.

Park, Robert E. "The Basis of Race Prejudice." *Race and Culture.* Volume I of *The Collected Works of Robert Ezra Park.* Edited by Everett C. Hughes et al. Glencoe, Illinois: Free Press, 1950.

————. "Blood Money of the Congo." *Everybody's Magazine.* XVI (January, 1907): 60-70.

————. "Cultural Conflict and the Marginal Man." *Race and Culture.* Vol. I of *The Collected Works of Robert Ezra Park.* Edited by Everett C. Hughes et al. Glencoe, Illinois: Free Press. 1950.

————. "The Etiquette of Race Relations." *Race and Culture.* Vol. I of *The Collected Works of Robert Ezra Park.* Edited by Everett C. Hughes et al. Glencoe, Illinois: Free Press, 1950.

————. "Human Migration and the Marginal Man." *Race and Culture.* Vol. I of *The Collected Works of Robert Ezra Park.* Edited by Everett C. Hughes et al. Glencoe, Illinois: Free Press, 1950.

————. "A King in Business." *Everybody's Magazine* XV (November, 1906): 624-33.

————. Manuscript Notes on Invasion, Conquest, Migration, Racial Mixture, etc. University of Chicago Library, Park Papers, Box II, Folder 4.

————. "Missions and the Modern World" *Race and Culture.* Vol. I of *The Collected Works of Robert Ezra Park.* Edited by Everett C. Hughes et al. Glencoe, Illinois: Free Press, 1950.

————. "The Nature of Race Relations." *Race and Culture.* Vol. I of *The Collected Works of Robert Ezra Park.* Edited by Everett C. Hughes et al. Glencoe, Illinois: Free Press, 1950.

————. "Our Racial Frontier on the Pacific." *Race and Culture.* Vol. I of *The Collected Works of Robert Ezra Park.* Edited by Everett C. Hughes et al. Glencoe, Illinois: Free Press, 1950.

————. "Politics and the 'Man Farthest Down'." *Race and*

Culture. Vol. I of *The Collected Works of Robert Ezra Park.* Edited by Everett C. Hughes et al. Glencoe, Illinois: Free Press, 1950.

———. "Race Prejudice and Japanese-American Relations." *Race and Culture.* Vol. I of *The Collected Works of Robert Ezra Park.* Edited by Everett C. Hughes et al. Glencoe, Illinois: Free Press, 1950.

———. "Race Relations and Certain Frontiers." *Race and Culture.* Vol. I of *The Collected Works of Robert Ezra Park.* Edited by Everett C. Hughes et al. Glencoe, Illinois: Free Press, 1950.

———. "Racial Ideologies." *Race and Culture.* Vol. I of *The Collected Works of Robert Ezra Park.* Edited by Everett C. Hughes et al. Glencoe, Illinois: Free Press, 1950.

———. "The Terrible Story of the Congo." *Everybody's Magazine* XV (December, 1906): 763-72.

———. "War and Politics." *Society.* Vol. III of *The Collected Works of Robert Ezra Park.* Edited by Everett C. Hughes et al. Glencoe. Illinois: Free Press, 1950.

Park, Robert E. and Ernest W. Burgess. *Introduction to the Science of Sociology.* Chicago: University of Chicago Press, 1921.

Small, Albion W. *Adam Smith and Modern Sociology.* Chicago: University of Chicago Press, 1907.

———. "The Church and Class Conflicts." *AJS* XXIV (March 1919): 481-501.

———. The Conflict of Classes. University of Chicago Library, Small Papers, Box II, Folder 4.

———. *General Sociology.* Chicago: University of Chicago Press, 1905.

———. "The Letters of Albion W. Small to Lester F. Ward." Edited by Bernhard J. Stern. *Social Forces* XII (December, 1933): 163-73.

———. *The Meaning of Social Science.* Chicago: University of Chicago Press, 1910.

———. "*The Process of Government* by Arthur F. Bentley." Review of *The Process of Government* by Arthur F. Bentley. *AJS* XIII (March, 1908): 698-706.

———. ."Sin and Society by Edward A. Ross." Review of *Sin and Society* by Edward A. Ross. *AJS* XIII (January, 1908): 566-568.

———. "Socialism in the Light of Social Science." *AJS* XVII (May, 1912): 804-19.

———. "*Sociologie und Politik* by Ludwig Gumplowicz." Re-

view of *Sociologie und Politik* by Ludwig Gumplowicz." *AJS* IV (July, 1898): 105-106.

Small, Albion W. and George, Vincent. *An Introduction to
the Study of Society.* New York: American Book Co.,
1894.

Ward, Lester F. "Contemporary Sociology." *AJS* VII (May,
1902): 749-62.

————. *Dynamic Sociology.* 2 vols. New York: D. Appleton &
Co., 1913.

————. "Ludwig Gumplowicz." *AJS* XV (November, 1909):
410-13.

————. *Outlines of Sociology.* New York: Macmillan Co.,
1913.

————. *Pure Sociology.* New York: Macmillan Co., 1914.

————. "Social and Biological Struggles." *AJS* XIII
(November, 1907): 289-99.

————. "Social Classes in the Light of Modern Sociological
Theory." *AJS* XIII (March, 1908): 617-27.

————. "Sociology and the State." *AJS* XV (March, 1910):
672-80.

————. "The Sociology of Political Parties." *AJS* XIII
(January, 1908): 439-54.

A Selected List of Relatively Contemporary Works on the Subject of Social Conflict

Adorno, T. W. *The Authoritarian Personality.* Studies in Prejudice Series. New York: Harper & Row Pub. Inc.,
1950.

Allport, Gordon. "The Role of Expectance." *Tensions That
Cause War.* Edited by Hadley Cantril. Urbana, Illinois: University of Illinois Press, 1950.

American Friends Service Committee. *In Place of War.* New
York: Grossman Pub., 1967.

Angell, Robert C. "Discovering Paths to Peace." *The Nature
of Conflict: Studies on the Sociological Aspects of International Tension.* Mayene, France: Joseph Floch for
the United Nations Educational, Scientific, and Cultural Organization, 1958.

Aron, Raymond. *The Century of Total War.* Boston: The
Beacon Press, 1963.

Bernard, Jessie. "The Sociological Study of Conflict." *The*

Nature of Conflict: Studies on the Sociological Aspects of International Tension. Mayene, France: Joseph Floch for the United Nations Educational, Scientific, and Cultural Organization, 1958.

————. "The Theory of Games of Strategy as a Modern Sociology of Conflict." *AJS* LIV (March, 1954): 411-24.

————. "Where Is the Modern Sociology of Conflict?" *AJS* LVI (July, 1950): 11-16.

Cantril, Hadley, ed. *Tensions That Cause Wars.* Urbana, Illinois: University of Illinois Press, 1950.

Coleman, James S. *Community Conflict.* Glencoe, Illinois: Free Press, 1957.

Coser, Lewis. *The Functions of Social Conflict.* New York: Free Press, 1955.

Dahrendorf, Ralf. *Class and Class Conflict in Industrial Society.* Stanford: Stanford University Press, 1959.

————. "Out of Utopia: Toward a Reorientation of Sociological Analysis." *Sociological Theory: A Book of Readings.* Edited by Lewis Coser and Bernard Rosenberg. New York: Macmillan Co., 1965.

Dollard, J. L. et al. *Frustration and Aggression.* New Haven: Yale University Press, 1939.

Fromm, Eric. *Escape From Freedom.* New York: Holt, Rinehart & Winston, Inc., 1965.

Germani, Gino. "Social Change and Intergroup Conflict." *The New Sociology: Essays in Social Science and Social Theory in Honor of C. Wright Mills.* Edited by Irving Louis Horowitz. New York: Oxford University Press, 1965.

Herz, John H. "The Territorial State in International Relations." *War and Its Prevention.* Edited by Amitai Etzioni and Martin Wenglinsky. New York: Harper and Row Pub., 1970.

Horowitz, Irving Louis. "Consensus, Conflict and Cooperation: A Sociological Inventory." *Social Forces* XLI (December, 1962): 177-88.

————. *Games, Strategy, and Peace.* Beyond Deterrence Series. American Friends Service Committee, 1963.

Horton, John. "Order and Conflict Theories of Social Problems as Competing Ideologies." *AJS* LXXI (May, 1966): 701-13.

Hoult, Thomas Ford. "Who Shall Prepare Himself to the Battle?" *The American Sociologist* III (February, 1968): 3-7.

Kahn, Herman. *On Escalation*. Baltimore, Maryland: Penguin Books, 1968.

———. *Thinking About the Unthinkable*. New York: Avon Books, 1968.

Klineberg, Otto. *Tensions Affecting International Understanding*. New York: Social Science Research Council, 1950.

Kornhauser, William. *The Politics of Mass Society*. New York: Free Press, 1959.

Lewin, Kurt. *Resolving Social Conflicts: Selected Papers on Group Dynamics*. Edited by Gertrude Lewin. New York: Harper & Bros. Pub. 1948.

Lipset, Seymour M. "Working Class Authoritarianism." *Political Man*. Garden City, New York: Doubleday & Co., Inc., 1960.

Lipset, Seymour M. and Altbach, Philip. "The Quest for Community on Campus." *The Search for Community in Modern America: Internpretations of American History*. Edited by E. Digby Baltzell. New York: Harper & Row Pub., Inc., 1968.

Mayo, Elton. *The Social Problems of an Industrial Civilization*. Boston: Graduate School of Business Administration, Harvard University, 1945.

McNeil, Elton B. "The Nature of Aggression." *The Nature of Human Conflict*. Edited by Elton B. McNeil. Englewood Cliffs, New Jersey: Prentice-Hall, Inc., 1965.

———. "Preface." *The Nature of Human Conflict*. Edited by Elton B. McNeil. Englewood Cliffs, New Jersey: Prentice-Hall, Inc., 1965.

The Nature of Conflict: Studies on the Sociological Aspects of Inter-National Tension. Mayene, France: Joseph Floch for the United Nations Educational, Scientific, and Cultural Organization, 1958.

Nisbet, Robert. *The Quest for Community*. New York: Oxford University Press, 1953.

Ofshe, Richard. "The Effectiveness of Pacifist Strategies." *The Journal of Conflict Resolution* XV (June, 1971): 261-69.

Schelling, Thomas C. *The Strategy of Conflict*. New York: Oxford University Press, 1963.

Secord, Paul F. and Backman, Carl W. *Social Psychology*. New York: McGraw-Hill, 1964.

Speier, Hans. *Social Order and the Risks of War*. New York: George W. Stewart Pub., Inc., 1952.

Szymanski, Al. "Toward a Radical Sociology." *Sociology in American Society.* Edited by New University Conference. Chicago. 1971.

Truman, David. *The Governmental Process.* New York: Columbia University Press, 1951.

Warner, Lloyd. *Yankee City.* One volume abridged edition. New Haven(Yale University Press, 1963.

Williams, Robin M. *The Reduction of Intergroup Tensions.* New York: Social Science Research Council, 1957.

Name Index

Adams, Henry B., 104
Adams, Henry C., 96
Adams, Herbert, 116
Adorno, T. W., 289
Allport, Gordon, 297
Andrews, C. M., 117
Angell, Robert, 296-97
Arendt, Hannah, 300, 311

Bagehot, Walter, 30, 40, 115
Bancroft, George, 95
Barnes, Harry E., 22, 58-59, 134
Bastian, Adolph, 267
Baumgarten, Hermann, 34, 52
Beck, Carl, 91
Becker, Carl, 19
Bentley, Arthur F., 14-16, 22, 88, 93, 122, 162-63, 241-78, 302; as muckraker, 243, 271; as optimist, 265, 278; as pacifist, 276-78; as philosopher of history, 262-63; as progressive, 23, 269-71, 303; as realist, 253, 255, 263, 265-66, 268; as sociologist, 241-46; at University of Chicago, 124; at Johns Hopkins, 116-17, 121, 242, 269; attitude toward revolution, 274-75, 303-4; basic unit of investigation for, 244-46; Dewey and, 124, 242, 266; Dilthey and, 118, 244; early life of, 113-14; Gumplowicz and, 247, 251-53,

258, 263-65, 267, 285; Ihering and, 247, 258, 263, 285; in Germany, 117-19; local society and, 23, 112, 113-14, 125-26, 129, 281; Marx and, 247, 251, 264-65; Menger and, 117, 242, 244; place of reason in, 266-68; Ratzenhofer and, 247, 251-53, 262-63, 266; Simmel and, 118-19, 244, 247, 285; Small and, 244, 245, 248, 262-63; social physics and, 254-55, 267; social psychology of, 245-46, 248-49. *See also Makers, Users, and Masters in America; Process of Goverment, The*
Berlin, Isaiah, 130
Bernard, Jessie, 279, 289, 296, 304
Bernhardi, Friedrich von, 15, 58
Bettelheim, Bruno, 311
Bismarck, Otto von, 61, 63, 93, 199
Blackmar, Franklin, 117
Bouglé, Celeste, 118
Brown, Charles R., 115
Burgess, Ernest, 122
Burgess, John, 91, 100-101, 103, 106, 107, 115, 151
Butler, Nicholas Murray, 101, 102, 107, 108

Calhoun, John C., 90
Carey, Henry, 89
Carey, Matthew, 89

Chipman, Alice, 120
Chugerman, Samuel, 127, 157, 161, 186
Comte, August, 40
Conrad, Johannes, 96, 107
Cooley, Charles H., 21-22, 110, 120, 212, 283
Coser, Lewis, 120, 210-11, 280
Coswell, Joseph, 95
Croly, Herbert, 151

Dahlmann, Friedrich, 34, 52
Darwin, Charles, 27, 30-31, 213-14; Park and, 211, 220, 223, 319
DeGrazia, Sebastian, 300
Dewey, John, 110, 123, 204; Bentley and, 124, 242, 266; Park and, 119-20, 205, 211, 218
Dilthey, Wilhelm, 26, 215; Bentley and, 118, 244
Dollard, John L., 289
Droysen, Johann G., 34
Durkheim, Emile, 252

Eichorn, Karl F., 66
Ely, Richard T., 96, 107, 108, 116, 241; Bentley and, 117
Everett, Edward, 95

Follen, Charles, 91
Ford, Franklin, 205
Freeman, Charles, 116
Freeman, John, 117
Fromm, Eric, 300, 303, 311

Galton, Francis, 213
Gandhi, Mohandis, 235
Gerland, Georg, 316
Gumplowicz, Ludwig, 14, 18, 24, 37, 62, 212, 255, 284, 316; as Jew, 25, 28, 39, 42; as national liberal, 44, 45-46, 64; as pessimist, 108-9, 157-60, 181, 185, 285; as Polish revolutionary, 39-41; Bentley and, 247, 251-53, 258,

263-65, 267, 285; conflict theory of, 38, 47-49, 51-52, 59-60, 70-74, 76-77, 258; methodology of, 26-28, 62n, 67n, 68, 237, 267n; morality and politics in, 295; Oppenheimer and, 41, 239; Ratzenhofer and, 43-44n, 171, 172-75, 176, 182, 185; Small and, 171-72, 175, 178, 265; social Darwinism and, 15-16, 213, 215-16, 222-23; Ward and, 129, 132-34, 137-39, 142, 143, 145, 147, 155, 157-60, 163, 168, 185, 265, 285
Gumplowicz, Maksymilian, 41

Haeckel, Ernst, 136
Hall, G. Stanley, 99-100, 102, 108, 113, 119, 121
Hapgood, Hutchins, 117-18, 119, 205
Harding, Warren G., 270
Hartmann, Eduard von, 109
Hayden, Ferdinand, 127
Hegel, G. W. F., 15, 16, 38, 109, 120, 128, 146, 285, 308; Idea of Right in, 31, 34, 161; morality and politics in, 32-33; realpolitik in, 31-34, 35, 36; Ward and, 161; World Spirit of Reason in, 34, 161
Heinzen, Karl, 91
Herz, John, 307
Hobbes, Thomas, 16, 132, 134
Hofstadter, Richard, 93, 94
Holst, Germann von, 114
Horkheimer, Max, 300
Hughes, Everett C., 212, 315-19
Hume, David, 214

Ihering, Rudolph von, 75; Bentley and, 247, 258, 263, 286

James, William, 120, 218
Jameson, John, 91
Jefferson, Thomas, 16, 160, 284, 287

Kant, Immanuel, 14, 34, 46, 160, 223
King, Clarence, 127
Kitiakowski, Bogden, 121
Knies, Carl G. A., 107
Kornhauser, William, 300

La Follette, Robert M., 269
Lazarus, Moritz, 123
Lenin, V. I., 274, 292
Leopold (king of Belgium), 208, 209
Lewin, Kurt, 168, 288, 294, 301, 304
Lieber, Francis, 91-92, 115
Lilienfeld, Paul von, 169
Lipset, Seymour M., 300, 303
List, Frederich, 89-90
Locke, John, 132, 223
Lynd, Robert, 125

Machiavelli, Nicolai, 31, 53, 308
McNeil, Elton, 292, 306-7
Marcuse, Herbert, 31
Marx, Karl, 42, 69, 157, 241, 274, 292; Bentley and, 247, 251, 264-65; Small and, 163, 191-92
Matson, Floyd, 247
Mayer, J. P., 54
Mayo, Elton, 288, 294, 300, 301, 303-4, 306
Mead, George H., 110, 120, 123, 318
Meinecke, Friedrich, 30-31
Menger, Karl: Bentley and, 117, 242, 244; Small and, 164-65
Merton, Robert K., 19, 125
Mill, John S., 132
Mills, C. Wright, 19
Moltke, Helmuth, 15, 58
Mommsen, Theodor, 53
Morris, George, 119-20
Mulford, Elisha, 91
Munsterberg, Hugo, 121, 211-12, 218

Napoleon I, 31, 61, 306
Niebuhr, Barthold G., 91

Nietzsche, Friedrich, 14, 59, 108
Nisbet, Robert, 289, 293, 300

Oppenheimer, Franz, 14, 15, 16, 18, 24, 30, 37, 41, 55, 62, 67, 216, 284, 299, 309; as Jew, 28, 41-42; as national liberal, 42-43, 44, 63; as optimist, 239; bureaucracy in, 79-80; career of, 39, 41-43; conflict theory of, 38, 49-51, 58-59, 69-70, 72-74, 76-77, 80-86; Freeman's Citizenship in, 87, 231, 239; Gumplowicz and, 41, 239; Park and, 212, 225, 226, 231, 236-38, 285, 316; sea state vs. plains state in, 56-57, 80-81

Park, Robert E., 14-16, 22-23, 88, 93, 105, 122, 123, 162, 163, 203-40, 241-43, 294, 315-19; as muckraker, 205-8, 209-11, 230; as optimist and pessimist, 230-32, 234-36, 239-40, 265; as philosopher of history, 223-25; as progressive, 205-8, 303-4; at University of Chicago, 123-24, 206, 209-11; concern of with social order, 236-38, 283, 285; early life and career of, 114, 119-21; Dewey and, 119-20, 205, 211, 218; in Germany, 121, 207, 219, 315; local society and, 23, 114, 125-26, 129, 281; Liberal World Society in, 235-36; objectivity of, 209-11; Oppenheimer and, 212, 225, 226, 231, 238-39, 285, 316; race relations in, 223-36; realpolitik in, 213, 219-36; Simmel and, 121, 163, 212, 219, 225, 285, 317; Small and, 124, 212, 225, 317, 318; Weber and, 318-19. *See also Introduction to the Science of Sociology*
Parsons, Talcott, 168
Paulsen, Frederick, 105

Pearson, Karl, 213
Philippovich, Eugen von, 66-67, 122
Polybius, 214
Potter, David, 19
Powell, John, 127

Ranke, Leopold von, 15-16, 38, 61,
    199, 215; realpolitik in, 35-37,
    308
Ratner, Sidney, 124, 246, 269
Ratzenhofer, Gustav, 14, 18, 24, 37,
    62, 122, 212, 284; as national
    liberal, 44-46, 64; as professional
    soldier, 44; as racist, 149n, at-
    titude toward history of, 29n;
    Bentley and, 247, 251-53, 262-63,
    266; conflict theory of, 38, 46,
    47-49, 78-79n, 176, 181-82, 229,
    285, 291; early life of, 43; Gump-
    lowicz and, 43-44n, 171, 172-75,
    176, 183, 185, 255; perpetual
    peace and, 46; positive monism
    in, 184, 266, 284; Small and, 163,
    164-65, 168-72, 175-85, 197-98,
    199, 266, 285; social Darwinism
    and 15-16, 30, 213, 215, 222-23;
    Ward and, 129, 138, 146, 147,
    149n, 151. See also Wesen und
    Zweck der Politik
Redfield, Robert, 123
Robbins, Henry E., 115
Roosevelt, Theodore, 151, 287
Root, Elihu, 101
Roscher, W. G. F., 215
Ross, Edward A., 21, 102, 104-5,
    107, 117, 123, 204, 241; as for-
    gotten American, 283; as op-
    timist, 109, 159; as racist, 282n,
    local society and, 281
Rousseau, Jean-Jacques, 16, 32, 160,
    223, 284
Royce, Josiah, 120, 121

Saint-Simon, Henri, 40

Savigny, Karl, 26, 66
Schäffle, Albert, 122, 164-65, 169
Schmoller, Gustav, 64, 65n, 69,
    80-81n, 95, 96; Small and,
    115-16, 118, 122, 163, 199
Schopenhauer, Arthur, 14, 109, 128,
    157
Schurz, Carl, 91
Seligman, E. R. A., 96
Simmel, Georg, 14, 121, 129, 294; as
    Jew, 28, 42; as lecturer, 103-4,
    119, 121, 122; Bentley and,
    118-19, 244, 247, 252, 258, 286;
    "hostility" in, 219, 291-92; Park
    and, 121, 163, 212, 219, 225, 285,
    317; social conflict in, 217, 258,
    305-6, 308
Sinclair, Upton, 205
Small, Albion, 14-16, 22, 88, 93,
    110, 153, 162-202; as apologist
    for order, 195-97, 199-201, 281;
    as Christian reformist, 183-85,
    197-99, 230; as non-Darwinist,
    213, 214, 222-23; as optimist, 20,
    185-87, 238-39, 265; at Univer-
    sity of Chicago, 123-24, 162; at
    Johns Hopkins, 116-17, 121, 242,
    317; attitude toward revolution,
    193-95, 301; Bentley and, 244,
    245, 248, 262-63; early life,
    112-13, 115; in Germany, 115-16,
    317; Gumplowicz and, 171-72,
    178, 265; Lieber and, 91-92,
    115-16; local society and, 23,
    112-13, 125-26, 129, 281; Marx
    and, 163, 191-92, 199, 317; Park
    and, 124, 212, 225, 317, 318;
    progressivism and, 23, 194-95,
    203-4, 205, 303-4; Ratzenhofer
    and, 163, 164-65, 168-72, 175-85,
    197-98, 199, 266, 285; Schäffle
    and, 122, 164-65, 169; Schmoller
    and, 115-16, 118, 122, 163, 199;
    value neutrality in, 183-84,

189-90, 203-4; Ward and, 131, 133, 162, 175, 194-95, 201, 317. *See also General Sociology; Introduction to the Study of Society*

Spencer, Herbert, 22, 213, 223, 248, 309

Stalin, Joseph, 311

Steffens, Lincoln, 205

Stern, Bernhard J., 129

Sumner, William G., 21-22, 221

Sybel, Heinrich von, 34, 52

Thomas, W. I., 110, 123, 209, 225, 229, 291, 318-19

Thwing, Charles, 106

Ticknor, George, 95

Tocqueville, Alexis de, 93

Tönnies, Ferdinand, 105, 122

Treitschke, Heinrich von, 15-16, 37-38, 52, 53, 61, 63, 65, 151, 181, 199, 215, 285, 308; as lecturer, 103; morality and war in, 57-60; the state in, 38, 46-47

Tufts, James, 123

Turgot, Robert Jacques, 214

Turner, F. J., 19, 117

Veblen, Thorstein, 21, 110, 117, 241, 283

Vincent, George, 164, 169, 170

Vincent, J. M., 117

Voltaire, Francois-Maria, 132

Wagner, Adolph, 64, 95, 96, 107, 115-16, 118, 199

Ward, Lester F., 14-16, 22, 88, 93, 123, 124-61, 162, 163, 224, 241-43, 248; as progressive, 23, 151-57, 194-95, 203-4, 303-4; attitude toward revolution, 149-52, 156-57; as optimist, 20, 157-61, 185-87, 238-39, 265, 285; conflict theory of, 134-45, 147-52, 156-57; education as panacea in, 154-57, 203-4, 205, 230, 277; Gumplowicz and, 129, 132-34, 137-39, 142, 143, 145, 147, 155, 157-60, 163, 168, 185, 265, 285; local society and, 23, 126-29, 281; vanity of, 128-29; Ratzenhofer and, 129, 138, 146, 147, 149n, 151; Small and, 131, 133, 175, 194-95, 201, 317; social Darwinism and, 213, 214, 222-23. *See also Dynamic Sociology; Pure Sociology*

Warner, Amos, 117

Warner, Lloyd, 125

Washington, Booker T., 207, 239-40

Wayland, Francis, 115

Webb, Walter P., 19

Weber, Max, 14, 16, 30, 61, 96, 212, 219, 241, 255, 318-19; as nationalist, 53-54; life and career of, 52-54; realpolitik in, 55-56, 58, 81-87, 217-18, 295-96, 299, 308

Webster, Daniel, 90

Wiese, Leopold von, 122

Willoughby, Westel, 91

Wilson, Woodrow, 117, 152, 287

Windelband, Wilhelm, 121, 212, 219

Woolsey, Theodore, 91

Wündt, Wilhelm, 121, 123

Subject Index

Absolute hostility, 48, 176-177, 179, 229, 266, 285, 291

Agression. *See* Realpolitik; Social conflict; Tension theory

American: Civil War, 90-91, 94, 150-51, 227, 307-8; college life, 105, 107, 110; political science, 91-92, 106, 107-8; social mobility, 265; social science professionalization, 106n; students in Germany, 97-109. *See also* Local society; Optimism; Progressive movement; Social classes, conflict between

American, The, 204

American Economic Association, 96-97, 106n

American Journal of Sociology, 122, 317

American Sociological Association, 96, 106n

Anomie, 293

Assimilation, 227

Austro-Hungarian Empire, 39-40, 45-46, 62-64

"Autobiographical Note" (Park), 224

Barbaric state, 187

Belgian Congo, 208

Belgian Congo Reform Association, 207-8

Berlin, University of, 34, 37, 101

Big business, 188-89, 270-74, 282-83

Bureaucracy, 79-87

Capitalist class, 188-89, 270-74, 282-83

Caste. *See* Social classes

Center for Group Dynamics, 301

Chicago, University of, 123, 209, 211, 231

Civilized state, 187

Civil War, 90-91, 94, 150-51, 227, 307-8

Clark University, 106

Class conflict. *See* Social class, conflict between

Colby College, 110, 115, 116, 131, 183

Colonialism, 208, 233-34

Columbia University, 106

"Coming Slavery, The" (Ross), 282

Communism, 270-71, 293, 311

Competition, 219-23

Condition of the Western Farmer as Illustrated by the Economic History of a Nebraska Township, The" (Bentley), 269

Conflict. *See* Social conflict

Conflict resolution, 277-78, 299. *See also* Tension reduction

"Conflict of Classes, The" (Small),

190-94

"Contemporary Sociology" (Ward), 132

Conquest state, 78-79n, 262, 309

Counter revolution, 275, 286

Cross section, 250n, 264. *See also* Interest group

Culture state, 78-79n, 262, 309

Darwinism. *See* Social Darwinism

Defense Department, 301

Democratic government, 260-63

Despotic government, 260-63

Dialectics in conflict, 182, 305

Disquisition on Government (Calhoun), 22

Distributive justice, 190, 192-93, 197-99, 231-32

Dynamic Sociology (Ward), 131, 133, 134-38, 141, 143

Education as panacea, 154-57, 203-5, 230, 285

Equality. *See* Democratic government; Distributive justice; Freeman's Citizenship; Liberal world society; Social classes; Socialism; Sociocracy

Everybody's Magazine, 208

Extremism. *See* Revolution; Violence

Franco-Prussian War, 100-101, 150, 307

Federal Reserve Bank, 287

Feudalism, 81-83

Freeman's Citizenship, 87, 231, 239

French Revolution, 31, 32

Friction, 254-55, 277. *See also* Social conflict

Game theory, 302n

Gemeinschaft und Gesellschaft (Tönnies), 122-23

General Sociology (Small), 22, 169-72, 175-82, 239; absolute hostility in, 176-77, 179; conflict within state in, 179-80; meaning of state in, 170; origin of state in, 175-76, 177-78; social process in, 170; telos of conflict in 181-82

Genesis of social forms, 139-40, 153-54

German: bureaucracy and militarism, 100-101, 294; cultural life, 98-99; immigration to America, 91; national economics, 89-90; social unrest, 62-65, 238; university life, 101-5. *See also* Berlin; Pessimism; Prussia; Prussian historical school

Glimpses of the Cosmos (Ward), 128-29

Government: as process, 250-53, 256; conflict within, 254, 256-58, 260-62, 272-74; defined, 250-51; despotic vs. democratic, 260-63; industrial, 271-72; law and, 256-58; revolution within, 261-62

Habsburg Dynasty, 45-46, 62-64

Hague Tribunal, The, 259

Harvard Department of Industrial Research, 301

Hatred. *See* Absolute hostility

Historicism, 26-28, 214-15

Historisch-Politische Zeitschrift, 35

Hostility. *See* Absolute hostility

Human society, 66-67, 221, 245

Idea of Right, 31, 34, 161

Imperialism, 208, 233-34

Inequality. *See* Social classes

Interest group, 251n, 254, 256-57, 263-66, 272, 275, 277

Introduction to the Science of Sociology, An (Park and Burgess), 122, 211, 237, 238, 316

Introduction to the Study of Society (Small and Vincent), 164-70; meaning of state in, 168, 170; social conflict in, 164-68; social physics in, 166-67, 170

Johns Hopkins University, 106, 116-17, 123
Journal of Conflict Resolution, The, 289, 292
Justice. *See* Distributive justice

Kraj, 40
Ku Klux Klan, 231

Law: meaning of, 256-57; origin of, 75-77, 257-58; significance of for violence, 74-75, 258-62
Law of Previous Accumulation (Marx), 42, 69
League of Nations, 269
Legal rights. *See* Law
Liberalism, 16-17, 34, 36, 76, 222-23, 284; modern sociology and, 303-4; total war and, 310-12. *See also* Hobbes; Jefferson; Kant; Locke; Mill; Rousseau; Voltaire
Liberal world society, 232-36
Local society, 23, 93-94, 95, 152; defined, 125-26; early sociologists as members of, 112-14, 126, 281; Ward as member of, 126-29. *See also* Progressive movement

McClures, 204
Machiavellianism, 15. *See also* Realpolitik
Makers, Users, and Masters in America (Bentley), 268-76; Bentley's biases in, 270-71; capitalist class in, 270-74; counter revolution in, 275-76; industrial government in, 271-72; non-partisan politics in, 275-76;

proletariat in, 270-71, 273-75; revolution in, 273-75
Man Farthest Down, The (Washington), 207
Man-society, 250n, 255. *See also* Human society
Marginal man, 227-28, 234; Oppenheimer as, 42
Michigan, University of, 119
Middle class. *See* Local society
Middle class counter revolution, 275-76, 286. *See also* Progressive movement
Monumenta Germaniae Historica, 35
Morality and politics, 17, 29, 32-33, 180-81, 253-55, 295-96
Muckraking, 204-8, 209-11, 243, 271

Nation, The, 204
National economics, 89-90
Nationalism: Gumplowicz and, 45-46; Oppenheimer and, 42-43; Ratzenhofer and, 44-46; Weber and, 53-54
National liberalism: American progressivism and, 95-97, 150-52, 153, 201; defined, 66; German social unrest and, 62-65; sociology and, 61-68; *Verein für Sozialpolitik* and, 64-65, 66
National liberation movements, 227-28, 234-34. *See also* Austro-Hungarian Empire
Naziism, 293, 311
Negro race, 226, 228, 231, 233, 234-36, 237, 239, 283
Non-Partisan League, 269, 276
Non-partisan politics, 275-76

Old middle class. *See* Local society
Optimism: in America, 17-20, 108-9, 186-87; in Bentley, 265, 278; in Oppenheimer, 239; in Park, 231-32, 234-36, 239-40; in Ross,

109; in Small, 185-87, 238-39; in Ward, 157-61, 238-39. *See also* Pessimism

Order. *See* Social order

Organicism, 169-70n

Oriental race, 228, 233, 234, 236, 283

Origin of law, 75-77, 257-58

Origin of social classes, 69-74, 155-56

Origin of the state, 32, 35-36, 46-51, 55-56, 134-45, 175-76, 225-26

Origin of the Species (Darwin), 30

Outlines of Sociology (Gumplowicz), 137, 267

Patrimonialism, 83n

Perpetual peace, 33, 46

Pessimism: in Germany, 20, 108-9; in Gumplowicz, 108-9, 157-60, 239; in Park, 230-31, 240; in Ratzenhofer, 149n; in Weber, 87. *See also* Optimism

Philosophy of Right, The (Hegel), 31, 34

Plains state, 56-57

Political science, 106, 107-8; Lieber's influence on, 91-92

Polish liberation movement, 39-40

Politics and morality, 17, 29, 32-33, 180-81, 253-55, 295-96

Positive monism, 184, 266, 285

Power struggles. *See* Social conflict

Prejudice: causes of, according to realpolitik, 228-30, 291-92; causes of, according to tension theory, 292. *See also* Absolute hostility,

Preussiche Jahrbücher, 34

Previous Accumulation, Law of (Marx), 42, 69

Process of Government, The (Bentley), 22, 246-68, 271, 274, 302; despotic vs. democratic govern-ment in, 260-63; domination and conflict in, 253-54; government defined in, 250-51; interest group in, 251, 254, 256, 264-65; "in-terest" in, 248-49; origin of law in, 257-58; political development in, 260-63; realism in, 253, 255, 263; revolution in 261-62; viol-ence in, 258-63

Progressive movement, 23, 93-97, 201, 203-8, 281-88; as reaction-ary, 275-76, 286-87, 303-4; edu-cation as panacea in, 154-57, 203-5, 230; German national liberalism and, 95-97, 150-52, 153, 201; imperialism and, 151-52, 287; muckraking and, 204-8, 210; non-partisan politics in, 275-76, 286; Park and, 205-8, 210, 269; Small and, 183-85, 194-95, 197-99, 203-4, 269; Ward and, 151-57, 194-95, 203-4, 269. *See also* Local society; National liberalism

Progressive Party, 152, 269

Proletariat, 188-89, 270-71, 273-75, 282-83

Prussia, 31, 32, 34-35, 53-54

Prussian-Franco War, 100-101, 150, 307

Prussian historical school: emphasis upon individual in, 61-62; his-toricism in, 26-28, 214-15. *See also* Hegel; Ranke; Treitschke

"Psychology of Race Prejudice" (Thomas), 229

Pure Sociology (Ward), 132, 134, 138-49, 239; genesis vs. telesis of social forms in, 139-40, 153-54; "intelligence" in, 141, 142, 143, 144-45; meaning of state in, 145-46; origin of state in, 140-45; revolution in, 153; social statics vs. dynamics in, 139-40; synergy in, 140n

Race relations: assimilation, 227; conflict, 227; emancipation, 228, 234-36; equality, 231-32; marginality, 227-28, 234; prejudice, 228-30. *See also* Origin of state

Races. *See* Negro; Oriental; Polish liberation movement; Slavic peoples

Race und Staat (Gumplowicz), 41, 132, 133, 134, 143

Rassenkampf, Der (Gumplowicz), 132, 134, 172

Realpolitik: causes of conflict in, 20, 290-92; game theory and, 302; liberalism and, 16-17, 34, 36, 76, 284; morality and politics in, 17, 29, 32-33, 87, 180-81, 253-54, 255, 295-96; optimism in, 305-6, 307-9; origins of, in Germany, 31-87; peace research and, 314; rationality in, 290; social Darwinism and, 15-16, 130, 213-23. *See also* Social class; Social conflict; Law; particular scholars; State

"Reason" (Ward), 159

Relativity in Man and Society (Bentley), 264, 276-77

Revolution: Bentley and, 274-75; bureaucracy and, 79-80, 86-87; causes of, in realpolitik, 227-28, 261-62, 273-74, 292-93; causes of, in tension theory, 293; German sociologists and, 63-66; of 1848, 34, 91; Small and, 193-99; Ward and, 149-52, 156-57. *See also* National liberation movements; particular revolutions

Russian Revolution, 193

Sea State, 56-57

Slavery. *See* Origin of social classes;

Origin of the state

Slavic peoples, 53, 316

Social classes: conflict between, 188-99, 270-75, 282-83; defined, 68; origin of, 69-74, 155-56; relative powers of different, 188-89. *See also* Equality; Revolution

Social conflict: as dialectical process, 181-82; between classes, 188-99, 270-75, 282-83; between races, 227-30; causes of, in realpolitik, 20, 290-92; causes of, in tension theory, 290-94; competition and, 219-23; disastrous consequences of, 306-7; early view of Small on, 164-68; meaning of, 214, 217-20, 254; sociology's avoidance of, 279-81; sociology's preoccupation with, 288-89; telos of, 181-82; unifying consequences of, 17, 140-45, 147-50, 181-82, 220-23; within the government, 254, 256-58, 260-62, 272-74; within the state, 147-50, 179-80, 187, 232. *See also* Realpolitik; Revolution; Social class; State; Tension theory; War

Social contract, 29, 32, 135, 138

Social Darwinism, 15-16, 30, 213-23, 284; Gumplowicz and, 213, 215-16; Park and, 219-23; Ratzenhofer and, 213, 216; Small and, 213-14, 216; Ward and, 213-14, 216

Social Democratic Party, 63

Social dynamics, 139-40

Socialism, 193-94, 273-75

Socialization, 285. *See also* Education as panacea

Social order: bias of modern sociology toward, 279-80, 288-89; basis of, in force, 31-32; Park and, 236-38, 283, 285; preoccupation of early sociologists with, 281-88,

305; Ross and, 281-83; Small and, 195-97, 199-201, 283, 285; Ward and, 149-52, 283, 285. *See also* Human society; Social conflict, unifying consequences of; State

Social physics: in Bentley, 254-55; in Small, 166-67, 170, 187

Social process: in Bentley, 245, 248-50, 266-68; in Small, 170

Social psychology: of Bentley, 245-46, 248-49; of Small, 164-65, 245, 248

Social statics, 139-40

Society, 66-67, 221, 245

Sociocracy, 232

Sociological organicism, 169-70

Sociologie und Politik (Gumplowicz), 171

Sociologische Erkenntnis, Die (Ratzenhofer), 169, 170

Sociologists of conflict: defined, 14n. *See also* Gumplowicz; Oppenheimer; Ratzenhofer

Sociology: avoidance of conflict in modern, 279-80; anti-liberal bias of, 201-2, 222; bias toward order of early, 281-88, 305; defined, 243-44; liberalism in modern, 303-4; preoccupation with conflict in modern, 288-89; roots of, in German national liberalism, 61-68; ties to dominant institutions of modern, 280, 301-3

Soziologie (Simmel), 317

Spontaneous cooperation, 304

Standard Oil Company, 288

State, the: barbaric vs. civilized, 187; bureaucratization of, 79-87; conflict within, 70-74, 80-86, 147-50, 179-99; conquest vs. cultural, 78-79n, 262, 309; expansion of, through war, 51-52, 187; meaning of, in realpolitik, 29, 35,

38, 55, 145-47, 168, 170, 182, 187; origin of, 32, 35-36, 46-51, 55-56, 134-45, 175-76, 225-26; sea vs. plains, 56-57. *See also* Government; Revolution

State, The (Oppenheimer), 87

Struggle for existence. *See* Competition

Struggle for power. *See* Social conflict

Synergy, 140n

Telesis of social forms, 139-40, 153-54

Tension, 290

Tension reduction, 296-98; weaknesses of, 312-14

Tension theory, 21, 290-307; avoidance of tactical thinking in, 296, 298-99; causes of conflict in, 290-94; liberalism and, 303-4; military-industrial complex and, 301-3; phobia of conflict in, 305-7; preoccupation with the individual follower in, 300, 312-14; sources of, 309-12. *See also* Realpolitik

"Terrible Story of the Congo, The" (Park), 208

"Thought News," 205

Totalitarianism, 304

Total war, 309-11

Ultimate Will in its Historical and Scientific Development, The (Gumplowicz), 40

University. *See* particular universities

UNESCO Tension Project, 289, 296

U. S. Steel, 288

Utilitarianism, 164-65

Verein für Sozialpolitik, 64-65, 66, 96, 150, 184, 201

Verstehen, 27, 215

Violence: causes of, 261-62; law and, 258-62. *See also* Revolution; War, as inevitable, 59-60; as progressive, 33, 36-37, 57-58, 147-52, 222, 307-8; as social interaction, 219-20; Bentley and, 276-78; dueling and, 308; Gumplowicz and, 59-60; Ratzenhofer and, 46, 308; total, 309-11; Treitschke and, 59-60, 308; Ward and, 147-52, 308. *See also* particular wars

Wealth of Nations (Smith), 192

Weimar Republic, 42-43

Wesen und Zweck der Politik (Ratzenhofer), 169, 172; absolute hostility in, 176, 178; books I and II in, 175-80; book III in, 180-82; dialectics in, 182; Gumplowicz's opinion of, 172-75, 183, 185; Small's opinion of, 175-85; telos of politics in, 180-82

"Where is the Modern Sociology of Conflict?" (Bernard), 279

Working class. *See* Proletariat

World Spirit of Reason, 34, 161

World War I, 42, 193, 269-70, 307, 309, 311

World War II, 20, 237, 301